Domesday Book
A Reassessment

Domesday Book
A Reassessment

Edited by
Peter Sawyer

Edward Arnold

© Edward Arnold 1985

First published in Great Britain 1985 by
Edward Arnold (Publishers) Ltd, 41 Bedford Square, London WC1B 3DQ

Edward Arnold (Australia) Pty Ltd, 80 Waverley Road, Caulfield East, Victoria 3145, Australia

Edward Arnold, 3 East Read Street, Baltimore, Maryland 21202, USA

British Library Cataloguing in Publication Data

Domesday Book: a reassessment.
  1. Domesday book
  I. Sawyer, P.H.
  333.3'22'0942   DA190

  ISBN 0-7131-6440-9

Text set in 10½/11½ pt Baskerville Compugraphic
by Colset Private Ltd, Singapore
Printed and bound in Great Britain
by Billings & Sons Limited, Worcester

Contents

Abbreviations

DB   Domesday Book
EHR   *English Historical Review*
Exon   *Liber Exoniensis*
GDB   Great Domesday Book, i.e. DB I
LDB   Little Domesday Book, i.e. DB II
TRHS   *Transactions of the Royal Historical Society*
VCH   *The Victoria History of the County of . . .*

In references to DB the established convention of distinguishing recto and verso as a and b will be followed here, except in Chapter 3 which follows palaeographical conventions. References to the contents of other manuscripts, including the Exeter Domesday, are given in the form fo. 1 (for 1 recto), 1^{rv} and 1^{v}.

Note on orthography

Spelling has been modernized throughout, substituting th, d or g where appropriate for the Old-English characters thorn, eth and yogh used in the manuscripts. The tironian nota has been replaced by 7.

Illustrations

Plates

Figures, Maps and Tables

Notes on Contributors

John Blair is a Fellow of The Queen's College, Oxford. His main research is on settlement and local organization in early medieval England, and he is preparing a book on the origins and formation of the English parochial system. He also has strong interests in medieval archaeology, architecture and church monuments, and edits the journal *Oxoniensia*.

Howard B. Clarke received his university education at Birmingham and Aix-en-Provence, and now lectures in the Department of Medieval History in University College Dublin. Dr Clarke is presently working on a series of Domesday-related topics, including the early surveys of Evesham Abbey and the uses of the English 'hide', as well as on an edition of the two Evesham cartularies for the Worcestershire Historical Society.

Sally Harvey was born in 1941, educated at King Edward VI High School, Birmingham and Birmingham University, where she wrote her thesis on Domesday Book. Dr Harvey has published many articles on Domesday Book and held Fellowships at Girton College, Cambridge, and St Hilda's College, Oxford, University Lectureships at Leeds and Oxford, and a Visiting Professorship at Keio University, Japan.

G.H. Martin has been Keeper of Public Records since 1982, and was formerly Professor of History in the University of Leicester. Educated at Merton College, Oxford, and the University of Manchester, he is the author of a number of works on urban history and the diplomatic of town records. He was awarded the Besterman Medal of the Library Association in 1973.

J.J.N. Palmer, BA and BLitt (Oxon) and PhD (London), is Senior Lecturer in History in the University of Hull. He is author of *England, France and Christendom 1377–1399* (1972), editor of *Froissart, Historian* (1981), and contributes to *English Historical Review*, *Transactions of the Royal Historical Society*,

Bulletin of J. Rylands Library, *Speculum*, and many other journals. His academic interests have recently changed to Domesday and computers and he has been awarded a grant of £21,000 by ESRC for computerizing Domesday Book, a version of which will be in use at the PRO Domesday Exhibition in 1986.

John Percival was educated at Colchester Royal Grammar School, and at Hertford and Merton Colleges, Oxford, where he read Greats. Since 1962 he has taught in the department of Classics in University College Cardiff, where he is now Professor. He is the author of *The Roman Villa* (1976), and editor (in collaboration with H.R. Loyn) of *The Reign of Charlemagne* (1975).

Alexander R. Rumble has been Lecturer in Palaeography in the University of Manchester since 1980. He was formerly employed successively by the English Place-Name Society and the Winchester Research Unit. Dr Rumble is the Editor of the Cambridgeshire, Essex, and Suffolk volumes of the Phillimore translation of Domesday Book.

Peter Sawyer was Professor of Medieval History in the University of Leeds from 1970 to 1982. His early research and first publications were on Domesday Book which has been a key source in his more recent work on Anglo-Saxon Charters, Scandinavian colonization and early English history. His main contribution to this volume is a development of a discovery made while preparing a book on Anglo-Saxon Lincolnshire.

Preface

Domesday Book is the most important single source for early English history and has long been used as a quarry by amateur and professional students of Anglo-Saxon and Anglo-Norman England. In recent years particular attention has been paid to the methods of the enquiry and this has led to an improved understanding of its purpose and a greater awareness of the limitations of Domesday Book as a source, and its possibilities. The present book, produced in preparation for the ninth centenary of the making of Domesday Book, has two main purposes. First, to review the present state of Domesday studies and to provide a guide to the voluminous and scattered literature on the subject. It is, however, not simply a retrospective survey but has, as its second purpose, the discussion of some questions that are of particular interest at present, and to indicate some of the potentially rewarding topics for future work.

As recent research on Domesday is discussed in all the following papers, the introductory survey of work done since the last centenary is very brief. The next three papers are devoted to general topics. John Percival's discussion of Roman and Frankish land registers is a step forward in understanding what William's officials meant when they described their achievement as a *descriptio*. Alexander Rumble provides the first comprehensive comment on the palaeography of the Domesday manuscripts since the publication in 1954 of *Domesday Rebound*. Howard Clarke's guide to the texts that derive from the preliminary stages of the enquiry, the so-called satellites, underlines their importance in understanding its methods and its purposes. The next four papers deal with substance rather than form. The editor's own contribution raises questions about the status of the pre-Conquest tenants and the scale of the tenurial revolution after 1066. Sally Harvey argues that the Domesday ploughlands represent taxation assessments made in 1086. Geoffrey Martin considers the problems apparently faced by the compilers, and consequently by modern students in dealing with the towns. John Blair's paper is not only an important contribution to the study of the English church, it also serves as a reminder that on many matters Domesday Book is most rewarding when studied along with the other available evidence. In the final contribution John Palmer describes one of the most significant recent developments, the application of computers to the study of Domesday Book.

Peter Sawyer

CHAPTER ONE

Domesday Studies since 1886

Peter Sawyer

The foundations of modern Domesday studies were laid in the last years of the nineteenth century by two scholars; F.W. Maitland and J.H. Round. For Maitland Domesday Book was a key to the Anglo-Saxon past and his *Domesday Book and Beyond*, published in 1897,[1] marked the beginning of the modern study of Old English society and is still one of the best books on that topic. In contrast Round regarded Domesday Book rather as the starting point for the study of Anglo-Norman feudal society. He was not, however, exclusively preoccupied with that and the full range of his interest in Domesday can best be seen in the many contributions he made to the Domesday sections of the Victoria County Histories, most of which were published between 1900 and 1908. He himself translated four county surveys, revised many others and also wrote 12 of the introductions as well as doing much preparatory work for others.[2] His most influential contribution to Domesday scholarship appeared as early as 1895 in *Feudal England*.[3] In the first section of that book he argued that the enquiry was conducted to produce not Domesday Book but 'Original Returns' in which the information was arranged by hundreds or wapentakes, the local units through which geld, that is tax, assessments were made and through which the geld was collected. According to Round the purpose of the enquiry was to review those tax assessments. None of the hypothetical 'Original Returns' has survived but Round claimed that they provided the basis for at least two later compilations, one of which, the *Inquisitio Comitatus Cantabrigiensis*, he described in the opening sentence of *Feudal England* as 'the true key to the Domesday Survey and to the system of land assessments it records'. Maitland accepted this argument and with characteristic lucidity drew the conclusion that 'Domesday Book is no register of title, no register of all those rights and facts which constitute the system of land-holdership. One great purpose seems to mould both its form and substance: it is a geld-book'.[4] Both Round and Maitland considered

---

[1]*Domesday Book and Beyond. Three Essays in the Early History of England* (Cambridge, CUP, 1897).

[2]W.R. Powell, 'J. Horace Round, the County Historian: the *Victoria County Histories* and the Essex Archaeological Society', *Essex Archaeology and History*, 12 (1981), pp. 25–38.

[3]*Feudal England. Historical Studies on the XIth and XIIth Centuries* (London, Swan Sonnenschein, 1895).

[4]*Domesday Book and Beyond*, p. 3.

1

Domesday Book itself to be a later rearrangement of the material, made some-time after the Conqueror's death.

On the last page of his essay Round drew attention to an omission that proved fatal to his argument; 'It will be observed that I do not touch the *Liber Exoniensis*'.[5] In 1912 F.H. Baring in effect undermined Round's whole thesis by demonstrating that the main text in the *Liber Exoniensis*, known as Exeter Domesday, was the direct source of the account of the south-western counties in Domesday Book.[6] Unfortunately Round's own work on Domesday was by then finished; he wrote his last contribution for the Victoria County Histories in 1908.[7] It was 30 years before the implications of Baring's work began to be more widely appreciated. This happened after V.H. Galbraith restated and developed Baring's argument in 1941 and suggested that the purpose of the enquiry was feudal rather than fiscal.[8] Galbraith showed that Domesday Book was not an afterthought but the intended result of the whole undertaking and that it was completed before William's death in 1087, probably already in 1086. Galbraith suggested that much of the information gathered was supplied in writing by the tenants-in-chief or their agents. Others, in particular Sally Harvey and R.S. Hoyt, have gone further and argued that the compilers also used official assessment lists, one of which, commonly but mistakenly called the 'Yorkshire Summaries', was copied on the last leaves of Great Domesday Book.[9]

Galbraith had a more general interest in the machinery of medieval English government and consequently he did not limit himself to the making of Domesday Book. He also studied the ways in which it was used later, an approach that is accurately reflected in the title of his last work *Domesday Book: its Place in Administrative History*.[10] He drew particular attention to the abbreviated versions of Domesday that were produced later and, with James Tait, edited one of them.[11]

It has been largely thanks to Galbraith that in recent years there has been a growing interest in the Domesday satellites, several of which have now been published.[12] He also put great emphasis on the importance of studying the manuscripts. Access to Domesday Book itself is necessarily very restricted but its structure is now determined thanks to the work done when it was rebound.[13]

[5]*Feudal England*, p. 146.

[6]F.H. Baring, 'The Exeter Domesday', *EHR* XXVII (1912), pp. 309–18.

[7]Powell, 'Round', p. 31.

[8]As Ford's Lecturer at Oxford, published in *Studies in the Public Records* (London, Thomas Nelson, 1948), pp. 89–121. The argument was presented in greater detail in 'The Making of Domesday Book', *EHR* LVII (1942), pp. 161–77 and in *The Making of Domesday Book* (Oxford, Clarendon Press, 1961).

[9]R.S. Hoyt, 'A Pre-Domesday Kentish Assessment List', in *A Medieval Miscellany for Doris Mary Stenton* ed. Patricia M. Barnes and C.F. Slade (London, Pipe Roll Society, 1962), pp. 189–202; Sally Harvey, 'Domesday Book and its Predecessors', *EHR* LXXXVI (1971), pp. 753–73; Harvey, 'Domesday Book and Anglo-Norman Governance', *TRHS*, Fifth series, 25 (1975), pp. 175–93.

[10]Oxford, Clarendon Press, 1974.

[11]*Herefordshire Domesday circa 1160–1170*, ed. V.H. Galbraith and the late James Tait (London, Pipe Roll Society, 1950).

[12]See below, pp. 69–70.

[13]*Domesday Rebound* (London, HMSO, 1954).

The most important discovery made at that time was that almost all the county surveys were written on separate gatherings. This means that the present order is not necessarily the order in which it was written. Another significant palaeographical discovery was made by R. Welldon Finn. He recognized some passages in the Exeter Domesday that are written in the same hand, and have the same formulas, as the Exchequer text of Domesday.[14]

The basic unit of the enquiry was the county and there has naturally been a tendency to study each county survey separately. This has been unavoidable in the Victoria County Histories. There have also been editions published by county societies, those for Cheshire and Lincolnshire being particularly valuable.[15] The same pattern was followed by John Morris in the series of parallel texts and translations that he edited.[16] Such locally based studies have contributed greatly to a better understanding of Domesday, not least by identifying many places, a task slowly being aided by the work of the English Place-Name Society. They also have disadvantages. The identification of many individuals named in Domesday, especially before the Conquest, commonly requires evidence drawn from several counties and many significant features are only revealed by a comparison of different county surveys.[17] There is, therefore, a need to balance and supplement local studies with others that are devoted to the systematic analysis of specific details throughout the whole text and the related manuscripts. This method has been particularly rewarding in the interpretation of terminology, for example, Sally Harvey's demonstration of the meaning of the formula '20 pence in the ora'.[18]

Several scholars have reviewed the evidence of Domesday as a whole with great profit. Welldon Finn, who had a remarkably detailed knowledge of the complete text, published a number of very helpful surveys of the material[19] and R.V. Lennard showed in *Rural England 1086–1135* how much could be gleaned by combining the evidence of Domesday with that of other sources of the period.[20] The most notable single achievement, however, is the Domesday Geography produced under the direction and leadership of H.C. Darby. This was based on separate county surveys but the full value of the enterprise was only brought out in the final volume in which the overall results and many of the problems of interpretation were clearly presented.[21] This remarkable undertaking was generally limited to the text of Domesday Book but some exceptions were made, and with revealing results. In particular the comparison of the places named in the Kentish Domesday with contemporary lists

[14]R. Welldon Finn, 'The Evolution of Successive Versions of Domesday Book', *EHR* LXVI (1951), pp. 561–4.

[15]J. Tait, *The Domesday Survey of Cheshire* (Manchester, Chetham Society, 1916); C.W. Foster and T. Longley, *The Lincolnshire Domesday and the Lindsey Survey* (Lincoln Record Society 19, 1924).

[16]29 volumes have been published (Chichester, Phillimore, 1975–83).

[17]See below, pp. 72–3.

[18]S. Harvey, 'Royal Revenue and Domesday Terminology', *Economic History Review*, Second series, 20 (1967), pp. 221–8.

[19]*An Introduction to Domesday Book* (London, Longmans, 1963); *Domesday Studies: The Liber Exoniensis* (London, Longmans, 1964).

[20]*Rural England 1086–1135. A Study of Social and Agrarian Conditions* (Oxford, Clarendon Press, 1959).

[21]H.C. Darby, *Domesday England* (Cambridge, CUP, 1977).

of Kentish churches clearly demonstrated that Domesday omitted many settlements, especially in the Weald.[22] This is a welcome reminder that the interpretation of Domesday evidence must always take account of the purpose, and the methods, of the enquiry. The compilers were not interested in settlements but in estates. Similarly, markets are only mentioned incidentally[23] and there is reason to believe that in some areas Domesday omitted large numbers of free men or *censarii*.[24]

Future students of Domesday Book will not only have the benefit of all the work that has been done in the past, they will also be able to take advantage of computer technology. Computers will make more sophisticated analyses possible and they will also facilitate the recognition and interpretation of internal features of the text.[25] They can, however, never replace the study of the texts and the manuscripts, even though most students have to be content with facsimiles. It is, for example, clear that the compression of some entries and the spaces left between groups of entries are significant clues to the procedures of the enquiry. Computers will undoubtedly help, not least by providing rapidly accessible indexes, but their value must depend on the reliability of the information fed into them. Even more important, the questions that are posed and the interpretation of the results of computer analyses must always be related to the texts.

Modern students of Domesday, and of eleventh-century England, are fortunate that since the last centenary so much thorough groundwork has been done and so many aids to the study of the text have become available.[26] We may be confident that the coming centenary will stimulate renewed interest in this tantalizing source and hope that as a result we may come closer to the realization of Maitland's dream that the common thoughts of our forefathers about common things will become thinkable once more.[27]

[22]H.C. Darby and Eila M.J. Campbell, ed., *The Domesday Geography of South-East England* (Cambridge, CUP, 1962), pp. 494–500.

[23]P.H. Sawyer, 'Fairs and Markets in Early Medieval England', in Niels Skyum-Nielsen and Niels Lund, eds., *Danish Medieval History New Currents* (Copenhagen, Museum Tusculanum Press, 1981), p. 156.

[24]J.F.R. Walmsley, 'The *Censarii* of Burton Abbey and the Domesday Population', *North Staffordshire Journal of Field Studies* 8 (1968), pp. 73–80.

[25]See below, pp. 169–70.

[26]Two of these merit specific reference: Olof von Feilitzen, *The Pre-Conquest Personal Names of Domesday Book* (Uppsala, Nomina Germanica 3, 1937); H.C. Darby and G.R. Versey, *Domesday Gazetteer* (Cambridge, CUP, 1975).

[27]Maitland, *Domesday Book and Beyond*, p. 520.

CHAPTER TWO

The Precursors of Domesday: Roman and Carolingian Land Registers

John Percival

In the sense that it was a single undertaking, resulting from a single decision at a particular point in time, the Domesday inquest was wholly without parallel in the earlier history of Europe. In this sense it is misleading, perhaps even a little impertinent, to speak of its precursors, as though it were part of some tradition of which the conventions and essential procedures had been worked out long before. Nor is it the purpose of this essay to suggest that this was so. Tempting as it may be to seek evidence for continuity over the centuries (a temptation, be it said, that will not be altogether resisted in what follows), one has to admit that a preoccupation with continuity can have a distorting effect on one's judgement and make one blind to many of the more valuable insights to which a sober comparison and contrast of one period with another can so often lead. It is with comparison and contrast, therefore, that we shall here be primarily concerned.

In this more modest vein, then, one could argue that there were two periods before the eleventh century when something similar to Domesday was put in hand and in due course achieved. In the first of these, beginning essentially with the emperor Augustus and continuing for some four centuries and possibly longer, the lands and peoples of the Empire were incorporated, by survey and formal register, into a system of taxation known to them and to us as the *census*. In the second, beginning in the late eighth century and extending into the ninth and beyond, the great ecclesiastical landowners of the Carolingian kingdoms, prompted in part perhaps by urging and example from their royal masters, undertook the detailed surveys of their estates which resulted in the polyptychs. In neither of these do we have an exact Domesday parallel, whether on the documentary, the institutional or the general historical level. But in each of them there are parallel features, which are numerous enough and significant enough to suggest that a comparison may be fruitful, and shed light, not only forwards from them to Domesday, but backwards from Domesday to them. Such an exercise is given an added interest by the long-held view, attacked on occasions but still widely entertained, that the polyptychs were in some sense derived from *census* records; and although this will not be a central concern in what follows a discussion of it may help to elucidate further the similarities and differences between the systems and periods that we shall be considering.

5

The *census*, as a system for registering citizens, assessing their property and assigning them to their appropriate property classes, had been known in Rome itself from earliest times.[1] Its extension to the provinces by Augustus[2] was intended, in part at least, as a means of replacing the iniquitous system of taxation under which the provincials had hitherto suffered – a system of tax farming whereby a syndicate of wealthy businessmen would contract for the taxes of a given region, pay the agreed sum to the central government, and then proceed to recover their outlay, and an appropriate margin of profit, as quickly and as efficiently as they could. In contrast to this the *census* was, in its developed form and to a large extent from its very beginning, a rating system: lands and people were surveyed and counted, an assessment of them was made, and it was on the basis of this assessment that taxes (or more properly *tributum*, that is 'contributions') were collected. The advantage to the individual tax payer was obvious enough: instead of being confronted with apparently arbitrary demands, he had the assurance that what was asked of him was in some measure related to his ability to pay, and that it was in this sense rational and consistent and (at least relatively) fair. For the central government the advantages were perhaps rather less tangible, and perhaps lay more in the reduction of ill will on the part of the provincials than in any significant improvement in the efficiency with which the revenues were collected.

It has to be said that we know far less than we would like to know about the *census* in these early stages of its history; of its later development we know a good deal more, and there is a serious danger, as has been rightly observed,[3] of projecting our evidence backwards in time in order to complete a picture. One obvious question is that of how, and by whom, the original survey and assessment were made. In the case of Gaul, as we know from a whole series of references,[4] it was supervised at any rate by members of the imperial family, among them Augustus himself, and this has led some scholars to suppose that it must have been centrally organized, and administered by officials answerable directly to the central government. Against this it has been pointed out that the presence of emperors and their officials seems to be linked in the sources with the difficulties encountered in persuading the Gauls to accept the new system –

[1]It was attributed to King Servius Tullius, who ruled in the mid-sixth century BC: cf. Livy I, 42, with R.M. Ogilvie, *A Commentary on Livy, Books 1–5* (Oxford, Clarendon Press, 1965), pp. 166–8. The bibliography on the Roman *census* is enormous, but the following will provide an introduction to work since the war, together with detailed references: A. Déléage, *La capitation du Bas-Empire* (Macon, 1945, repr. New York, Arno Press, 1975); A.H.M. Jones, 'Census Records of the Later Roman Empire', *Journal of Roman Studies* 43 (1953), pp. 49–64 (repr. in *The Roman Economy* (Oxford, Basil Blackwell, 1974), pp. 228–56); F. Lot, *Nouvelles recherches sur l'impôt foncier et la capitation personnelle sous le Bas-Empire* (Paris, Bibl. École des Htes. Études, fasc. 304, 1955); A.H.M. Jones, '*Capitatio* and *Iugatio*', *Journal of Roman Studies* 47 (1957), pp. 88–94 (repr. in *The Roman Economy*, pp. 280–92); A.H.M. Jones, *The Later Roman Empire, 284–602* (Oxford, Basil Blackwell, 1964), ch.xx; W. Goffart, *Caput and Colonate: towards a History of Late Roman Taxation* (Univ. Toronto Press, 1974).

[2]The only province where it is known to have been conducted in Republican times is Sicily: cf. Cicero, *in Verrem* II, 131. For Augustus' own activities see below, note 4; and for the Republican tax-farmers, E. Badian, *Publicans and Sinners: Private Enterprise in the Service of the Roman Republic* (Oxford, Basil Blackwell, 1972).

[3]Goffart, *Caput and Colonate*, p. 4.

[4]Livy, *Periochae* 138, 139; Tacitus, *Annals* I, 31; II, 6; Dio Cassius LIII, 22, 5.

difficulties arising, perhaps, from the imposition of a pattern implying individual ownership or tenure upon a people traditionally accustomed to tenure by kinship groups. In this sense Gaul, and perhaps other areas in the West, might be somewhat special, and the organization elsewhere might more reasonably be supposed to have been the responsibility of the local *civitas*.[5] There is no doubt that the actual collection of the taxes, once the system had been established, was through the community rather than the individual: that is, the community was given an overall assessment, which it then had to raise from the lands and people in its territory. We know this from, among other passages, a clause in the *Digest*[6] which says that a landowner who had properties in more than one *civitas* would have to register these properties separately; only much later was it possible for him to register all his lands in a single package. In other words, it was the *civitas*, as intermediary, which dealt with the central government on the one hand and with the individual tax payer on the other. Indeed, it was the *civitas*, or more particularly its council, or *curia*, which underwrote the *tributum*: individual councillors, or *curiales*, had to undertake the task of collecting it and were required to make good any arrears or non-payments out of their own pockets, with the council as a whole being liable if any of its members defaulted. In this sense there was no need for the central government to involve itself in the actual survey and assessment – unless, of course, there were difficulties connected with these for which the local community needed assistance. Ultimately, as we have said, it was for the central government to say how much it wanted, and for the *civitas* to decide how best to raise the amount required.[7] A likely implication of this, at least in the early stages, was that the *census* need not have been universally adopted, and need not have been uniform in the areas where it was, though there will no doubt have been central advice and guidance for the communities which felt the need of it.

It would be as well as emphasize this point at this stage, because there is an obvious temptation, as with so much of what went on in the Roman Empire, to assume that there was a uniform and universal system, centrally devised and everywhere faithfully adhered to. Even if such a picture were to emerge from the lawbooks we would be wise to retain a degree of scepticism, if only on the general grounds that, given the scale and diversity of the Empire, it would be surprising if administrative (not to say academic) theory were totally reflected in practice. In fact, however, there is no uniformity in the lawbooks themselves, which quite frequently refer to specific local variations or make more general allowance for such variations as may exist. As examples of this we may cite the different formulae for calculating the assessment units known as *capita* (of which more later), or the ruling given in AD399 to the Praetorian Prefect of the Gauls, which was to apply only to those regions 'in which this method of registration is observed'.[8]

[5]The evidence is set out by Goffart, *Caput and Colonate*, pp. 14–17; as he says, the question is what precisely the imperial officials' role was – the actual survey and register, or simply a forceful official presence?

[6]L, 15, 4, 2.

[7]This is not to deny that the central government, in making its demand, would need to have some idea of what, and how much, the *civitas* was able to supply: cf. Jones, *Roman Economy*, p. 177.

[8]*Codex Theodosianus* XI, 1, 26.

This said, and with the appropriate qualifications, it may be helpful to attempt an outline history of the *census* as a first step towards assessing its interest in relation to later exercises of a similar kind. It would appear from the beginning that, as we have already noted, the surveys in the various provinces were of both land and people, and that they formed the basis of two distinct taxes, a *tributum soli*, or land tax, and a *tributum capitis*, or poll tax.[9] Both appear to have been levied at this stage in money, the land tax as a percentage of the valuation of the land, and the poll tax as a simple *per capita* charge. Precisely how the land was valued we do not know, but it seems clear that once the valuation had been carried out both it and the percentage levied remained more or less indefinitely the same. That this was so for the poll tax at any rate is clear from an inscription from Tenos, an island in the Aegean,[10] in which a benefactor sets up an endowment fund to pay the *tributum capitis* of his local community; this would hardly have been practicable if the amount required was liable to frequent fluctuations. The reasons for this apparently rather benevolent attitude on the part of the central government are not immediately obvious: A.H.M. Jones remarks, in noting that Vespasian was the only one of the early emperors known to have raised the rates of *tributum*, that to do so involved 'very great difficulty', though whether this would arise from administrative complications or from hostility on the part of the tax payers we are not really in a position to decide.[11]

Whatever the reasons, a system as static as this would face severe problems in a period of inflation, and it seems clear that in the frightening inflation of the third century, when the value of the *denarius* fell to around a tenth of what it had been a century earlier, the system was virtually abandoned.[12] What appears to have happened during this time is that emperors resorted to irregular requisitions in kind in order to feed and equip their armies, thus by-passing the 'money' stage altogether and so avoiding the trap of an ever decreasing revenue. And when, with Diocletian, the recovery eventually came, it was upon a fairer assessment of these requisitions in kind that the revival and reconstruction of the *census* was based.

The main reform attributed to Diocletian was the institution of the *iugum*, which was an assessment unit intended to standardize, or at least make rather more objective, the calculation of a landowner's tax liability. Instead of working on the valuation of the land in money terms, officials now noted the extent of arable, vineyard, etc. that an individual owned, converted each of these into *iuga* by reference to a given formula, and arrived at a total – the 'rateable value', as it were, of the holding in question. We have, in the so-called Syro-Roman Lawbook of the late fifth century,[13] a statement of the con-

[9]These are most lucidly described by Jones, *Roman Economy*, pp. 164–5; strictly speaking *tributum* is applied, not to the tax itself, but to the total amount produced by it – see Goffart, *Caput and Colonate*, pp. 9–14.

[10]*Inscriptiones Graecae* XII, v, 946.

[11]'Inflation under the Roman Empire', *Economic History Review* 5 (1953), p. 296 (= *Roman Economy*, p.193); the reference is to Suetonius, *Vespasian* 16.

[12]Jones, *Roman Economy*, pp. 168–70.

[13]S. Riccobono, ed., *Fontes Iuris Romani Antejustiniani* (2nd edn, Firenze, 1940), II, pp. 795–6. The most explicit evidence for Diocletian's reform is the papyrus *P. Cair. Isidor.* 1 (A.E.R. Boak

version formula defined by Diocletian for Syria: property is assessed at one *iugum* for every 5 *iugera* of vineyard, 20 *iugera* of arable, 220 *perticae* of old olive trees, and so on (there are different assessments for poorer land or for 'mountain' olives). It is important to recognize, since failure to do so can lead to some very basic confusions, that the *iugum* was an abstract unit on paper rather than a fixed area of land: the Lawbook does not say that a *iugum* consists of 20 *iugera* of arable, but that ownership of 20 *iugera* of arable renders a man liable to pay whatever is the amount corresponding to one *iugum* – the exact phrase is '20 *iugera* of arable gives the *annona* of one *iugum*', *annona* being the word most commonly used to describe the range of foodstuffs and either items provided by the system.[14]

In other parts of the Empire other formulae applied. Inscriptions from the Greek islands and from Asia Minor[15] make it clear that the distinctions between the different qualities of land were not everywhere maintained; and in other regions still it seems to have been customary to treat all land, whether arable or vineyard or whatever, on the same basis. In Africa the standard unit was the *centuria* of 200 *iugera*, which was equated to a *iugum*, and in Italy (in the fifth century at least) the *millena*.[16] There were similar variations in the *caput*, which under Diocletian seems also to have become an assessment unit rather than an actual individual: this is an inference from the Asia Minor and Greek inscriptions already referred to, in which people (and indeed animals, it would appear) are sometimes converted into whole or fractional *capita*. The formula used in these cases is not at all clear – it has been suggested that it might be one *caput* = 1 man = 2 women, with animals perhaps counting as smaller fractions –,[17] but in any case we have evidence that it was different in different parts of the Empire. In some areas a woman counted as one *caput* alongside a man, while in others (such as Egypt) she appears not to have counted at all. One of the most striking variations appears in a ruling given in 386 to the Praetorian Prefect of the East that instead of the existing equations of a *caput* with one man or two women he should now equate it with two and a half men and four women.[18]

Another point that emerges from these same inscriptions is that *iuga* and *capita* seem to have been added together to give an overall total, implying, first, that as assessment units they were equal in value, and second, that we are dealing here, not with two separate taxes, but with a single composite one.[19]

---

and H.C. Youtie, *The Archive of Aurelius Isidorus* (Ann Arbor, 1960), p. 29), the edict of Aristius Optatus, prefect of Egypt in 297: cf. Goffart, *Caput and Colonate*, p. 34, n. 10.

[14]Pointed out, forcefully, by Goffart, *op.cit.*, p. 33, who provides a translation of the passage in question.

[15]Most readily available in Déléage, *Capitation*, pp. 163–96; for a discussion of them see Jones, 'Census Records', and (in more detail) Goffart's *Appendix* I.

[16]*Codex Theodosianus* XI, 28, 13 (*centuria*); *Novellae Valentiniani* V, 1, 4 (*millena*). On the doubtful reference to *millena* in a fourth-century inscription from Volcei (*Corpus Inscriptionum Latinarum* X, 407) see Goffart, p. 113.

[17]Jones, 'Census Records', pp. 50–1 (= *Roman Economy*, pp. 230–1), disputed (with good reason) by Goffart, pp. 119–20.

[18]*Codex Theodosianus* XIII, 11, 2.

The Greek, indeed, conflates the two words ζυγά and κεφαλαί (i.e. *iuga* and *capita*) into a single word ζυγοκεφαλαί, and although this appears not to have happened in Latin texts the phrase *iuga vel capita* is so common that it can be taken as more or less the same thing.[20] This equation of *iuga* with *capita* is a little crude, to say the least, since it would mean (for example) that a small estate with a lot of people on it could be liable for as much as a large estate with few people; and some have therefore felt that this cannot have been part of the original plan of Diocletian but a rather later development of it – an acknowledgement, that is, that the plan as first conceived was rather too subtle. Jones, indeed, argued[21] that in some areas, 'certainly Egypt and probably Africa and part of the Gallic prefecture', the combined system did not operate and therefore that the continuation of the *caput* as the basis of a separate poll tax should not be ruled out. It would seem, however, that the combined system was the normal, if not the universal one, and that *capitatio* is to be seen, in spite of its name, as an integral part of the assessment of land.[22]

The importance of the Diocletianic system, as has been pointed out, was that it made possible a degree of budgetary planning from year to year. Calculations could be made of the likely needs of the armies and other parts of the imperial service, and by an annual *indictio* (in our terms a rate declaration) these needs could be supplied with a minimum of inefficiency and duplication. To use Jones's convenient example, 'if x pounds of pork were required in Palestine, and Palestine was rated at y *iuga*, it was clear that a levy of x/y pounds of pork per *iugum* would meet the case'.[23] In this sense Diocletian, as we have already noted, was simply regularizing the payments in kind which had been irregularly levied during the period of economic instability earlier in the third century. How much further he went is a matter of some dispute: the introduction of the new system would seem to imply a programme of new *census* surveys throughout the Empire, and this is normally assumed to have happened. It has, however, been pointed out that the evidence for this in the sources is less than strong, and it may be that there was a dusting-off and token up-dating of the old records rather than a full-scale attempt to produce new ones.[24] If this was so there will have remained in the system a large measure of inequity, depending on the extent to which the situation on the ground had changed since the original registration. There is evidence, after Diocletian's retirement, of great activity in respect of the *census* by Galerius, part of the motive for which seems to have been to bring more categories of people into the assessment.[25] The hostility which this appears to have aroused may indicate

[19]There is independent evidence for this in *Codex Theodosianus* VII, 6, 3, where *iuga* and *capita* are explicitly equated. The particular Greek inscriptions are those from Astypaleia (*Inscriptiones Graecae* XII³, 180–2) and apparently also one from Thera (*ibid.*, XIII³, 343).

[20]For a list of references see Jones, 'Capitatio and Iugatio', p. 88 (= *Roman Economy*, pp. 280–1).

[21]'*Capitatio* and *Iugatio*', pp. 91–3 (= *Roman Economy*, pp. 286–91).

[22]Goffart, *Caput and Colonate*, pp. 35–40.

[23]'*Capitatio* and *Iugatio*', p. 94 (= *Roman Economy*, p. 292).

[24]New surveys: Jones, *Later Roman Empire*, p. 62; A.C. Johnson and L.C. West, *Byzantine Egypt: Economic Studies* (Princeton, 1949), p. 230; for the alternative view, Goffart, *Caput and Colonate*, pp. 44–6.

[25]Lactantius, *de Mortibus Persecutorum* 23.

that the tax payers in general found the inequities of an out-of-date survey more bearable than those of a new one ruthlessly applied.

The other main development after Diocletian of which we need to take note is the tendency, from the mid-fourth century onwards, for payments in kind to be commuted once again into money payments.[26] This is likely to have been a direct result of Constantine's re-establishment of a stable gold-based currency, and the evidence is that by the beginning of the fifth century the change-over to money payments, in the western Empire at least, was more or less complete.

Such, in outline, is how the Roman system developed and operated. Even in this very general statement, it should be said, there are items which would not be universally agreed to. It is partly, as we have noted, that there were important regional variations in the system itself; partly also that our evidence is spread over several centuries, so that geographical variations can easily be confused with changes over the course of time; and partly again that the references to the *census* and its operations in the sources are often very imprecise – not least in the legal codes themselves, whose authors seem to have paid as much attention to the literary qualities of what they were writing as to its administrative usefulness. For our present purposes, however, a detailed discussion of all the points of dispute would be inappropriate.

One of the main disappointments in all this, from the point of view of later analogies, is that we are so poorly provided with examples of the *census* registers themselves. Outside of Egypt, and apart from a single rather unhelpful fragment from Italy, we are limited to the small collection of inscriptions from the Aegean islands and the Asia Minor coast already referred to.[27] Even from these, however, a number of points emerge, the most important being that they differ considerably from one another, both in the information they contain and in their method of setting it out: some record actual measures of land, others enter it in *iuga*, while others again give both; some distinguish between qualities of land, others do not. To some extent this might be explained by arguing that the inscriptions represent different stages in the registration process: that is to say, some are the preliminary declarations by owners, while others have already begun their transformation into the official record. But even allowing for this it is hard to believe that the official record itself was entirely consistent and standardized, and if this was so for one small area of the Empire it is likely to have been much more so for the Empire as a whole. What seems very clear is that there were no detailed guidelines, let alone instructions, available to either landowners or *census* officials; they were aware of the general principles of the system, they knew the kind of information that the returns would need to contain, and they no doubt had formulae whereby the individual returns could be processed, but there was clearly no *pro forma* to ensure that the returns themselves were standardized.

It is interesting in this context to consider the entry in the *Digest* which at first sight would seem to disprove this assertion.[28] 'This', it begins, 'is how lands

---

[26] Jones, 'Inflation', p. 314 (= *Roman Economy*, p. 220), citing *Codex Theodosianus* XI, 1, 19; 32; 34; 37; Theodoret, *Epistulae* 42.

[27] Above, note 15.   [28] L, 15, 4.

should be registered for the *census*', and it refers to a *forma censualis*, or formal *census* procedure. There follows a list of items that have to be included: the name of the farm concerned, and the names of the *civitas* and *pagus* in which it lies, together with the names of its two nearest neighbours; the amount of arable, in *iugera*; the number of vines and olive trees; the amounts of meadow and pasture, again in *iugera*, and so on. All of this has to be valued, and there are instructions to the registering officer (the *censitor*) as to what action to take regarding farm land lost in landslides or trees that have died. In other words the guidance, though detailed enough, is essentially in the form of a list of items that will be needed, and although the overall layout of the return could be said to be implied we are clearly not being presented here with a *pro forma*, let alone a specimen return. When, later on in the instructions, we read that 'in registering slaves it should be ensured that their nationality, age, duties and particular skills are also registered', it is rather like the instructions familiar to us nowadays from the purchase of goods – 'in the event of a complaint about this product be sure to give your name and address, the invoice number, and say when and where you bought it'. It may be, of course, that the *censitores* under Diocletian and later emperors had something more helpful than this; but there is no evidence to suggest that they had, and if they did not it is hardly surprising that the few actual returns that we have are so different from one another in both form and content.

Of the registration procedures themselves we have seen something already, and there is little more to add. The *censitores* were local officials who actually went to the individual tax payer and carried out the survey on the spot; a declaration, or *professio*, of the property concerned would be drawn up, and it was on the basis of these *professiones* that the main assessment documents were produced. In other words, the instructions in the *Digest*, and any later equivalent of them that there may have been, were instructions to the official rather than to the person whose property was being assessed. In the likely absence of anything other than the kind of general guidelines that we have seen, one imagines that there will have been room for a certain amount of discussion, or even negotiation, between tax payer and official, before the *professio* was finally sent for entry on the official roll. The normal word for this would appear to have been *census*, as in the expression *censibus adscriptus* which means literally 'entered on the *census* register.[29] The word *polyptychum* or *poleticum* appears later in the Empire and indicates something like our modern book, that is, a number of pages fastened together as opposed to a scroll.[30] The word is of course a highly evocative one for students of the Carolingian period, and we shall need to consider later whether there is any significance to be attached to its use in these two contexts; for the moment we may simply make the uncontroversial point that it indicates that the registers were normally of a perishable rather than a permanent form. The inscriptions on stone to which we referred earlier would appear, therefore, to have been the exception – perhaps, as has been suggested, a temporary fashion, and appropriate anyway to a period when a

---

[29]*Codex Justinianus* I, 3, 20, 1; *Codex Theodosianus* V, 6, 3; XI, 3, 2, etc.

[30]Below, note 56; for the format itself, see L.D. Reynolds and N.G. Wilson, *Scribes and Scholars* (2nd edn, Oxford, 1974), pp. 30–2.

man's appearance on the registers was an indication of status which he might well see fit to advertise by reproducing it in a more public and more durable form.[31] Whatever their form, however, they were essentially local documents, the concern of local communities and presumably lodged in local archives. We have no reason to suppose that the records of even a single province, let alone the Empire as a whole, were ever collected together in a kind of Roman Domesday; indeed, everything that we know about the machinery of the *census* would suggest that this was not the case. The nearest equivalent of Domesday in this sense might be a kind of summary document, in the office of the provincial governor or the Praetorian Prefect, listing the various communities under his authority with the totals of *iuga* or *capita* against them.

The mention of the term *polyptychum* leads naturally to a consideration of its later resurgence as applied to the ecclesiastical estate registers of the ninth century, which have provided the material for an enormous range of studies since they first began to appear in printed editions a century and a half ago.[32] If we accept brief fragments on the one hand or survival in later manuscripts on the other we have nearly two dozen documents to which the term could reasonably be applied – documents, that is, which within a broadly similar framework record the estates of the church or abbey in question, giving details of their location, nature and extent, the pattern of their tenure and administration, and the income (in money, kind or labour) derivable from them. They come from two main regions: from north-eastern France and the Rhineland; and from northern Italy. In general the ones from Italy are less detailed and less carefully compiled than the others, though in both regions there is such variation in this respect that generalizations of this kind may not be particularly helpful. The majority of the documents are from the ninth century, and the best of them can be dated to about 850 or soon after; there is one exception, the so-called polyptych of Irminon, relating to the lands of St-Germain-des-Prés in Paris, which has to be earlier than 828, the year of the death of the abbot who

[31]Goffart, *Caput and Colonate*, pp. 29–30, 121.

[32]The most convenient list of polyptychs is in C.H. Taylor, 'Note on the Origin of the Polyptychs', *Mélanges d'histoire offerts à Henri Pirenne* (Bruxelles, 1926), pp. 475–81, which can be supplemented for the Italian examples from D. Herlihy, 'The History of the Rural Seigneury in Italy, 751–1200', *Agricultural History* 33 (1959), p. 58, n. 4. Details of those referred to in this essay are as follows:

St-Germain des Prés: B. Guérard, *Polyptyque de l'abbé Irminon* (Paris, 1836–44); A. Longnon, *Polyptyque de l'abbaye de St-Germain des Prés* (Paris, 1886–95).

St-Rémy de Reims: B. Guérard, *Polyptyque de l'abbaye de St-Rémi de Reims (Paris, 1853).*

Prüm: H. Beyer, *Urkundenbuch zur Geschichte der . . . mittelrheinischen Territorien* I (Coblenz, 1860), no. 135, pp. 142–201.

Montiérender: C. Lalore, *Le polyptyque de l'abbaye de Montiérender* (Paris, 1878).

Lobbes: J. Warichez, 'Une *descriptio villarum* de l'abbaye de Lobbes a l'époque carolingienne', *Bull. Comm. Roy. d'Hist.* 78 (1909), pp. 245–67.

St-Bertin: B. Guérard, *Cartulaire de l'abbaye de St-Bertin* (Paris, *Coll. de docs. inédits pour l'hist. de France*, 1ère serie III (1841)); G.W. Coopland, 'The Abbey of St-Bertin and its Neighbourhood, 900–1350', in P. Vinogradoff, ed., *Oxford Studies in Social and Legal History* IV (1914), pp. 1–166.

Bobbio: C. Cipolla, ed. *Codice diplomatico del monasterio di S. Colombano di Bobbio* (Rome, *Fonti per la storia d'Italia* 52–53 (1918)), no 63, pp. 184–217.

compiled it and after whom it is named. As well as being the earliest example (indeed, the only reasonably complete one which can be regarded as more or less contemporary with Charlemagne himself), it is also by far the fullest and most detailed, and for this reason is the one to which scholars most naturally turn in the first instance as a guide to the rest.[33]

The form and content of this remarkable document are immediately apparent from its first complete section, which relates to *Palatiólum*, now Palaiseau, a commune on the southern outskirts of Paris itself.[34] This section, like the other 24 that we have, is in the form of a *breve*, or brief, describing a single administrative unit, or *fiscus*, of the abbey's lands. It begins with a detailed description of the demesne, noting the existence of a house, or *casa*, and giving the amounts of arable land, vineyard, pasture and woodland associated with it. The arable is said to comprise six main fields, or *culturae*, and we are told the amount of grain required to sow it; for the vineyard and pasture we are given the expected yield of wine and hay, and for the woodland an estimate of the number of pigs that can be fattened within it. There is mention of three mills, with their combined income, and of two churches, one at Palaiseau itself and one at Gif, some eight kilometres away to the west; for each of these we are given the associated holdings, again with the amounts of the various types of land, and the dues and services rendered by their tenants. There follow the entries for the dependent *mansi*, 117 entries in all, five of them servile and the rest free (*ingenuiles*). In each case we are given the names of the holder and his wife (in the majority of them there are in fact more than one couple), their status (*colonus*, *servus*, etc.), and the names of their children. This is followed by the amounts of arable, vineyard and pasture attached to the holding, and after this come details of payments in money and kind and of the various types of service. At the end of the Palaiseau section there is a brief list of those who pay the head tax known as *capaticum*, a list of the 21 people, led by the *major*, who have sworn to the accuracy of the entries, and finally a brief summary giving totals of manses, payments and so on. The whole section takes up just over 20 pages of Longnon's edition of 1886, and relates to close on 650 named individuals and a total area probably in excess of 1,000 hectares. The same basic format is followed for the other *fisci*, the main variations occurring in those where the abbey's lands are dispersed among several centres rather than clustered around one.

Of the other polyptychs that we have only a handful come anywhere near the Irminon one in length or detail, the nearest in both respects being those of St-Remy at Reims and of Prüm in the Rhineland. More typical of the rest are those of Montiérender in Haute-Marne, Lobbes in the Hainault province of Belgium, and St-Bertin, near St-Omer in the Pas-de-Calais, which describe the demesnes in each fisc in a fair amount of detail and then summarize the dependent holdings by giving totals of free and servile manses and indicating the dues and services appropriate to each type. It is a measure of the bounty of

---

[33]As an example (and also as a useful introduction to the document) see R. Latouche, *The Birth of Western Economy* (London, Methuen, 1961, translation of French edn., Paris, 1956), pp. 190–208.

[34]Text in Guérard II, pp. 6–23; Longnon II, pp. 7–28.

Irminon that these 'lesser' polyptychs, which themselves contain a wealth of extremely valuable information, and which in any other period would be regarded as sources of central importance, have tended to be somewhat neglected. There is, clearly, a danger here – not so much that we may forget the others and regard Irminon as unique, but rather the converse, that we may think of him as typical. He is in fact very special, and only by considering the collection of polyptychs as a whole can we appreciate the wide variation in quality that they display and so attempt to assess their significance in the broader context.

There is, as we have seen, a concentration of documents of the polyptych type in two distinct regions, and this might be thought to preclude the possibility that they were a response to any central directive or initiative, that is, from the court itself. We do, nevertheless, need some explanation why so many of them should have appeared within a few decades of one another, and it may indeed be that they were prompted in some way or other by Charlemagne and his immediate successors. It is only in recent years, indeed, that such a view has come to be seriously doubted, and the traditional view, certainly, was that they were part of the wider economic programme of Charlemagne himself.[35] In support of this one could cite the capitularies in which the great ecclesiastical landlords were exhorted to compile inventories of their estates,[36] and if further proof were needed there was the capitulary *de Villis*,[37] which showed the scrupulous concern of Charlemagne for his own estates, and the so-called *Brevium Exempla*,[38] which was seen as an official model provided by him as a guide to others. It is in connection with these last two documents, however, that doubts have arisen, since neither can be securely dated and neither can be firmly assigned to Charlemagne. The capitulary *de Villis* is thought by some scholars, on linguistic grounds, to be an enactment of Louis the Pious relating to his kingdom of Aquitaine, and although this has been disputed there is sufficient doubt on the matter to lessen its value in this context. The *Brevium Exempla*, which does indeed appear to be a model inventory of a series of miscellaneous

[35]The theory of a royal origin goes back to Guérard and particularly to K.T. von Inama-Sternegg, *Deutsche Wirtschaftsgeschichte* (Leipzig, 2nd edn, 1909). The latter's notion of a large-scale programme of economic reform on the part of Charlemagne has been attacked by (among others) A. Dopsch, *The Economic and Social Foundations of European Civilization* (London, Kegan Paul, 1937, abridged translation of German 2nd edn, Vienna, 1923-4); L. Halphen, *Études critiques sur l'histoire de Charlemagne* (Paris, 1921); J. Calmette, *Charlemagne, sa vie et son oeuvre* (Paris, 1945).

[36]*Monumenta Germaniae Historica, Legum II, Capitularia Regum Francorum I* (A. Boretius, ed., Hanover, 1883), no. 49, 4; no. 80, 5-7.

[37]Boretius, no. 32, translated in H.R. Loyn and J. Percival, *The Reign of Charlemagne* (London, Edward Arnold, 1975), pp. 64-73, and discussed in general terms by Latouche, *Western Economy*, pp. 176-89. For the arguments about its date, authorship and purpose see K. Verhein, 'Studien zu den Quellen zum Reichsgut der Karolingerzeit: das *Capitulare de Villis*', *Deutsches Archiv* 10 (1954), pp. 322-94, and T. Mayer, 'Das *Capitulare de Villis*', *Zeitschrift der Savigny Stiftung für Rechtsgeschichte, German. Abt.* 79 (1962), pp. 1-31, both of which give detailed references to earlier work. There is now a facsimile edition, edited by C. Brühl (*Dokumente der deutschen Geschichte in Faksimile*, Reihe 1, Bd 1, Stuttgart, 1971).

[38]Boretius, no. 128, translated in Loyn and Percival, pp. 98-105. For detailed discussion see W. Metz, 'Zur Entstehung der Brevium Exempla', *Deutsches Archiv* 10 (1954), pp. 395-416, and the second part of Verhein's article, *ibid.* 11 (1955), pp. 333-92.

estates, and in some respects is strikingly similar to a polyptych,[39] has nothing overtly royal or official about it and could as easily come from a private source. Again, as has been pointed out, the ecclesiastical landlords had long been accustomed to the keeping of efficient records, and there are references as early as Pope Gregory the Great (590–604) to the compilation of estate inventories, apparently on a quite large scale.[40] In this respect it could be maintained that they had more to teach Charlemagne than he them, and far from giving a lead the capitulary *de Villis* might be seen as an attempt to bring his own estates up to the standard of theirs. On this extreme view, then, the appearance of the polyptychs is the result of private enterprise rather than central direction, explicable perhaps in terms of local fashions or possibly as a response to particular threats or challenges. Nevertheless, the notion of some official influence is difficult to dismiss from one's mind entirely, and it may yet, though unprovable, be correct.

Whatever the motivation, the decision to compile such a register can hardly have been taken lightly, since even the more modest ones, let alone that of Irminon, will have involved a very considerable amount of work and organization. The way in which this was managed will no doubt have differed from place to place, but a close examination of one example has given a fairly clear picture of its manner of compilation, and it may be of interest to look at this a little more closely. The register of the estates of the abbey of Prüm, in the Rhineland north of Trier,[41] is preserved for us in a manuscript of 1222, which purports to be a copy, with commentary, of the 'original' register of 893. There are some complications arising from doubts about the faithfulness of the copy, and from the possibility that the supposed original may itself have been copied from an even earlier document, but for our present purposes these are not too serious. The first point to note is that the entries for the various *fisci* of the abbey are arranged in a recognizably geographical order, beginning with those in the immediate neighbourhood and then moving round in a clockwise direction beginning in the south-east. Exceptions to this, which are few, can readily be explained, either on the view that entries arrived late, or, more probably, that parts of the manuscript got out of order at some stage in the transmission. The second point is that there are differences of detail in the way that the different entries are set out, and that these differences seem also to be explicable in geographical terms. Thus, to take a specific example, in entries XXX–XXXII, which refer to three *fisci* close to one another in the Glahn and Nahe valleys south-east of Trier, the regular beginning is of the form 'In N. est terra dominicata ad seminandos modios . . .'; whereas in entries XXXIV–XLIII, referring to

[39]Compare, for example, the second part of the entry for Staffelsee with the standard entries in the Prüm register.

[40]Below, note 66. For an interesting suggestion that a number of passages in Flodoard's *History of the Church of Reims*, the earliest relating to the first quarter of the seventh century, are references to documents of the polyptych type see W. Goffart, 'From Roman Taxation to Medieval Seigneurie', *Speculum* 47 (1972), pp. 165–87, 373–94 (the Flodoard suggestion is first stated on pp. 375–6).

[41]Discussed, as his first and most important item, by C.-E. Perrin, *Recherches sur la seigneurie rurale en Lorraine d'après les plus anciens censiers* (IXe–XIIe siècle) (Paris, *Publ. de la Fac. des Lettres de l'Univ. de Strasbourg*, Fasc. 71, 1935), pp. 2–98.

a whole series of *fisci* in the Metz region of northern France, we have 'Est in N. mansus indominicatus, ubi aspicit terra arabilis ad seminandos modios . . .' In other words, we are given the same basic information but in subtly different ways. The clear conclusion from this is that different people were responsible for the different districts, presumably being sent out to them to collect the necessary information and record it for transcription into the main register. For the purposes for which the register was intended these small variations of wording were not important, and there was no need to standardize the entries provided they contained the right categories of information. Essentially, that is, the task of the central 'office' was to assemble the entries in order and to copy them out more or less as they stood, altering only such first-person expressions as 'Invenimus ibi . . .', and so on – and even these slipped through on occasions. How far the procedure identified for Prüm can be assumed for the other registers one cannot say; even for Prüm it has been argued that one group of entries may have been prepared, not by a commission sent out from the centre, but locally by monks from two dependent priories,[42] and it may be that what was exceptional here was the rule elsewhere. The estates in the polyptych of Irminon are geographically arranged in the sense that the *fisci* which are close to each other on the ground are frequently described in consecutive entries, and that the *fisci* which are at some distance from the abbey are all grouped together in entries VIII–XIII; but there is no overall geographical arrangement as seems to be the case at Prüm. Again, though there are some variations in wording from one entry to another, such as the uncertainty between *dominicatus* and *indominicatus*, there is a far greater degree of standardization – which may, of course, simply reflect a more careful collator at the centre. What we do have in Irminon's register, as we have already noted, are the lists of local jurors, who will presumably have sworn to the entry at the point when the commissioners left the district to return to the abbey. In the St-Remy polyptych of Reims there is no detectable geographical pattern, but a quite striking variation in wording: 'In N. est mansus dominicatus . . .', 'In N. habet mansum dominicatum . . .', 'In N. habetur mansus dominicatus . . .', and so on, suggesting something like the arrangements identified at Prüm.

Variations of wording and detail apart, the basic format of the polyptychs is fairly standard: all but the slightest of them consist of a series of entries, or chapters, each devoted to a single estate unit, the appropriate term for which is clearly *fiscus*, even though this is not always (or indeed often) specifically applied to them. The standard *fiscus* comprised a demesne, with its associated lands, churches, mills and personnel, and a number of dependent *mansi*, free and servile, held by people described as *coloni* or *servi* (though not necessarily matching the status of their holdings), plus in some cases a number of *hospitia* and other minor holdings. In many cases the abbey's lands in a given *fiscus* appear to be consolidated, with the result that the *fiscus* is effectively a village. Thus the demesne and 54 *mansi* held by St-Germain at *Spinogilum* (Épinay-sur-Orge, Essonne)[43] may well have been, more or less in their own right, the

[42]Perrin, pp. 54–7.
[43]Guérard II, pp. 52–9; Longnon II, pp. 66–76.

village which gave the *fiscus* its name, except of course that there are likely to have been some lands in the village's territory which were owned by persons other than the abbey. Clearly, however, there will have been many cases in which this was not so, most notably in areas where the abbey's possessions were not so numerous: thus the $11\frac{1}{2}$ *mansi* dependent on the demesne at *Colridum* (Coudray-sur-Seine, some 20 kilometres south-east of Épinay)[44] are no evidence that *Colridum* was at that time a small village, but simply that the abbey had less land there than at *Spinogilum*. Indeed, it is not even a valid inference that *Colridum* was a village at all, since it seems clear that a *fiscus* was an administrative unit, territorially based certainly, but not implying any one pattern of settlement. This becomes most evident when we see such a *fiscus* as *Villamilt*, identified with Villemeux, Eure-et-Loir,[45] and significantly among the more distant of the abbey's possessions; here the *mansi* are dispersed over several dozen localities, a handful in each, and it is clearly administrative convenience rather than any territorial unity which gives the *fiscus* its raison-d'être.

In other words, we have a problem very familiar to students of Domesday, that of interpreting a document which imposes a seigneurial pattern upon a territorial one; the only difference is that, whereas in Domesday we have all (or most of) the information and can reconstruct the vills, albeit laboriously, by rearranging it, with the polyptychs we have only one section of the information, so that the task of reconstruction is that much more difficult. The mention of vills, moreover, reminds us that even at the territorial level there are problems of interpretation. In the polyptychs, as in Domesday, the standard unit of settlement above the individual holding is the *villa*, or its apparent diminutive *villaris*: holdings are listed as being 'in villa N.', and several of the *fisci* of the French abbeys have names of which *villa* or *villaris* is a part.[46] This is hardly the place for a detailed discussion of the history of this most fundamental term, which in the Roman period has a distinctly seigneurial flavour and means essentially a farm or estate, later develops a more territorial meaning approaching that of a parish, and eventually narrows down to denoting a nucleated village (one simplifies, of course, no doubt excessively).[47] At its meaning in the ninth-century polyptychs we can at the moment do little more than guess: it seems possible that in the majority of cases where it occurs it actually refers to a village, and to this extent the *villae* of the polyptychs may normally be villages, but this is not the same as saying that 'village' is the meaning of the term.

Nor is this the only problem confronting the student who attempts to look through the documentary record to the situation on the ground. Being compiled for the use of particular people, the documents naturally tend to omit

[44]Guérard II, pp. 197–8; Longnon II, pp. 256–7.

[45]Guérard II, pp. 76–116; Longnon II, pp. 98–154

[46]St-Germain VII, *Villare*; XV, *Villanova*; XXV, *Mansionis Villa*; St-Remy XV, *Villaris*; XIX, *Beconis Villa*; XXVII, *Longa Villa*, etc.

[47]For an introduction to the Roman material see J. Percival, *The Roman Villa* (London, Batsford, 1976), pp. 13–15; and for an exhaustive discussion of this and related terms in the medieval period G. Fournier, *Le peuplement rural en Basse Auvergne durant le haute moyen-age* (Paris, Publ. de la Fac. des Lettres de Clermont-Ferrand, 2me série, Fasc. 12, 1962), pp. 218–327.

matters which those people knew already or in which they had no interest, and there are any number of pitfalls to trap the unwary modern reader, who may interpret silence in quite the wrong way.[48] It was possible, for example, for a man to hold a manse in one locality and live in another: occasionally the more detailed registers tell us this,[49] but one suspects that it is normally not thought worth recording. Even the overall distribution of manses within a given *fiscus* may not be indicated, with the result that it is at best detectable only from chance references to individual items[50] or at worst not detectable at all. More fundamentally, it seems likely that in the majority of cases what the registers comprise is a list of those *fisci* which were directly concerned with the maintenance of the church or abbey in question; the ones that were not so concerned, but were (for example) held as *beneficia*, may either be listed in summary form only, as in an annexe to the St-Remy register,[51] or not referred to at all.

There is also the question of whether, in the details of land areas and so on, we are dealing with real or notional units. One's impression, certainly, so far as the fullest of the registers are concerned, is that we are dealing with real ones, if only because of the wide variations from one holding to another and the comparative lack of suspiciously 'round' figures. Turning again to the entry for *Palatiolum* in the Irminon register,[52] and looking simply at the numbers of *bunuaria* of arable attached to individual manses, we get the following series: 7, 10, 4, 12, 12, $2\frac{1}{2}$, 2, 3, 3, 6, 3, 3, 5. . ., and similar series emerge from the *fisci* that follow. The rather high frequency of the figure 3, and multiples of 3, may cause us to hesitate somewhat, but this is much more likely, one would have thought, to be explicable in terms of a three-field system, with holdings distributed over the main fields, than as the result of some notional assessment. The figures from St-Bertin are of interest in this context, since the standardization there is much more striking. Of the 250-odd manses referred to in the register some 136 are of 12 *bunuaria*; in nine of the 14 *fisci* all manses are of this size, in two others they are all of 10 and 20 *bunuaria* respectively, and only in three *fisci* is there any variation. Again, it is the multiples of 3 which dominate, and again we are probably dealing with holdings in the form of dispersed parcels rather than consolidated blocks.[53] It is difficult, in any case, to see what the purpose of a system of assessment units would be, since the dues and services of each holding are fixed already and appear, where we have sufficient evidence to check this, to have little or no correlation with the holding's size. This is a matter which needs further examination, however, and it would be unwise to adopt too firm a position at this stage in our understanding of it.

[48]See, for example, J. Percival, 'Ninth-century polyptyques and the Villa-system', *Latomus* 25 (1966), pp. 134–8, replying to S. Applebaum, *ibid.* 23 (1964), pp. 774–87.

[49]St-Germain IX, 44; XXI, 3; XXII, 4, etc.

[50]For an example see C.-E. Perrin, 'A propos d'une redevance en *fossoirs* inscrite au Polyptyque d'Irminon', *Études d'histoire du droit privé offertes à Pierre Petot* (Paris, 1959), pp. 431–40.

[51]The *beneficia* appear as chapter XXVI, one of a series of miscellaneous chapters at the end of the register. There is a similar reference to *beneficia* in one of the *fragmenta* added by Guérard to the St-Germain register: in this case they may have been the subject of a second volume (cf. Longnon's edition, pp. 10–11).

[52]Above, note 34.

[53]For a similar point see A. Déléage, *La vie rurale en Bourgogne jusqu'au début du onzième siècle* (Macon, 1941), p. 466.

The aim so far in this essay has been to consider two periods in the earlier history of Europe when something like the Domesday survey can be said to have taken place, in the hope that similarities between one or other of them and Domesday itself will suggest themselves – and, indeed, that the dissimilarities may in their own way be equally enlightening. It may be helpful, in conclusion, to ask how far these earlier episodes represent a continuous tradition in the surveying and registering of estates, or whether we are to see them as isolated phenomena and as the responses to particular situations and needs.

We have noted already that the compilation of estate inventories was not a ninth-century innovation so far as the great ecclesiastical landowners were concerned, in that they had at least been encouraged to compile them, not only by earlier temporal rulers, but by popes as far back as Gregory the Great. It would be very surprising, in any case, if the stream of bequests and donations great and small had not prompted some at least of them to contemplate the construction of a composite list of their estates, not necessarily as something to confirm title (which the original charters could do equally well, or better), but as an overall indication of their wealth and of where they might look for returns of one kind or another. What the likely form of such documents may have been we can only guess: it has been suggested by Perrin[54] that they will have been very different from the registers with which we have so far been concerned, but his reasons for this view are not particularly convincing. What, in the earlier capitularies, the churches were being asked to provide were *descriptiones*, and Perrin sees this as implying that they were something less than polyptychs, for which the term *polyptycha* would by this time have been the regular one. This seems a particularly weak argument in the sense that *descriptiones*, though no doubt a specific and technical term in some contexts, could well have been here a more general one, and have included polyptychs as well as other forms of inventory; and it will seem a rather ironic argument to students of Domesday Book, which is the greatest of all the polyptychs and refers to itself as a *descriptio* on a number of occasions.[55]

This particular discussion of terms is in any case only part of a greater one, which concerns the ultimate origins of registers of the polyptych type. *Descriptio*, and more significantly *polyptychum*, are terms which appear to have been regularly applied to the *census* records of the later Roman Empire,[56] and scholars have long been tempted to see this as an indication that the one kind of document is in fact the ancestor of the other. Some have gone further, and argued, not merely for the survival of documents and a continuing documentary tradition, but for the survival in some sense of the *census* system itself, and have sought to derive units such as the manse or the hide from Roman

---

[54]*Seigneurie rurale*, pp. 605–6.
[55]Fol.II, 3ai, 252ai, 269a2, etc.; cf. R. Welldon Finn, *The Domesday Inquest* (London, Longmans, 1961), p. 34; V.H. Galbraith, *The Making of Domesday Book* (Oxford, 1961), pp. 180–5.
[56]*Polyptychum*: Vegetius, *Epitome rei militaris* II, 19; Cassiodorus, *Variae* V, 39, 44; *Codex Theodosianus* XIII, 11, 13; XIII, 28, 13, etc. (cf. Goffart, 'Medieval Seigneurie', pp. 376–9). *Descriptio*: *Codex Theodosianus* VIII, 11, 1; XII, 4, 1, etc.

prototypes.[57] This more radical view, which becomes steadily less attractive the more we come to understand the way in which the *census* worked, is fortunately outside our present concern, but the more modest one, concerning the documents alone, is rather more attractive. It is, of course, a very old view, and there is little to be gained from merely going once more over the old ground. It has, on the other hand, tended to suffer somewhat from the way in which it was presented by its early exponents, and we are now in a position, precisely because of the clearer picture which is emerging at the Roman end of the process, to see it in somewhat better perspective.[58] Whether or not this brings us any closer to a final judgement on its validity is still doubtful, but a consideration of it in an up-dated version may at least shed light on some of the more general themes with which we have been concerned.

The end of the Roman *census*, like the end of the Roman Empire, is not something to which one can assign a single, everywhere applicable date. In some areas it will have fallen into disuse while the Empire was still officially flourishing, while in others it may well have survived the Empire by many generations. There is in antiquity no lack of examples of conquering powers continuing to collect the tributes and taxes of their predecessors, and in parts of the former Empire where there was a strong local authority we must expect the same thing to have occurred. In the Gothic kingdoms of the early sixth century the machinery of the *census* is still visible: there is still an annual *indictio*, appeal can still be made to the *polyptycha publica*, and when there are abuses in the provision of *paraveredi* or unduly harsh exactions of tribute it is by reference to these, and not simply by arbitrary reductions, that the grievances are dealt with.[59] For the Merovingian kings the evidence is less explicit and the machinery less clear: here too there are *descriptiones*, which provoke violent reaction if they are *novae* or *iniquae* (or if there is an attempt to apply them to a community which believes itself to be immune), but which otherwise appear to be a normal and accepted thing.[60] More than this it is difficult to say: the new ones ordained by Chilperic, which were destroyed by an angry populace at Limoges, were sufficiently detailed to enable dues to be exacted in respect of both lands and people, and for a charge of an amphora of wine from each *aripennis* of vineyard. Of the form of these documents, or of how they were compiled, we know nothing beyond what we can reconstruct from these brief refer-

[57]The classic statement of the theory of documentary continuity is by J. Susta, 'Zur Geschichte und Kritik der Urbarialaufzeichnungen', *Sitzungsberichte der Kaiserlichen Akademie der Wissenschaften, Phil.-hist. Classe* 138 (1897), pp. 1–72; this was attacked by C.H. Taylor, 'Origin of the Polyptychs' (above, note 32). As examples of the more radical view, see M. Bloch, *French Rural History* (London, Routledge & Kegan Paul, 1966, translation of French edn., Oslo, 1931, repr. Paris, 1960), pp. 155–6; F. Lot, 'Le *jugum*, le manse et les exploitations agricoles de la France moderne', *Mélanges Pirenne* (above, note 32), pp. 307–26; and more recently D. Herlihy, 'The Carolingian Mansus', *Economic History Review* 13 (1960–1), pp. 79–89.

[58]For a very thorough survey of the evidence, and a statement of the present position, see Goffart, 'Medieval Seigneurie', pp. 373–94; cf. also his two most recent contributions, 'Merovingian Polyptychs. Reflections on Two Recent Publications', *Francia* 9 (1981), pp. 57–78, and 'Old and New in Merovingian Taxation', *Past and Present* 95 (1982), pp. 3–21.

[59]Cassiodorus, *Variae* IV, 38; V, 39; IX, 10; IX, 12, etc.

[60]Gregory of Tours V, 21, 26 (Chilperic); IX, 30 (Childbert II), etc.; cf. Jones, *Later Roman Empire* I, pp. 261–2.

ences – which is very little: but there is enough about them that is familiar to make it hard for us to believe that either they or the system to which they are related are something utterly new and not simply the latest phase of something decidedly old. 'System', of course, is a word which assumes a great deal, and it seems likely that it is somewhat over-complimentary as applied to the *census* in either Gothic Italy or Merovingian Gaul. Taken in their wider political and economic context, what these references seem to reveal is not so much a system as a miscellaneous collection of documents, procedures, customs, which are made use of if it is profitable or convenient to do so. There is no evidence that they were everywhere in existence, or that where they did exist they were applied consistently or in the manner for which they had been devised. Their continuing existence is the result of their usefulness to certain people for certain purposes, and it is unlikely to be more deeply significant than this.

The same must be true, incidentally, of the quite frequent mention in the polyptychs of dues and services which seem to be reminiscent of *census* procedures. The most obvious is the provision of *paraveredi*, which is still a requirement on the estates of St-Germain and Montiérender, though not apparently St-Remy.[61] There is also the very common requirement to provide beef and pork for the army (*hostilitium* and *carnaticum*), which might indicate the survival of some aspects of the Roman *annona*;[62] and also (though here one is entering something of a minefield) the occasional references to 'capital' payments (*capitale, census de capite, capitalicium* and so on), which are most naturally interpreted as the remains of a system in which *capita* were the units of assessment.[63] But it is clearly the remains with which we are dealing, and fragmentary remains at that, rather than the system itself in any meaningful sense; and there is, even more clearly, a considerable risk involved in assuming that because the technical terms are still being used the institutions for which they were originally devised must still be in existence.

A more tenable line of argument, then, is roughly as follows: the practice of compiling estate registers, whether by lay or by ecclesiastical landowners, was in large measure a by-product of the *census* and its various procedures. The motivation for the practice, which could well have begun within the Roman period, is likely to have been complex rather than simple: one could envisage a situation, for example, in which a landowner, in assisting in the preparation of the *census* return for his estate, might keep a copy, as it were, for his own use (one thinks, in an analogous context, of some of the suggestions which have been made concerning the *Inquisitio Eliensis*[64]); equally, one can imagine a church or monastery, enjoying immunity for its estates from the demands of the *census*, recognizing the value of such registers and turning to the census records as the obvious and appropriate models. Ferdinand Lot, indeed, was tempted by the

[61] St-Germain I, 38; II, 6; IX, 48, etc.; Montiérender III, etc. For the workings of the system in the Roman period see Jones, *Later Roman Empire* II, pp. 830-4.
[62] *Hostilitium*: St-Germain I, 42; II, 121, etc.; St-Remy VII, 2; IX, 5, etc. *Carnaticum*: St-Germain IV, 35; XXII, 70, etc.
[63] St-Germain I, 42; IX, 4; XII, 20, etc.; St-Remy VII, 2; XVII, 2. etc.
[64] Galbraith, *Making of Domesday Book*, p. 141; cf. the similar comments in D.C. Douglas, ed., *The Domesday Monachorum of Christ Church Canterbury* (London, Royal Historical Society, 1944), p. 20.

idea that a grant of immunity might have been marked by the handing over of the *census* records for the estate in question,[65] but what little evidence we have seems to be against this, and it is not a necessary part of the hypothesis in any case. As the *census* gradually disintegrated (so the argument goes), these 'private' registers would be its only legacy, appropriating its terms and evolving over the generations to meet particular needs.

But how can such a hypothesis be tested, and what evidence is there, apart from the apparent development in terminology, to back it up? Have we any indication of what these 'private' registers may have been like, and how early are they? The evidence from the time of Gregory the Great is somewhat ambivalent: there is a statement in the *Life* of Gregory by Johannes Diaconus that he had the *reditus* of all the *patrimonia* and *praedia* of the church inscribed in a *polyptychum*, with details of the various payments that were made at certain times of the year; the use of the word *polyptychum* suggests a sizeable document, and thus something rather more than a summary list and probably a register of the individual estates with the amounts due from each.[66] In one of the *Letters*, on the other hand, there is a *polyptychum* of a rather different kind: Gregory's instructions to restore to one Calixenus a *domus* which had been donated to the church by his grandmother have been disobeyed on the grounds that the *notitia* of the donation had not been deleted from the *polyptychum*, which in this case appears to be, not a register of the kind suggested, but simply a collection of individual *notitiae*.[67]

More helpful (and interesting, too, on a number of other grounds) is the mid-sixth-century papyrus from north Italy known nowadays as *P. Ital.* 3,[68] which appears to be part of a register of the estates of the church of Ravenna. The text as we have it concerns two estates, and although the entry for the first of them lacks a beginning there is enough remaining to show that the layout in each case was a the same. In each there is a series of holdings, or *coloniae*, identified by name and by the names of the people responsible for them; the rest of the information, apart from an occasional note regarding a particular farm's condition, concerns payments and services due from the holders, that is to say the *coloni*, to the landlord. At the head of the entry for the second estate is the description: *Terr(itorio) Patavino*, which suggests that the first estate may have belonged to a different 'territory', and that what we have here is a mere fragment of a rather extensive document covering all the lands under the one ownership within a given region. This is further suggested by the note at the end of the document which gives totals for the various items of food: the 8,880

---

[65] *L'Impôt foncier et la capitation personelle sous le Bas-Empire et à l'époque franque* (Paris, Bibl. École des Htes. Études, Fasc. 253, 1928), p. 119.

[66] *Vita Greg. Max* II, 24 (in Migne, *Patrologia Latina*, vol. 75); the document is in fact attributed to Pope Gelasius (492-6).

[67] *Ep.* IX, 199 (in *Monumenta Germaniae Historica, Epp.* II, = IX, 40 in Migne, *Patrologia Latina*, vol. 77).

[68] J.-O. Tjäder, *Die nichtliterarischen lateinischen Papyri Italiens aus der Zeit 445-700* (Lund, *Skrifter utgivna av Svenska Institutet i Rom*, 4° XIX: 1, 1955), no. 3, pp. 184-9 (text), 408-10 (commentary). Among recent discussions see L. Ruggini, *Economia e Società nell' Italia Annonaria* (Milano, 1961), pp. 407-25; Jones, *Later Roman Empire* II, pp. 803-8; J. Percival, '*P. Ital.* 3 and Roman Estate Management', *Hommages à Marcel Renard* (Bruxelles, *Collection Latomus* 102, 1969), pp. 607-15; Goffart, 'Medieval Seigneurie', pp. 384-7.

eggs and 3,760 pounds of pork recorded in this note compare with 1,810 and 820 pounds, which are the totals actually contributed from the holdings we have, and must imply something like half a dozen other estates of roughly the same size as the two contained in the papyrus as it now exists.

Now, although this is not a polyptych in the technical sense (since it is part of a roll rather than a *codex*), its form is very similar to some of the Italian *polyptychs*, in particular that of Bobbio,[69] and it is not at all difficult to see it as a prototype of the later registers, as well as an example of the kind of thing referred to rather earlier in connection with Gregory. But is it anything like a *census* record? One's immediate reaction, perhaps, is that it is not, in the sense that the emphasis is wrong: the *census* records will have been concerned primarily with the land itself and the people living on it, while the papyrus, like the polyptychs, gives primary emphasis to the dues and services obtainable. In the early debates on the origins of the polyptychs this matter of dues and services was seen as a major problem:[70] neither the extant examples of *census* records nor the instructions in the *Digest* for the preparation of a *census* return make any mention of them, and it would indeed be rather surprising if they did; the *census* record, to use the modern terminology, was a detailed statement of rateable value, and the rate demand (that is, the demand for dues and services) was something else. How then, if *census* registers and polyptychs were so radically different in their emphasis, could the one be derived from the other? One way out of this problem was to suggest that the polyptychs must in fact be a conflation of *census* records with another type of document for which there is some evidence in the Roman period, the *lex praedii* or estate customal, the point being that we know from one of the references to such a *lex* that services were part at least of its concern.[71] It is not, perhaps, very surprising that this idea has failed to convince the sceptics: quite apart from the obvious doubts about how common these *leges praedii* were, it does have an air of desperation about it, as though a Roman origin for the polyptychs were being maintained at almost any cost. It also implies a rather strange view of the early polyptych compilers, who were apparently incapable of adapting one kind of document to their own use unless every adaptation was already provided for them in another.

One wonders, in any case, whether such a refinement is necessary. Granted that the *census* records themselves were unlikely to mention dues and services, the fact remains that they were part of a system, the whole purpose of which was to exact such dues and services. It will be recalled that, in the later Empire, a levy of (say) so many pounds of pork per *iugum* would be decided upon, and a given community would be instructed to provide its quota on the basis of the known total of *iuga* in its territory. In order to do so it would presumably need to consult the *census* records lodged in the municipal archive in order to discover

[69]Above, note 32; there is a translated extract in G. Duby, *Rural Economy and Country Life in the Medieval West* (London, Edward Arnold, 1968, translation of French edn., Paris, 1962), p. 377.

[70]Perrin, *Seigneurie rurale*, pp. 593–4.

[71]*Codex Justinianus* XI, 48, 5; *Corpus Inscriptionum Latinarum* VIII, 25902, 25943, etc. The connection with dues and services is in 25902, i, lines 10f., 22f. For the suggestion see Perrin, *Seigneurie rurale*, p. 594, n. 1.

the amounts to be levied from the individual landowners. In other words, it is not hard to envisage a situation (and a relatively frequent one at that) in which the census records would be closely and actively associated with dues and services. The two things went together, and each implied the other. There is, indeed, some evidence which suggests that dues and services may in fact have been incorporated into the documents at the end of the Roman period,[72] and whether this indicates a deliberate change of policy or was simply part of the breakdown of the system it is not, in general terms, unexpected. One can, of course, take fancy a little too far, but if we were ever to have the good fortune to discover part of a *census* record with the individual amounts and sub-totals jotted down, as it were, in the margin, we would have something very close to *P. Ital.* 3 and so to the polyptychs themselves.

In this connection, and as part of the wider search for possible intermediary documents between *census* registers and polyptychs, it may be helpful to consider briefly a recently published collection, datable to the late seventh or early eighth century and emanating (apparently) from the abbey of St-Martin of Tours.[73] They appear to be fragments of a land register, and though less detailed than *P. Ital.* 3 they are of the same basic format, with the names of holders of land grouped under named *colonicae*, and with payments of farm produce, mainly cereals, listed against each. Again there are sub-totals from time to time, presumably at the end of larger administrative units. They lack any details of the holdings themselves, but the same is true of many of the polyptychs, and it would not be unreasonable to apply the label of polyptych to them, albeit with some reservations in view of their fragmentary nature.

It is just possible that we can go further than this; as their editor has noted, there are signs in some of them that the payments have been scored through, presumably as an indication that they have been duly made and collected, and if this is so we are probably to see the documents, not as permanent records for reference purposes, but as working lists for use in the collection process.[74] The significance of this should be immediately plain: there must have been master registers, probably rather more detailed, from which these working documents were copied, and although it would be foolish to speculate about their likely form and content they can hardly have been less informative than *P. Ital.* 3 and may well have borne a closer resemblance than it does to the polyptychs of a century later.

Certainly, if we are looking for a documentary tradition behind the polyptychs, it is to documents like this that we need to turn, rather than to the various other kinds of document in which estates may have been listed. It was suggested earlier that it would have been natural for great landowners to compile check-lists of their estates as a guide to potential income: such lists appear from time to time in rudimentary form in the *Chronicles* of the great reli-

---

[72]Goffart, 'Medieval Seigneurie', pp. 380–1.

[73]P. Gasnault, *Documents comptables de St-Martin de Tours à l'époque mérovingienne* (Paris, *Coll. de docs. inédits sur l'hist. de France*, Serie in-4°, 1975).

[74]Gasnault, p. 20; discussed further by Goffart, 'Merovingian Polyptychs', pp. 71f., who links the documents with the late Roman tax procedure known as *peraequatio*.

gious houses,[75] and they are implied, at the individual level at least, by the highly detailed Merovingian wills of which we have a number of fine examples.[76] It is worth noting, too, that there was a practice of recording one's will in the *gesta municipalia*:[77] indeed, the Formularies imply that any transaction involving the donation of land could be so recorded.[78] In other words, there would appear to have been many kinds of document in which lists of estates might appear, and one may be tempted to ask whether, in view of the obvious difficulties associated with them, we really need to bring *census* documents into the discussion at all. But there is a difference, surely, between these other kinds of lists, whose primary function is to confirm title, and documents of the polyptych type, which are chiefly concerned with the income to be derived. It may indeed be that some of these other sources are evidence that a 'polyptych' tradition existed, but it would appear that they are not themselves part of it, and that their relevance to the discussion is in this sense only peripheral.

This said, it would be foolish to pretend that the direct link between *census* documents and polyptychs is anything more than a hypothesis. Some of the earlier worries, admittedly, can now be seen to be unfounded – or, at least, less serious than they were once thought to be. It should not worry us unduly, for example, if we cannot point to a very close resemblance between a given *census* document and a given polyptych, since it would seem that there was no standard and prescribed form for either. Nor need we be long detained by the thought that *census* documents were in some sense 'private', and by the question of how they could have passed from public to private hands. Even if we accept this as a meaningful distinction in theory, there is no chance of persuading any but the most blinkered lawyer that it meant much in practice, and there are any number of ways in which the public and private user of the document could be one and the same person.[79] But some worries still remain, not least that of the gap in the dates between the latest *census* records (let us say, generously, the mid-sixth century) and the earliest polyptychs (realistically, the late eighth), and there seems little likelihood of this being completely closed. Attractive as it may be, particularly for a Roman historian, to trace a line of influence from Augustus through to Charlemagne, it has to be admitted that at some points the line is, to say the least, a little thin, and there is nothing to be gained from pretending otherwise.

For the Domesday scholar, in any case, it is probably the next stage in the process which is of most concern – the stage, that is, between the polyptychs

[75]e.g. the *Chronicon S.Benigni Divionensis* (Migne, *Patrologia Latina*, vol. 162, pp. 768, 802, etc.)
[76]For a detailed study see U. Nonn, 'Merowingische Testamente. Studien zum Fortleben einer römischen Urkundenformen im Frankerreich', *Archiv für Diplomatik* 18 (1972), pp. 1–129.
[77]Nonn, 'Merowingische Testamente', pp. 93–100, citing in particular the will of St Bertram of le Mans (G. Busson and A. Ledru, *Actus pontificum Cenomannis in urbe degentium*, le Mans, *Archives historiques du Maine* 2, 1902, pp. 101–41).
[78]e.g. Marculf, *Formulae* II, 3; II, 37, etc. (*Monumenta Germaniae Historica, Legum* V, ed. K. Zeumer, Hanover, 1886, pp. 75, 97).
[79]Even officially, the *census* documents seem in the late Empire to have moved from the archives into the hands of the collectors (Goffart, 'Medieval Seigneurie', pp. 381–2); unofficially, they could have strayed even further.

and Domesday itself, and the question of how strong is the historical link between them. To this question we cannot, at the moment, give more than a tentative answer, and it seems likely that any more definite conclusions will be reached by Domesday specialists working backwards in time rather than by others working forwards.[80] What this essay has sought to show is that Augustus and Charlemagne may have something, by way of analogy and example, to teach these specialists: whether either of them had anything to teach William and his ministers has yet to be established.

[80]For the 'tentative answer' see James Campbell, 'Observations on English Government from the Tenth to the Twelfth Century', *TRHS* 25 (1975), pp. 39–54; and for the first steps backwards Sally Harvey, 'Domesday Book and its Predecessors', *EHR* 86 (1971), pp. 753–73; and 'Domesday Book and Anglo-Norman Governance' *TRHS* 25 (1975), pp. 175–93.

CHAPTER THREE

The Palaeography
of the Domesday Manuscripts

Alexander R. Rumble

In descending order of seniority, the three surviving manuscripts contemporary with the Domesday Inquest are the Exeter Domesday in the *Liber Exoniensis* (Exon), Little Domesday Book (LDB), and Great Domesday Book (GDB).[1] As V.H. Galbraith first demonstrated in 1942, each was the product of a different successive stage of an editorial process whose ultimate aim was to organize the mass of information which had been collected in different parts of the country by the Domesday commissioners into a format easily usable by officers of the royal government.[2] Further description and comparison of certain physical features in the three MSS, by Galbraith and others, has served to highlight some of the differences between them as to status and immediate purpose, since each MS, in its external characteristics, bears witness to its place in the pedigree of the final Domesday record.[3] In particular, the varying amounts of flexibility apparently acceptable in the order and make-up of quires reflects the degree of finality accorded to each MS as a textual composition, as does the number, competence, and autonomy of the scribes entrusted to copy the text in each.

Although each one of the three Domesday MSS is now both bound up and commonly thought of as a separate volume, it is important to remember that each, like any other manuscript book, began its existence as a large number of individual loose sheets of material (here parchment) on to which a text was

[1]The MSS are, respectively: Exeter, Cathedral Library, MS no. 3500 described in N.R. Ker, *Medieval Manuscripts in British Libraries* II, *Abbotsford-Keele* (Oxford, Clarendon Press, 1977) pp. 800–7; London, Public Record Office, E 31/1 and E 31/2. There is no complete published facsimile of Exon, but see *Palaeographical Society*, 2nd series (London 1884–94), II, plates 70–1 (fos. 103, 313). For facsimiles of both GDB and LDB, see the photozincograph copy (Southampton, Ordnance Survey, 1863); although this has been touched up in places, it is the only published photograph of the whole of the two volumes to date.

[2]'The Making of Domesday Book', *EHR* LVII (1942), pp. 161–77.

[3]V.H. Galbraith, *The Making of Domesday Book* (Oxford, Clarendon Press, 1961) and *Domesday Book: Its Place in Administrative History* (Oxford, Clarendon Press, 1974), especially pp. 18–22, 47–72; *Domesday Re-Bound* (London, HMSO for the Public Record Office, 1954); R. Welldon Finn, 'The Immediate Sources of the Exchequer Domesday', *Bulletin of the John Rylands Library* XL (1957), pp. 47–78, 'The Exeter Domesday and its Construction', *Bulletin of the John Rylands Library* XLI (1959), pp. 360–87, *The Domesday Inquest and the Making of Domesday Book* (London, Longmans, 1961), pp. 160–91, and *Domesday Studies: The Liber Exoniensis* (London, Longmans, 1964), pp. 26–54, 130–58.

added one page at a time. These sheets and pages of text were planned however from the beginning so as to fit together to form quires and they were subsequently collected together as such. The quires so made were often kept unbound for quite a while before being collated into final volume form. Until that time, a single quire, or a group of quires containing a self-sufficient piece of text, might be used independently as a 'booklet', sometimes protected by a temporary cover. P.R. Robinson has recently defined such a booklet as 'a small but structurally independent production containing a single work or a number of short works', and has shown that they were used from at least the late eighth century.[4] Within a large collection of material, numbers of booklets could be filed in various different sequences, according to design or accident. Depending on the care with which a manuscript volume was eventually bound, and often re-bound more than once, the present sequence of text in it may or may not thus represent any order intended by the person who had planned its writing. It will have proved difficult, and sometimes impossible, to put into flowing sequence the contents of a collection of booklets whose planners had never intended them to be bound as a single volume. The general concept of the booklet is a useful one to keep in mind when considering the three Domesday MSS. It will be seen that in Exon the booklets discernible are basically feudal and provincial in type, each fief within the Domesday circuit covered by Exon forming a self-sufficient unit of text. In both LDB and GDB the booklets are county units, although consisting of many more quires in LDB than in GDB.

As might be expected, the Exeter Domesday, first shown by F.H. Baring in 1912 to be the several remains of a draft of the Domesday circuit return relating to the south-western counties of England,[5] has presented great difficulties to those who have attempted to bind it in a book. The arrangement of even the surviving portion (532 folios) of its text at the time of its first binding is not now retrievable, except perhaps for about half (see below). Nor is it known exactly when the missing booklets for fiefs in most of Wiltshire and parts of Devon and Dorset were lost, but this had apparently occurred before the late fourteenth century when the collection that now survives was bound up as two volumes of fairly similar size.[6] The leaves in these volumes were foliated i–xii, 1–520 in the early sixteenth century, but when Exon was re-bound as a single volume in 1816 its constituent booklets were rearranged in an order which had been worked out by Ralph Barnes, the chapter clerk at Exeter Cathedral, principally as part of his considerable contribution to the Record Commission edition of the text which appeared in that year.[7] Guided by the order of GDB for the south-western counties, Barnes had identified 103 self-contained sections of

[4]'The "Booklet": a Self-Contained Unit in Composite Manuscripts', *Codicologia* III (1980), pp. 46–69, p. 46.

[5]'The Exeter Domesday', *EHR* XXVII (1912), pp. 309–18.

[6]Ker, *Medieval Manuscripts* II, p. 800, states that the two volumes consisted of 258 and 275 leaves. T.W. Whale, 'History of the Exon "Domesday" ', *Transactions of the Devonshire Association* XXXVII (1905), pp. 246–83, quotes (p. 246) a note in the MS, dated 1810, which however gives the number of leaves in the volumes as 258 and 274.

[7]*Libri Censualis Vocati Domesday Book* IV, *Additamenta*, ed. Sir H. Ellis (London, Record Commission, 1816); Whale, 'History', pp. 246–9.

text in the MS and had distinguished each section (except the final one) by a letter-mark in the sequence *a–5g*, added on the first leaf of each section. In 1977, N.R. Ker expanded these 103 textual sections into 106, and suggested that originally they may have formed 110 quires.[8] Ker's suggestions regarding the physical make-up of the 106 textual sections may be summarized as follows:

> a^6 (probably associated with one leaf of *5e*), b^6, c^4, d^8, e^2 (four leaves), $f^?$ (seven leaves, including two bifolia), g^4 (fourth leaf missing), $h^?$ (eight leaves, including two bifolia), i^4 (fourth leaf missing), $k^?$ (four leaves, including one bifolium), $l–m^4$, $n^?$ (one leaf, probably associated with *5f*), o^4 (third leaf missing), p^8 (eighth leaf missing), $q^?$ (two leaves), $r–s^8$, t^2, u^8 (seventh and eighth leaves missing), w^8, $x^?$ (one leaf), y^8 (sixth, seventh and eighth leaves missing), z^4 (fourth leaf missing), $2a^?$ (one leaf), $2b^?$ (four leaves, perhaps associated with *2x*), $2c^4$, $2d^8$, $2e^6$, $2f^8$, $2g^4$, $2h^4$ (third leaf missing), $2i^?$ (one leaf), $2k^6$, $2l^8$, $2m^?$ (seven leaves, including three bifolia), $2n^6$ (sixth leaf missing), $2o^?$ (two leaves), $2p^?$ (one leaf), $2q^?$ (three leaves), $2r^4$, $2s^2$, $2t^?$ (one leaf), $[2u + 2w]^8$ (sixth, seventh and eighth leaves missing), $2x^?$ (three leaves, perhaps associated with *2b*), $2y–2z^8$, $3a^8$ (seventh and eighth leaves missing), $3b^{10}$, $3c^8$, $3d^8$ (fifth, sixth and seventh leaves missing), $3e^8$, $3f^{20}$, $3g^8$ (eighth leaf missing), $3h^4$, $3i^?$ (two leaves), $3k–3m^8$, $3n^4$, $3o–3p^8$, $3q^?$ (three leaves), $3r^8$, $3s^?$ (two leaves), $3t^8$, $3u^4$ (fourth leaf missing), $3w^8$, $3x^?$ (two leaves), $3y^6$ (second leaf missing), $3z^5$ (two bifolia, and one leaf after the fourth leaf), $4a–4b^6$, $4c^4$, $[4d + 4e]^{?8}$ (eighth leaf missing), $4f^?$ (four leaves), $4g^4$, $[4h + 4h2 + 4h3]^{?6}$ (fifth and sixth leaves missing), $4i^?$ (four leaves), $4k^4$, $[4l + 4l2]^{?6}$ (fourth, fifth and sixth leaves missing), $4\dot{m}^8$, $4n^8$ (eighth leaf missing), $4o^{2+2}$ (probably two quires), $4p^6$ (sixth leaf missing), $4q^4$, $4r^2$, $4s^4$, $4t^8$, $4u^4$, $4w^8$ (seventh leaf missing), $4x^8$ (seventh and eighth leaves missing), $4y^8$, $4z^6$, $5a–5c^8$, $5d^8$ (eighth leaf missing), $5e^?$ (four leaves, one probably associated with *a*), $5f^?$ (two leaves, probably associated with *n*), $5g^?$ (one leaf).

The number of leaves now missing from Exon, particularly at the end of sections, is noteworthy and probably reflects the removal of blank leaves at various times for use in other medieval MSS. The fact that there seem to have been so many blank leaves in Exon, some of which are still in place at the end of sections (cf. Plate 3.5), was thought by Ker to be the result of scribes following a specific instruction as to normal method of procedure, such as 'take a bifolium; when you have filled the first leaf do not go on to the second leaf, but take another bifolium and continue on that; and so on, up to four bifolia.'[9] This procedure would account for the many sections consisting, or formerly consisting, of quires of four bifolia. Modifications of it, to take into account abnormally large or small textual units, must also be allowed however, to explain those sections consisting of one, two, three, five, and even ten, bifolia. In these cases, the scribes must have been free to respond to significant varia-

---

[8]Ker, *Medieval Manuscripts* II, pp. 801–7.
[9]*Op. cit.*, p. 806.

tions in the amount of associated text to be copied.[10]

A roughly contemporary table at fo. 532[rv] lists the subject-matter of about half of the surviving textual sections in Exon, in an order which might possibly be that of the collection's first binding or even that in which the loose booklets were normally filed before they were bound together. This order relates to the textual sections in the following manner:[11]

> *e, s–x* (king's land in Dorset, Devon, Cornwall, Somerset)
> *f*[part], *y* (Queen Matilda; Dorset, Devon, Cornwall)
> *f*[part] (countess of Boulogne; Dorset)
> *3i* (Earl Hugh; Devon and Somerset)
> *2z–3g* (count of Mortain; Devon, Cornwall, Somerset)
> *2y* (lands of various Cornish churches)
> *2c–2h* (bishop of Coutances; Devon and Somerset)
> *2i* (Osmund, bishop of Salisbury; Somerset)
> *2t* (abbess of Shaftesbury; Somerset)
> *2k* (Giso, bishop of Wells; Somerset)
> *2m* [part] (Walkelin, bishop of Winchester; Somerset)
> *2b, 2x* (bishop of Exeter; Devon, Cornwall)
> *p–r, d* (geld documents; Devon, Cornwall, Somerset, Dorset)
> *2u–2w* (almsland in Devon and Somerset)
> *2p* (abbot of Horton; Devon)
> *g* (Cerne Abbey; Dorset)
> *h*[part] (Milton Abbey; Dorset)
> *h*[part] (Abbotsbury Abbey; Dorset)
> *h*[part], *2s* (Athelney Abbey; Dorset and Somerset)
> *2q* (Bath Abbey; Somerset)
> *h*[part], *2n* (Tavistock Abbey; Dorset, Devon, Cornwall)
> *2o* (Buckfast Abbey; Devon)
> *2l, 2m*[part] (Glastonbury Abbey; Devon)
> *2r* (Muchelney Abbey; Somerset)

The first item in the table is *Dominicatus REGIS*, with a half-formed letter *S* between the two words. Rather than take this letter to stand for *S(TEPHANI)*, as suggested by Ker,[12] it is probably better to interpret it as an unerased error: it may be that the scribe had begun to write *Dominicatus Suus* for the section on the king's demesne and then decided to define it closer by the word *REGIS*, but did not erase his false start.

Fragments of an even older order for a few intermittent parts of the contents of Exon are indicated by the textual links between sections, in which the sense runs on from one section to the next. These links are as follows:[13]

---

[10]Section *3b* (five bifolia) is the first of four quires containing the lands of the count of Mortain in Cornwall, section *3f* (ten bifolia) is the first of two quires containing the same count's lands in Somerset.

[11]Compare Ker, *Medieval Manuscripts* II, pp. 806–7, 801–5, and Galbraith, *Domesday Book*, Appendix, 'Exon Domesday: List of Contents'.

[12]*Medieval Manuscripts* II, p. 806, n. 5.

[13]*Op. cit.*, pp. 801–5; and Galbraith, *Domesday Book*, Appendix.

l–m (the widow of Hugh son of Grip; Dorset); *s–t* (king's land; Devon and Somerset); *w–x* (king's land; Cornwall and Somerset); *2d–2e* (bishop of Coutances; Devon and Somerset); *2f–2h* (bishop of Coutances; Somerset); *2u–2w* (almsland in Devon and Somerset); *2z–3a* (count of Mortain; Devon); *3c–3d* (count of Mortain; Cornwall); *3f–3g* (count of Mortain; Cornwall and Somerset); *3k–3n* (Baldwin the sheriff; Devon and Somerset); *3r–3s* (Ralph of La Pommeraye; Devon and Somerset); *3t–3u* (Walscelin of Douai; Devon and Somerset); *4c–4e* (Jocelyn and Walter; Devon and Cornwall); *4f–4g* (W. Goat [*Capra*]; Devon); *4h–4h3* ((Tetbald son of Berner; Devon); *4l–4l2* (Robert of Aumâle; Devon); *4y–4z* (English thegns; Devon and Somerset); *5a–5d* (*Terrae Occupatae*; Devon, Cornwall, Somerset).

These last associations of a few individual sections of text are probably the only sections of Exon which can be said to have ever had a correct sequence. The rest of the text, before first binding, was made and used as a large collection of booklets of varying size whose order could be changed at will, allowing particular component parts of the collection to be used or checked by different people at the same time. It was an *ad hoc* group of texts produced by and for a team of administrators as a stage in the production of a more definitive and formal record. As such, it is evidence of a bureaucratic method in use in late eleventh-century England which was fairly sophisticated in its flexibility.

The highly pragmatic flexibility of the large collection of feudal booklets which has now ossified to form Exon presents a contrast to the more stable relationship between the physical make-up and the text in LDB. This MS consists of 451 parchment folios gathered in 57 quires. It is a fair copy and represents the final version of the return for the Domesday circuit consisting of Essex and East Anglia, as sent in to the royal treasury at Winchester in 1086.[14] The text is distributed between the quires in the following way: Essex, quires 1–14; Norfolk, 15–36; and Suffolk, 37–57.[15] There are no quire-signatures, but in each county the order of text follows that of the preceding table of contents. Although there is no reason to suppose that the order in which the three counties now appear is different from that when the volume was first bound (by at least 1320, when it was re-bound by William le Bokbyndere of London, for 3s 4d),[16] there is equally no reason why, before that time, individual counties could not have been kept and used as separate booklets. The blank spaces which occur at the end of counties are suggestive of this.

In 1954, the Public Record Office first issued the pamphlet *Domesday Re-Bound*[17] which, although it has since become dated in certain aspects of interpretation, has lasting value as a record of the investigation into the physical make-up of both GDB and LDB carried out prior to a modern re-binding of the two volumes. From the information given in the pamphlet, it may be seen that the quires of LDB are more regular in composition than those of GBD (see

[14]Galbraith, 'Making of Domesday Book', and *Making of Domesday Book*, pp. 3–6, 30–1; R. Welldon Finn, *Domesday Studies: The Eastern Counties* (London, Longmans, 1967), pp. 64–78.
[15]*Domesday Re-Bound*, Appendix I, B.
[16]*Op. cit.*, p. 38.
[17]See note 3, above. It reached its third impression in 1966.

below). Except where leaves have been added, as here listed in brackets, the quires of LDB are constructed of normally-collated bifolia, and may be summarily described in the following way:[18]

> 1–4[8], 5[9] (third leaf [fo. 35] is a half-sheet), 6–12[8], 13[2], 14[9] (fourth [fo. 103] is a half-sheet), 15–23[8], 24[2], 25[8] (first and second [fos. 183, 184] are half-sheets), 26[10], 27–29[8], 30[10] (fifth and sixth [fos. 229–30) are an additional bifolium), 31–35[8], 36[6], 37[11] (eighth [fo. 288] is a half-sheet; ninth and tenth [fos. 289–90] are an additional bifolium), 38–57[8].

Most of the additional leaves indicated above were probably needed in order to effect the insertion of text to rectify an omission, due usually rather to the chance unavailability of an exemplar booklet than to any carelessness on the part of the copyist. Thus, fo. 35 is a half-sheet containing the whole of chapter 21 of Essex, the lands of Count Alan of Brittany; and fos. 288–90 are additional leaves containing a potentially self-sufficient group of three sub-sections of text at the end of the *Terra Regis* chapter of Suffolk.[19] Fo. 103, the last folio of the Essex *Invasiones*, should probably be related to quire 13, a bifolium (fos. 98–9), which contains the end of the Essex Domesday proper and the beginning of the same *Invasiones*: it may be that the text of these *Invasiones* and of the Colchester section (fos. 104–7), also in quire 14, were still coming to hand while this part of LDB was being copied, making planning of the last quires of the Essex booklet difficult. However, fos. 183 and 184 may be associated with the preceding quire (24; fos. 181–2), a single bifolium, which seems to be making good the omission of exactly one folio of the text of Norfolk (that running from *ual'* on fo. 181, line 1, to *Totu'* on fo. 181[v], last line: cf. *totu'* on fo. 180[v], last line, and *hals* on fo. 182[r], line 1, and note that the text on fo. 182[rv] is generously spaced to avoid having a blank page on the verso). Fos. 229–30 also appear to be rectifying an omission, since the text copied is not self-contained (see Plate 3.3); it may also be noted that, since there are twice as many lines written on these folios as usual, the omitted text may have taken up four folios in the draft.

It was apparently intended that there should be a continuous flow of text within each county booklet in LDB. There are some small blank spaces left between chapters within each county (usually of a few lines, but once consisting of a whole page [fo. 156[v]]), but there is also a run-on of text between quires therein. Behind LDB was probably a draft version compiled for each of the three counties by extracting information from a collection of provincial feudal booklets similar to Exon.[20] At this draft stage, it may be that what became chapters, and sub-sections of chapters in the *Terra Regis* and elsewhere, within each county in LDB were then in the form of separate booklets. The four partial lists of contents which survive in LDB may belong to the stage when the

---

[18]*Domesday Re-Bound*, Appendix I, B and p. 42.

[19]The sub-sections are: lands formerly held by Archbishop Stigand, now in the custody of William of Noyers; lands in the custody of Picot; and the borough of Ipswich, in the custody of Roger Bigot.

[20]Welldon Finn, 'Immediate Sources', pp. 64–6.

fair copy was being made from such booklets (see below).

The make-up of GDB is also illustrated in *Domesday Re-Bound*.[21] This shows how the volume is now gathered in 47 quires, consisting of 383 parchment folios (foliated 0–382). These quires are of varying size and composition. Except where half-sheets occur or where irregular leaves have been added, as here listed in brackets, the quires in GDB are composed of normally-collated bifolia and may be summarily described as follows:

1^8, 2^8 (third and sixth leaves [fos. 10, 13] are half-sheets), 3^8, 4^6 (second and fifth [fos. 25, 28] are half-sheets), 5^7 (fourth [fo. 33] is a half-sheet), 6^9 (sixth [fo. 42] is an irregular leaf), 7^6, 8^4, 9^8, 10^{11} (eleventh [fo. 74] is a half-sheet), 11^{11} (second and seventh [fos. 76, 81] are irregular leaves; eleventh [fo. 85] is a half-sheet), 12^8, 13^6, $14–15^8$, 16^{10} (eighth and ninth [fos. 123, 124] are half-sheets), 17^6, 18^{11} (third, fourth, and tenth [fos. 134, 135, 141] are half-sheets), 19^{11} (tenth [fo. 152] is a half-sheet), $20–21^8$, 22^9 (eighth [fo. 177] is a half-sheet), 23^{10}, 24^8, $25–26^6$, 27^{10} (eighth and ninth [fos. 216, 217] are half-sheets), 28^{11} (eleventh [fo. 229] is a half-sheet), $29–30^8$, 31^6, 32^8, $33–34^6$, 35^8, 36^9 (third [fo. 282] is a half-sheet), 37^8, 38^{10} (fourth and fifth [fos. 300, 301] are half-sheets), $39–41^8$, 42^{10}, $43–46^8$, 47^{10}.

The three irregular leaves listed above (fos. 42, 76, 81) and one of the half-sheets (fo. 33) represent the addition of previously omitted text, in the same way that half-sheets were used in LDB (see above). The three irregular leaves are parts of spoiled bifolia turned sideways so that the unaffected part of the sheet might be used and not wasted.[22] Two of the other half-sheets in GDB (fos. 13 and 28) may also replace spoiled folios which had been conjoint with the half-sheets fos. 10 and 25, in quires 2 and 4 respectively. In contrast, fos. 134 and 135 may each be the first half of adjacent sheets whose conjoint second halves were both spoiled during the copying of the latter part of quire 18. Fos. 300 and 301 contain part of a sub-section of the *Terra Regis* chapter in Yorkshire which had probably been copied from geld documents earlier than the Domesday Inquest and whose length may have been difficult to assess in terms of the folios of GDB because of its unusually summary nature.[23] Fo. 282 follows the *Terra Regis* section in Nottinghamshire and is blank on the recto, suggesting perhaps that further material about royal lands was anticipated. The remaining half-sheets in GDB occur either at the end of a county (fos. 74, 85, 229) or immediately before the last folio of a county (fos. 123, 124; 141; 152; 177; 216, 217) and are probably the result of a desire to produce a series of quires none of which consisted either of singletons or of single bifolia.

The arrangement of the text in GDB by counties, and some groups of counties, is reflected in the following textual links between quires: 1–2 Kent; 3–4 Sussex; 6–8 Hampshire; 12–13 Somerset; 14–16 Devon and Cornwall;

[21]Appendix I, A and pp. 20, 26–7.
[22]*Op. cit.*, p. 27.
[23]For this sub-section of text, see S. Harvey, 'Domesday Book and its Predecessors', *EHR* LXXXVI (1971), pp. 753–73, pp. 762–3.

21–2 Gloucestershire and Worcestershire; 24–5 Cambridgeshire; 32–4 Shropshire, Cheshire, Between Ribble and Mersey; 35–7 Derbyshire, Nottinghamshire, Rutland; 38–47 Yorkshire and Lincolnshire. These groups of quires as units, and maybe at one stage as booklets, are probably not now in the order in which they were written, either in relation to each other or to the remaining quires which cannot be grouped together by textual links. These latter quires, which consist of a single county, are: 5 Surrey; 9 Berkshire; 10 Wiltshire; 11 Dorset; 17 Middlesex; 18 Hertfordshire; 19 Buckinghamshire; 20 Oxfordshire; 23 Herefordshire; 26 Huntingdonshire; 27 Bedfordshire; 28 Northamptonshire; 29 Leicestershire; 30 Warwickshire; and 31 Staffordshire. The only surviving quire-signatures in GDB are a sequence of 10 letters (A, B, C, etc.) running in reverse order from the end of the MS and further linking the text of Yorkshire and Lincolnshire.[24]

It is likely that the present order of counties in GDB is still that imposed at first binding. As Galbraith observed, it presents a logical sequence which covers England in four 'bands' of neighbouring counties from south to north: the southern counties westwards from Kent to Cornwall; Middlesex westwards to Herefordshire; Cambridgeshire westwards to Cheshire, then eastwards to Derbyshire and Nottinghamshire; and finally Lincolnshire and Yorkshire.[25] Parts of this sequence can be related to the internal order of the seven circuits postulated by Carl Stephenson for the work of the Domesday commissioners,[26] but there are some inconsistencies, and it is best seen as an early and functional rearrangement of the collection of county booklets represented by GDB.

The relative order of writing of part of the text of certain of the individual counties in GDB is governed by the textual links listed above. Since, however, on several occasions further entries or extra details seem to have been added, as they became available, on to folios already written, there was probably some temporal overlap between the writing of other parts of different counties and any absolute statement as to the order of writing of each whole county as a unit would be inaccurate. Nevertheless, a rough chronological order of writing individual counties, grouped within Stephenson's circuits, as representative of the provincial returns such as LDB, may be suggested by a study of differences in the amount of writing-space allowed for, and in that actually used, in each county booklet. *Domesday Re-Bound* reports significant variations in the number of horizontal lines ruled per page, the number of lines written per page, and the occurrence of blank spaces, as between the record of different Domesday circuits in GDB.[27] The conclusions drawn from this information by the authors of the Record Office pamphlet were however affected by their belief that the present order of counties in GDB is probably the one in which they were written.[28] A more open-minded approach allowed Galbraith to use the same

[24]*Domesday Re-Bound*, p. 24.
[25]*Domesday Book*, p. 55.
[26]'Notes on the Composition and Interpretation of Domesday Book', *Speculum* XXII (1947), pp. 1–15.
[27]Appendix II, and pp. 24–9.
[28]*Domesday Re-Bound*, pp. 27–9, 32 n. 1. On p. 35 however is the suggestion that the work was planned to start with Kent (as it does) but that the actual writing began with Middlesex.

information to better effect. In 1961, he observed that, when the text of the various circuits was put in a certain sequence, the variation in number of horizontal rulings was a progressive one, from basically 44 lines per page rising to nearly 50, then to 50 itself, until finally these rulings were abandoned altogether.[29] The order in which Stephenson's circuits have to be put to give this effect is the following one:

III (Middlesex, Hertfordshire, Buckinghamshire, Cambridgeshire, Bedfordshire) [44 × 47 rulings, mostly 44]

VI (Huntingdonshire, Derbyshire, Nottinghamshire, Rutland, Yorkshire, Lincolnshire) [38 × 52, mostly 44]

I (Kent, Sussex, Surrey, Hampshire, Berkshire) [45 × 52, mostly 50]

IV (Oxfordshire, Northamptonshire, Leicestershire, Warwickshire) [50 × 59, and unruled]

II (Wiltshire, Dorset, Somerset, Devon, Cornwall) [52 × 54, mostly unruled]

V (Gloucestershire, Worcestershire, Herefordshire, Staffordshire, Shropshire, Cheshire, Between Ribble and Mersey) [unruled].

Increases in the amount of general compression of individual entries, and decreases in the number of blank spaces left within counties, match the progressive increase in amount of text per page as indicated by the changes in the horizontal rulings shown above[30] (see Plates 3.1 and 3.2). These variations together mostly reflect, in Galbraith's words, 'the scribe's growing sense of urgency to complete his task, even at the cost of some lowering of standards',[31] but some part of them may also be due to a natural increase in speed of work as the scribe became more confident in the handling and editing of his exemplars. The general order of writing as between circuits was very likely that suggested by Galbraith, although there is still some doubt about the exact composition of certain circuits. Galbraith himself was of the opinion both that Yorkshire and Lincolnshire may have formed a single circuit and that, of the two counties, Yorkshire was written last.[32] There is also the possibility that Staffordshire formed part of circuit IV rather than V, particularly since there are some Staffordshire entries misplaced in the text of counties in circuit IV, an error which could have occurred at the drafting stage of a circuit return.[33]

From the above discussion of the present order of the booklets in each of the surviving MSS of the Domesday Inquest, and of various possibilities as to their previous order, it may be seen that a comparison between the over-all physical structure of each of the MSS and theories as to the provincial organization of the Inquest has, in the last 30 years, led to some important general conclusions, still capable however of some refinement in points of detail. The same period

---

[29]*Making of Domesday Book*, pp. 203–4; reprinted in *Domesday Book*, pp. 55–6. For the rulings, see *Domesday Re-Bound*, Appendix II, column 10.

[30]*Op. cit.*, Appendix II, columns 14, 12 respectively.

[31]*Domesday Book*, p. 55.

[32]*Op. cit.*, pp. 38, 55–6; *Making of Domesday Book*, p. 203.

[33]In Oxfordshire (Drayton, fo. 160ᵛ), Northamptonshire (Lapley, Marston, fo. 222ᵛ; West Bromwich, fo. 226), and Warwickshire (Essington, fo. 243).

has also witnessed some investigation of the reasons behind the order of text within individual booklets, both of the feudal and the county type.

Individual feudal booklets, as found in Exon and to be presumed as a source of the chapters within each county in both LDB and GDB, appear in general to have been arranged firstly by circuits, then by county, then by individual entries grouped (but not always explicitly) by hundred, wapentake, or other sub-division of the county. The order in which the various counties of the circuit occur within feudal booklets seems to have been fairly consistent, so that, for example, in Exon, Devon was placed first, followed by Cornwall and Somerset, but material for these three counties was apparently segregated from that for Wiltshire and Dorset.[34] The order in which the hundreds, wapentakes, etc. of each county occur seems to have been also fairly consistent from one feudal booklet to the next.[35] The individual entries within each hundred, wapentake, etc. appear to have been ordered by reference to the arrangement of earlier documents associated with the payment of geld.[36]

The county booklets that make up both LDB and GDB were arranged in a broadly similar manner to each other. Although the usual arrangement in GDB begins with an account of the county borough, while in LDB these were not placed first, counties in both MSS are preceded by a list of tenants-in-chief, and then a description of the *Terra Regis*, and these are followed by a series of chapters, each containing the description of the lands held by one of the tenants-in-chief in a county. There are some occasional variations in relation to the placing, or omission, of the county borough, or omission of the list of tenants-in-chief,[37] but most counties are ordered as here described. The sequence in which each tenant-in-chief's chapter appears within a county is usually strictly hierarchical, beginning with the archbishops, then the bishops, abbots, abbesses, earls, and lesser barons, and often ending with groupings of the king's thegns, servants, or other officers; within the lesser baronage there is often an attempt to place adjacent to each other those individuals with the same forename (*Walterus, Willelmus, Robertus*, etc.) but this is by no means rigidly sustained.

It was noted by Galbraith that the sequence of chapters within counties in GDB is rarely exactly the same as that given in the preceding list of tenants-in-chief, but that in LDB the sequence in each county matches similar lists precisely.[38] He explained the first of these facts as a result of changes made by the scribe of GDB to the order of the text he was copying and editing from the (now lost) circuit returns of the same type as LDB; presumably, in these returns, as in LDB, the order of chapters and the list of tenants corresponded, but since the list was always, from its position, one of the first items to be copied into GDB, it was not able to be changed to take account of subsequent editorial

[34]Welldon Finn, *Liber Exoniensis*, p. 33; Galbraith, *Domesday Book*, Appendix.

[35]P.H. Sawyer, 'The "Original Returns" and Domesday Book', *EHR* LXX (1955), pp. 177–97.

[36]Harvey, 'Domesday Book', pp. 755–63.

[37]There is no list of tenants in Cheshire since all land, except that of the bishop of Chester and the church of St Werburgh, was held from the king by Earl Hugh.

[38]*Making of Domesday Book*, pp. 33–4.

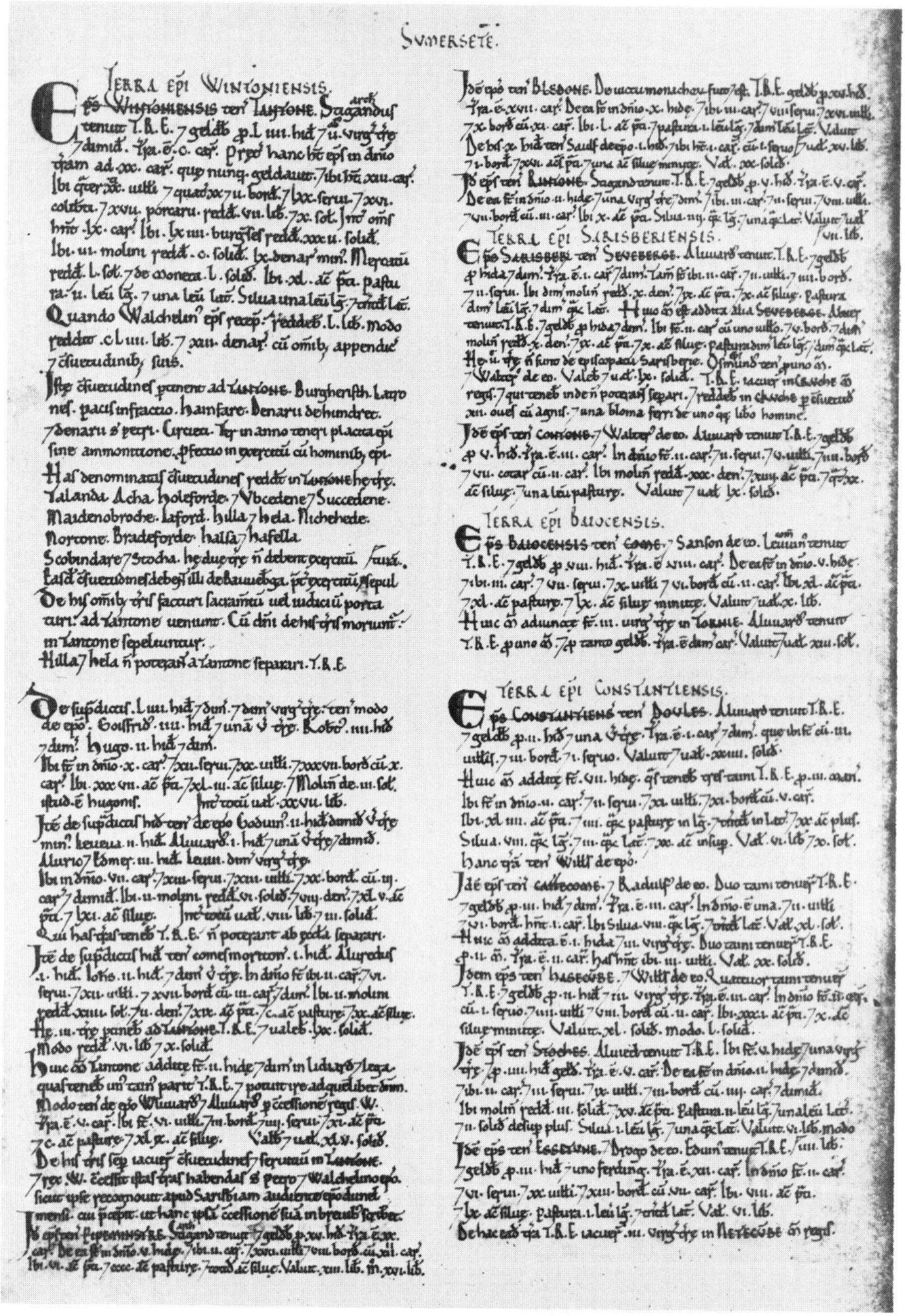

Plate 3.1 Great Domesday Book (London, Public Record Office, E 31/2), fo. 87ᵛ [actual size *c*. 380 × 280 mm]. A page from the Somerset folios, containing the final version of the Domesday record for lands in Somerset held by the bishops of Winchester, Salisbury, Bayeux, and Coutances. The amount of compression of text exhibited here is characteristic of certain of the Domesday circuits as recorded in this MS (see pp. 35–6). For an enlargement of part of col. 2, see Plate 3.4. For the description of the same land of the bishop of Bayeux, as written in the Exeter Domesday Book, see Plate 3.5.

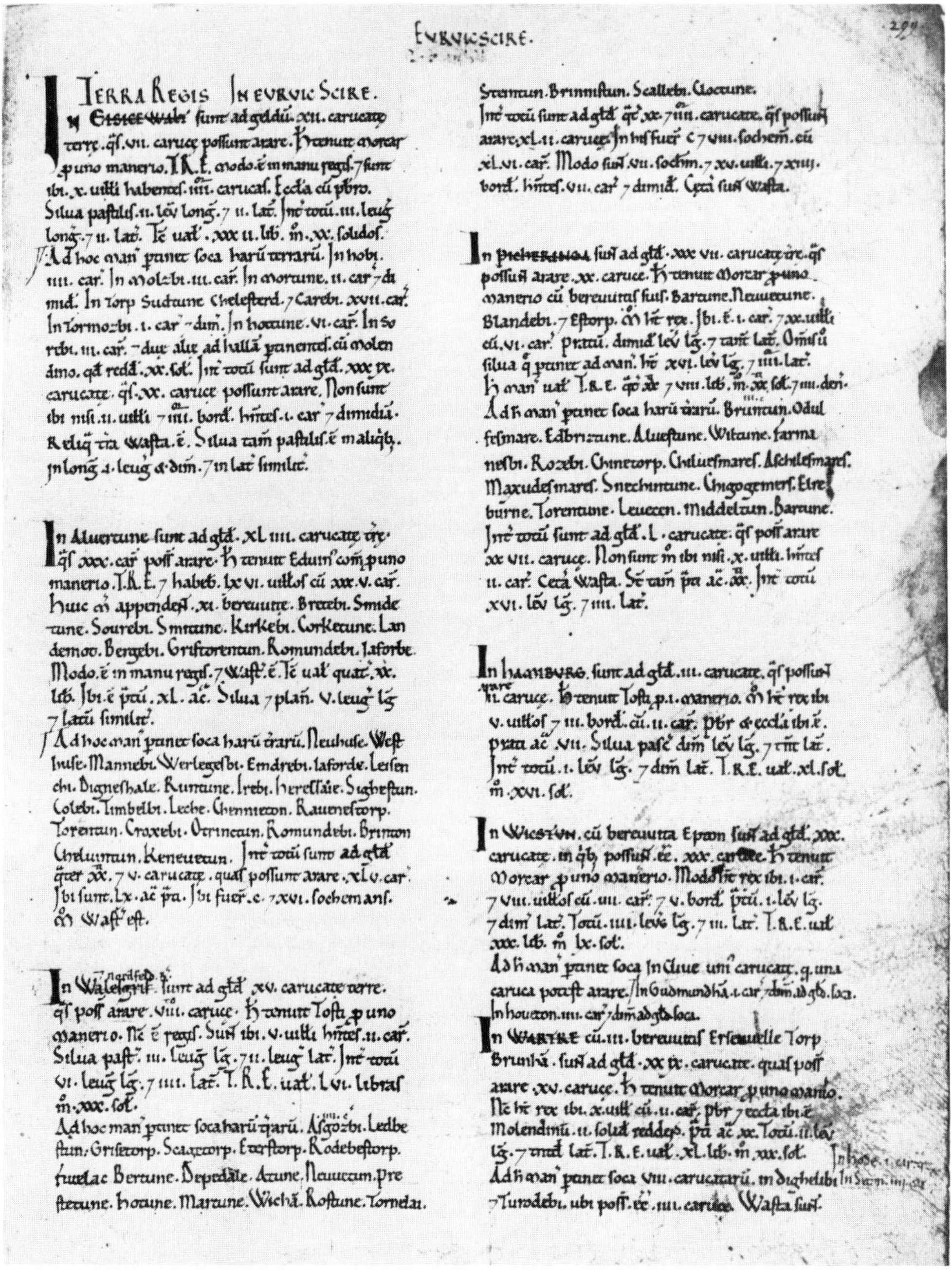

TERRA REGIS IN EVRVIC SCIRE.

Plate 3.2 Great Domesday Book, fo. 299ʳ [actual size *c.* 380 × 280 mm]. The opening page of text for the *Terra Regis* in Yorkshire. The writing is formal, upright, and well-spaced except where additions have been made; see pp. 36–7, 45.

changes made within each county booklet. The reason why the lists in LDB, and presumably in other circuit returns, matched the text was probably not however, as Galbraith suggested,[39] because the copyists were slavishly following the order as laid down for them by the prefatory lists, but rather because the list for each county was constructed only after the text in that county had been written up as a fair copy.[40] This would give some point to the four partial lists of tenants which occur in LDB, which otherwise would be otiose.[41] Also, if the lists for Norfolk and Suffolk were constructed first, why were they not, like that for Essex, arranged in proper order, with all the ecclesiastics together immediately after the *Terra Regis*, rather than after several of the king's secular barons?

While, as regards the general order of text within booklets, described above, it is LDB and GDB which present a contrast to Exon, in relation to the initial planning of the layout of individual pages of text it is Exon and LDB which differ from GDB. A major difference is presented by the size of the leaves in Exon (280×165 mm) and LDB (*c.* 280×205 mm) when compared to those in GDB (*c.* 380×280 mm).[42] The larger amount of space available in GDB is fully utilized by a double column arrangement of text as against the single column of the other two MSS[43] (see Plates 3.1–3.5). The various horizontal rulings found in GDB and their possible significance has been discussed above; in Exon, there are 20 horizontal lines ruled, and usually the same number written, although in the geld documents the number of written lines varies;[44] in LDB, the number of horizontal lines ruled and written in 40 of the 57 quires is 24 per page, the number in other quires ranging from 22 to 28.[45] Comparison between the three MSS as regards normal presentation of text upon a page may be summarized under the following features:

(i) The *running-title* at the top of both facing pages of an opening in GDB is the name of the county concerned;[46] in LDB, the left page has an abbreviated form of the county name, and the right page an indicator of the person or institution forming the subject of the chapter; none in Exon.

(ii) The *chapter-title* at the beginning of each chapter is written in rustic capitals in GDB and usually so in the other two MSS, but occasionally there in minuscules.

(iii) The *hundred-headings* are written in rustic capitals, at the latter end of a column-line in GDB; in LDB, they are at the beginning of a column-line and are usually in rustic capitals but sometimes in minuscules, depending

[39]*Op. cit.*, p. 34.

[40]Welldon Finn, *Eastern Counties*, pp. 66–7.

[41]On fos. 9, 17, 292, and 372. The first two and the last one have been deleted, but not the third.

[42]Ker, *Medieval Manuscripts* II, p. 807; *Domesday Re-Bound* (measurements given in inches), pp. 4–5.

[43]Except that in LDB the folios (1, 109, 281) which contain the lists of tenants-in-chief are ruled for four, three, and three columns respectively, *Domesday Re-Bound*, p. 43.

[44]Ker, *Medieval Manuscripts* II, pp. 806, 804.

[45]*Domesday Re-Bound*, p. 43.

[46]However, as noted *op. cit.*, p. 33, in Lincolnshire the right page of each opening has 'Lindsey' as the title; while on fos. 40^v–42, the county-name of Hampshire is written once in each opening, divided *HANTE/SCIRE*.

on the scribe concerned; none in Exon. Their position at the end of a column-line in GDB allows the first part of it to be used for any run-over of text from the previous line.

(iv) *Individual entries* in GDB are signalled by the use of an enlarged, sometimes calligraphic, versal-letter; in LDB and Exon, entries are signalled by the gallows-mark or *paragraphos*, at times more elaborately made than others.[47]

(v) *Significant names and titles*, such as the place-names of individual entries, and the names or titles of tenants-in-chief (and some major subtenants, for example those in Cheshire and Cornwall) at first occurrence, are in rustic capitals in GDB; in LDB and Exon, they are in minuscules.

(vi) *Rubrication*: in GDB, full rubrication is used for the running-titles, chapter-titles, chapter-numbers (both next to the chapter-title and in the list of contents), and for certain large initials at the beginning of counties;[48] red-lining, or the ruling of a single red horizontal line through a word or words, is used for the hundred-headings and for significant names and titles; and the entry-indicators (iv, above), as well as the initial letters to sub-paragraphs within entries, are touched with red. In LDB, full rubrication is used for the running-titles, the chapter-numbers (as in GDB), and the colophon (see below); some, but not all, of the chapter-titles have been red-lined; hundred-headings are either red-lined or the initial *H* has been touched with red. None in Exon, apart from one red initial on fo. 173v.

Originally, the pages of Exon and LDB were very similar in appearance and contrasted sharply to those of GDB, but the addition of rubrication to LDB, probably as an unplanned extra in 1087 (see below), has gone some way to distance LDB from Exon and seems to have been intended to harmonize it somewhat with GDB. The addition of the colophon to LDB (fo. 450) as part of this rubrication process may have been meant as a specific reminder of the essential unity of the final Domesday text now that it was to be in 'mongrel form', consisting of two rather different volumes.[49]

Just as the original intended page-layout of Exon and LDB contrasts them to GDB, so also does a consideration of the handwriting in the three MSS. Such a consideration needs to take into account at least three aspects: the accurate definition of the work produced by particular scribes; their place of work both in 1086–7 and at other times; and any evidence which might suggest the name of individuals amongst them.

The definition of handwriting should be both general and specific. General definition entails the classification of the complete alphabet of letter-forms used by a particular scribe within the system, or full range, of scripts used in a precise geographical area – here north-western Europe – within a meaningful period of time – here from *c*.800 to 1600. In fact, all of the scribes whose work

---

[47]Such gallows-marks occur in GDB with two functions – firstly, as a paragraph-marker within a long multiple entry (such as a borough) and, secondly, to mark the run-over of text at a line-end.

[48]In the Yorkshire Summary (fos. 379–82), the names of tenants are written in red ink, as interlineations.

[49]The colophon states: ANNO MILLESIMO OCTOGESIMO SEXTO. AB INCARNATIONE DOMINI. VIGESIMO VERO REGNI WILLELMI FACTA EST ISTA DESCRIPTIO. NON SOLVM PER HOS TRES COMITATVS. SED ETIAM PER ALIOS For the description, 'mongrel form', see Galbraith, *Making of Domesday Book*, p. 205.

occurs in the three MSS under discussion used the same alphabet, that of caroline minuscule script, although with different degrees of attainment. This script had been developed on the Continent under the patronage of Charlemagne but was not used in England until the mid-tenth century, as an outward expression of the Continental influence embodied in the Benedictine Reformation. A peculiarly English variety is found in late Anglo-Saxon England, employed for the writing of texts in Latin as opposed to the vernacular (for which Anglo-Saxon minuscule was retained), but between 1066 and *c.*1100 this English variety came under the influence of the Norman style of the script and the Anglo-Norman period was one in which some quite distinctive styles of caroline minuscule were written in England.[50]

The specific definition of handwriting entails the recognition and description of any idiosyncratic features, within the general alphabet as used by an individual scribe, which may be used to distinguish his work from that of others. While one or two unusual letter-forms, abbreviation- or punctuation-marks might be used by all the members of an early medieval scriptorium, the consistency of scribal production to be found in the writing-offices of the later Middle Ages was not yet rigidly enforced, and quite different *combinations* of unusual graphs are to be found in the work of particular scribes in Anglo-Norman England.

A superficial attempt to distinguish between the work of 'Saxon' and 'Norman' scribes in Exon was that made by T.W. Whale in 1896.[51] This appears to have been based solely on the occurrence of the tironian nota (7) for Latin *et*, which Whale erroneously called 'Runic' and use of which, instead of the ampersand, he believed to be the mark of a 'Saxon' scribe. Although this abbreviation, in combination with others, has been taken as evidence of insular as opposed to Continental origin for Latin MSS of the eighth and ninth centuries,[52] it can certainly not be so taken at the time of the Domesday Inquest, after two centuries of considerable literary and political contact between the countries of western Europe.[53] A more recent division of Exon into the work of two major and at least 11 minor scribes (one of them probably being the scribe of GDB, see below and Plate 3.5) was made by R. Welldon Finn in 1959,[54] and although his description of the individual scribes lacks precise palaeographical definition, no refinement of it has been made to date. As a group, the men who wrote Exon were described by Galbraith as writing a 'variety of non-curial and non-calligraphic scripts'.[55] Ker thought that they worked at a 'large centre' and characterized their writing as 'many rather poor hands of Norman type'.[56] From the frequent interchange of hands in Exon,

[50]See T.A.M. Bishop, *English Caroline Minuscule* (Oxford, Clarendon Press, 1971) and N.R. Ker, *English Manuscripts in the Century after the Norman Conquest* (Oxford, Clarendon Press, 1960).
[51]'Analysis of Exon. Domesday', *Transactions of the Devonshire Association* XXVIII (1896), pp. 391–463, especially p. 391.
[52]For example, by E.A. Lowe, *Codices Latini Antiquiores* (11 volumes and Supplement, Oxford, Clarendon Press, 1934–72).
[53]Bishop, *English Caroline Minuscule*, pp. xii–xiii.
[54]'Exeter Domesday', pp. 362–8.
[55]*Making of Domesday Book*, p. 6.
[56]*Medieval Manuscripts* II, p. 807.

several scribes often occurring and recurring within the same feudal booklet,[57] it appears that the writing-office was also a well-organized one. It has been assumed that this writing-office was at Exeter,[58] where the MS has been kept since at least 1669,[59] but this cannot yet be said to have been proven. One scribe, who wrote most of the geld documents known as Wiltshire Geld Accounts B and C, has been shown by Ker to have also written in 14 different surviving MSS copied for the library of the cathedral which was founded at Salisbury in 1075.[60] The work of one of the two major scribes distinguished by Welldon Finn was considered by him to be very similar to the hand which wrote the Domesday 'satellite' in the Bath Abbey cartulary.[61] However, it may be that, in each circuit, scribes were gathered from various local monastic and episcopal scriptoria into one writing-centre in order to work together on the production of the return relating to their own group of counties, and Exeter cannot be ruled out as the location of the centre where Exon was written.

Although, unlike Exon, LDB is a fair copy of material mostly already drafted, it is probable that it too was written at a writing-centre in one of the counties with which it deals. Galbraith called it 'the work of many non-curial penmen',[62] because of its contrast to GDB, whose advanced style of handwriting is usually taken as a reflection of its production at Winchester, the site of the royal treasury. About half a dozen hands occur and recur in LDB, with some frequency of interchange in Norfolk and Suffolk, but most of Essex was written by one scribe.[63] No serious attempt has yet been made to define the specific characteristics of each scribe, although both Welldon Finn and the authors of *Domesday Re-Bound* listed points in the MS where apparent changes of hand occur.[64] One of these points, at fos. 229–30 (see Plate 3.3), was listed by both, but there is in fact no change of hand: these folios, an additional bifolium containing previously omitted text (see above), merely present a visual contrast to those before and after because of the doubling of the number of lines written per page and consequent compression of writing. Another place, fo. 35, is listed only by Welldon Finn as marking a change of hand, but here again he was misled by a difference in spacing of the writing associated with an additional leaf: the folio is a half-sheet rectifying an omission of text

[57]*Op. cit.*, p. 806, n. 3; Welldon Finn, 'Exeter Domesday', pp. 368–83. Sir Henry Ellis, in his 'Introduction' to the Record Commission edition of Exon (see above, note 7), p. ix, n. 1, refers to a note on fo. 316 which apparently names one of the scribes as 'Richard'.

[58]Galbraith, *Making of Domesday Book*, p. 103 and *Domesday Book*, p. 20.

[59]Ker, *Medieval Manuscripts* II, p. 807, referring to a note (on fo. 534ᵛ) concerning the loan of Exon to the bishop of Salisbury in that year.

[60]N.R. Ker, 'The Beginnings of Salisbury Cathedral Library', *Medieval Learning and Literature: Essays Presented to Richard William Hunt*, edd. J.J.G. Alexander and M.T. Gibson (Oxford, Clarendon Press, 1976), pp. 23–49, especially pp. 34–8 and plates IIIa and IIIb.

[61]'Exeter Domesday', p. 368. The cartulary (Cambridge, Corpus Christi College, MS 111, pp. 55–131) is dated however as mid twelfth-century by G.R.C. Davis, *Medieval Cartularies of Great Britain: A Short Catalogue* (London, Longmans, 1958), no. 23. For the text, see R. Lennard, 'A Neglected Domesday Satellite', *EHR* LVIII (1943), pp. 32–41.

[62]*Domesday Book*, p. 59.

[63]He wrote fos. 1–8ᵛ, 9ᵛ–16ᵛ, 17ᵛ–99, 99ᵛ–103ᵛ. Another scribe wrote the partial lists of tenants on fos. 9 and 17; and a third scribe wrote the Colchester section, fos. 104–7ᵛ, and most of the lower half of fo. 99.

[64]*Eastern Counties*, pp. 66–8 and *Domesday Inquest*, pp. 174–8; *Domesday Re-Bound*, pp. 44–5.

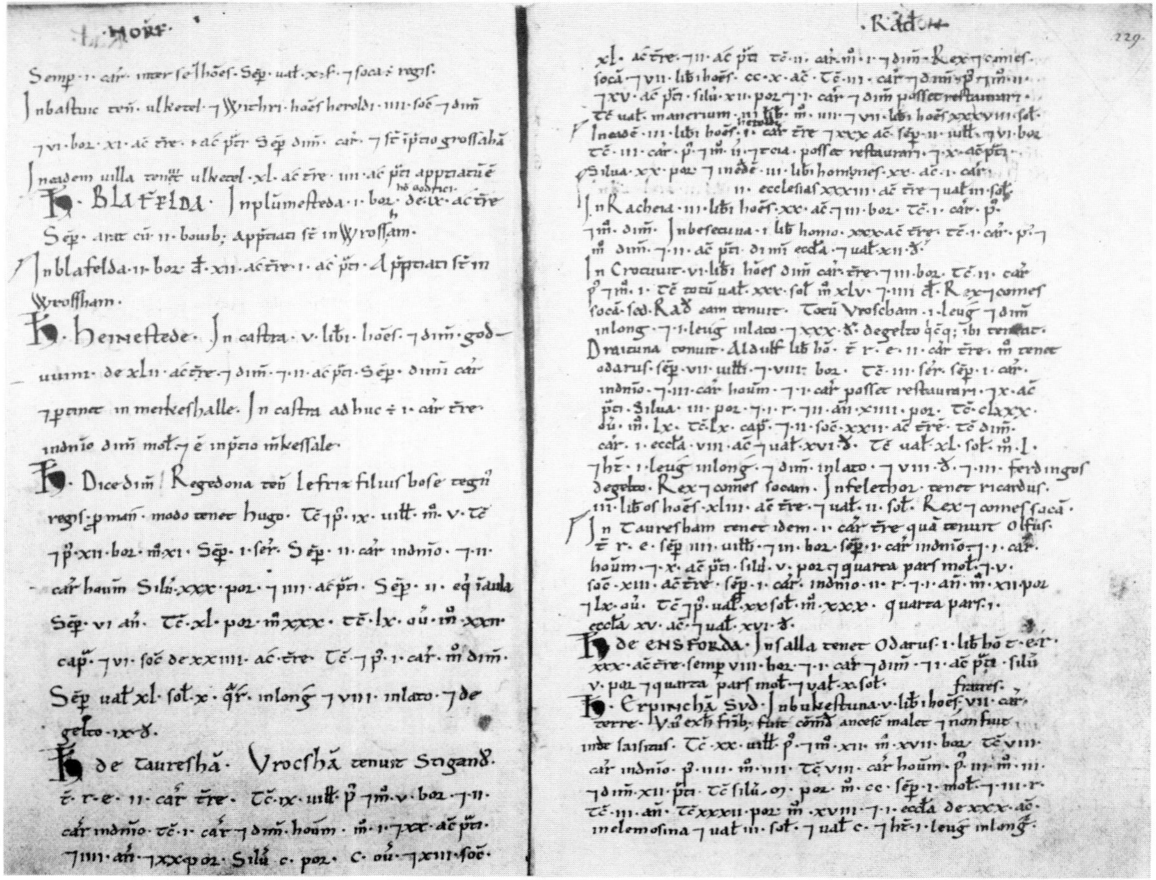

Plate 3.3 Little Domesday Book (London, Public Record Office, E 31/1), fos. 228ᵛ–229ʳ [actual size of each page *c*. 280 × 205 mm]. Description of part of the land of Ralph of Beaufour (*de Bello Fago*) in Norfolk. The right-hand page is part of an inserted bifolium (fos. 229–30) containing text apparently omitted in error during copying of this MS (see p. 33). There is a substantial increase in the number of written lines in this bifolium as compared to the preceding and following folios, but there is no change of hand (see pp. 43–4).

(see above), and on the recto the writing is generously spread and enlarged to fill the page, but is by the same scribe as fos. 34ᵛ and 35ᵛ. A clearer definition of the work of individual scribes in LDB will probably allow the dismissal of some other suggested changes of hand, as well as providing a corpus of data which may be compared to surviving contemporary MSS to see whether any of the scribes of LDB, like those of Exon, can be associated with a particular scriptorium.

Of the three MSS under discussion, GDB, though never completed, represents the latest stage in the editing of the Domesday record. Although its actual exemplars do not survive, it has been shown by Galbraith that they must have consisted of individual circuit returns similar to LDB but probably lacking rubrication.[65] There can be no doubt that the record of the Domesday Inquest in GDB was both edited and written by a single scribe. Suggestions that more than one scribe was involved have been helped by the fact that the record, still in its county booklets, was added to and corrected over a period of several months in a variety of shades of ink and sizes of writing.[66] All of the Domesday text in GDB however exhibits an over-all consistency of letter-forms, abbreviations, and formulae, which in combination force one to agree with Galbraith's considered judgement that there is 'no page or passage which could not have been written by the same scribe.'[67] The general character of the writing is semi-cursive and highly abbreviated (see Plate 3.4), but retaining in many passages quite a high degree of formality. It tends to be most formal at the beginning of a county booklet (see Plate 3.2) and then to become more compressed as the end of the allotted amount of parchment approaches; a greater degree of currency also occurs where text has been added in a small amount of space. In both its formal and its current modes it is more modern (that is, closer to the protogothic scripts of the twelfth century) than any of the examples of writing in LDB or Exon. However, since it is the work of one man, even though he was probably intimately associated with the royal treasury at Winchester, it may yet be anachronistic to term it 'curial', with so few contemporary royal documents surviving with which to compare it. Each of the three scribes identified by T.A.M. Bishop and P. Chaplais as members of the permanent staff of the Anglo-Norman chancery (because each of them wrote documents issued by the king on behalf of different beneficiaries at different times and locations) wrote quite distinctive styles of caroline minuscule script.[68] They do not appear to have had any unusual palaeographical features in common which might be used to show their sharing of the same place of work. It may also be unwise to use the term 'curial' since it begs the question of the exact nature of the royal secretariat under William I, for which the Domesday MSS are themselves a prime exhibit.[69]

[65]Most recently, *Domesday Book*, pp. 56–9, 62–3. See also Welldon Finn, 'Immediate Sources'.

[66]A recent example of such a suggestion is Welldon Finn, *Domesday Inquest*, pp. 179–87.

[67]*Domesday Book*, p. 48. Alfred Fairbank, speaking from practical experience as a modern scribe, was also of the opinion that only one scribe was involved, *Domesday Re-Bound*, p. 34.

[68]*Facsimiles of Royal Writs to AD 1100 Presented to Vivian Hunter Galbraith* (Oxford, Clarendon Press, 1957), pp. xviii–xix, and plates listed there.

[69]See P. Chaplais, 'The Anglo-Saxon Chancery: From the Diploma to the Writ', *Prisca Munimenta: Studies in Archival and Administrative History Presented to Dr A.E.J. Hollaender*, ed. F. Ranger (London, University of London Press, 1973), pp. 43–62, especially pp. 61–2.

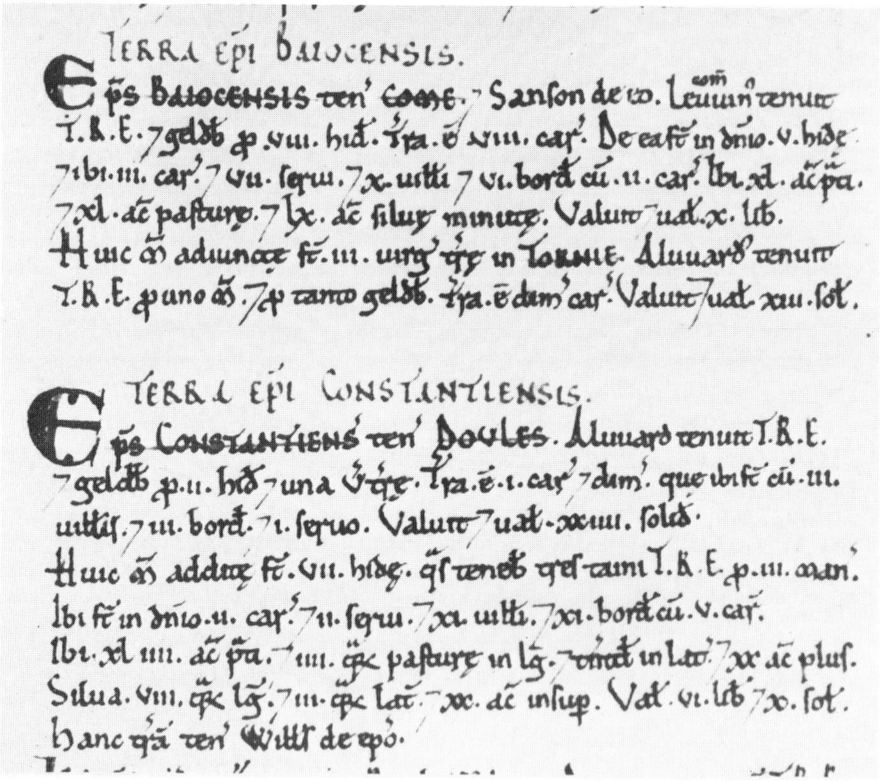

Plate 3.4 Great Domesday Book, fo. 87ᵛ, col. 2, lines 24–39 [actual size *c.* 100 × 140 mm]. Lands of the bishops of Bayeux and Coutances in Somerset (for the remainder of this page, see Plate 3.1). This example of the writing of the scribe of Great Domesday Book exhibits many of the abbreviations, formulae, and letter-forms characteristic of his work (for a general description of which, see pp. 45–6). See Plate 3.5 for the text in the Exeter Domesday of the first seven lines shown here.

The still quite widespread reluctance on the part of historians to admit that a single scribe wrote the Domesday record in GDB has been for reasons which are not wholly palaeographical. These reasons relate to the logistical feasibility of conducting the Domesday Inquest and editing most of its findings into the form found in GDB within a period of time which they limit to that between Christmas 1085, when the Inquest was decided upon, and late summer of 1086, when William I left England never to return and before which 'all the writings' (*ealle tha gewrita*) were brought to him.[70] There is, however, no reason why these 'writings' should be taken to refer to GDB rather than to the several

[70] *The Peterborough Chronicle*, ed. C. Clark (Oxford, Clarendon Press, 2nd edn 1970), p. 9, s.a. 1085.

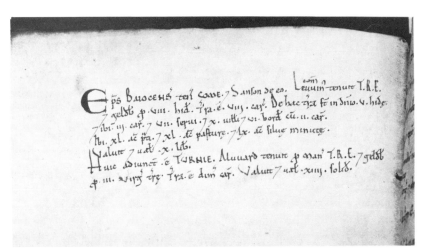

Plate 3.5   Liber Exoniensis (Exeter Cathedral Library), fo. 153ᵛ [actual size *c.* 280 ×
165 mm]. An addition of text on to a leaf which had been left blank at the end of section *2h*
(see p. 30). This text in the Exeter Domesday is almost the same as part of that shown on
Plates 3.1 and 3.4, from Great Domesday Book, and similarities of letter-form, formulae,
and abbreviation suggest that it was written by the same scribe (see pp. 47–8). Reproduced
by permission of the Dean and Chapter of the Cathedral Church of Exeter.

circuit returns, such as LDB.[71] This would then allow about a year for the
writing and editing of GDB, as far as it reached, before William's death on 9
September 1087. It is probable that work stopped then, leaving the contents of
LDB still awaiting compression into GDB form; this is the most likely explanation of the cobbled-together two volume arrangement of Domesday Book as we
know it, and also of the hasty addition to LDB of both rubrics and explanatory
colophon. D.C. Douglas's suggestion that GDB was not completed until the
reign of Henry I is very unlikely,[72] considering Sir Frank Stenton's observation
that certain information in it was rendered out of date by the confiscations of
1088.[73] Alfred Fairbank's opinion that 12 columns of GDB could be both prepared and written in two days,[74] would allow someone approaching an auto-
maton to complete GDB in 240 days, so the period of about a year suggested
above is not unreasonable for a well-trained scribe who might well have had
other duties to perform in the royal administration.

The contention made by Welldon Finn in 1951 that three (additional)
entries in Exon were written by the scribe of GDB,[75] taken with some items of
circumstantial evidence, led Galbraith to suggest that Samson, a royal

---

[71]As suggested by Welldon Finn, 'Immediate Sources', p. 60.

[72]'The Domesday Survey', *Time and the Hour: Some Collected Papers of David C. Douglas* (London,
Eyre Methuen, 1977), pp. 223–33, especially p. 228; this article first appeared in *History*, New
Series, XXI (1937), pp. 249–57.

[73]*Anglo-Saxon England* (Oxford, Clarendon Press, 3rd edn 1971), p. 655, n. 3.

[74]Quoted in *Domesday Re-Bound*, p. 34.

[75]'The Evolution of Successive Versions of Domesday Book', *EHR* LXVI (1951), pp. 561–4.
The entries are on fos. 153ᵛ and 436ᵛ. For the former, see Plate 3.5.

chaplain to William I and William II and later bishop of Worcester (1096–1112), who is mentioned in two of the said entries, should be identified as the compiler, and hence almost certainly as the scribe, of GDB.[76] Although the three entries in Exon are very probably the work of the GDB scribe,[77] there is still nothing but circumstantial evidence to identify him as Samson. Nevertheless, whatever his name, the occurrence of writing by the GDB scribe in Exon would be important, both in making it certain that he and two of the Exon quires (containing sections *2h* and *4n*) were at one time in the same place, and in suggesting that Exon was regarded as being worthy of being added to, at least after the time that the formulae and abbreviations used in GDB had been settled (since the three entries in Exon also use them), and perhaps even after they had been employed in the compression into GDB of the final returns sent in by some of the other circuits. The order of writing of GDB suggested by the evidence of the horizontal rulings, discussed above, may support this, the counties in Exon being apparently the fifth circuit to be edited in final form. Evidence of contemporary checking of information in Exon may be reflected by the words *Consummatum est* on otherwise blank leaves in 10 of its quires:[78] perhaps this should be taken literally, to mean 'it has been added up', rather than 'it has been completed'. The words may indicate that the fiscal statistics have been added up and checked to other information; in LDB there occur some marginal summaries, apparently of hidage, which may have had a similar purpose.[79] In all three of the Domesday MSS there are contemporary marginalia or notes such as these, whose purpose has not yet been investigated, many of them being omitted from printed editions.[80]

A recent investigation by Gillian Fellows Jensen of the place-name spellings in a survey of the lands of the fief of Robert de Bruce, which may be dated to between 1120 and 1129 and which was added to previously blank folios (332ᵛ–333) of GDB in a contemporary hand, shows that the text of the return for the Domesday circuit containing Yorkshire may still have been extant in the early twelfth century.[81] Had it and its fellows survived today, we would be in a far better position to judge the accuracy and editorial practices of the GDB scribe, by comparing his actual exemplars to the GDB text.[82] An indication of the advantages which such a comparison would have given us was provided by

[76]'Notes on the Career of Samson, Bishop of Worcester (1096–1112)', *EHR* LXXXII (1967), pp. 86–101.

[77]Ker, *Medieval Manuscripts* II, p. 805: 'His hand is very like and may well be the same as the main hand of the Exchequer Domesday'. Compare Plates 3.4 and 3.5.

[78]*Op. cit.*, p. 804. Note also the word *probatio* in the right margin of fo. 317; two entries have been corrected by interlineations on this page (lines 8, 13).

[79]Fos. 8, 20, 87 for example. The first two appear to match the hidages in the adjacent chapters 2 and 11 of Essex, respectively; the last one does not seem to tally with chapter 42, however.

[80]For example, the series of letters (usually *f* or *fr*, but also *m*, *n*) which occur beside entries in LDB and GDB, as well as beside Devon and Cornwall entries in the count of Mortain's fief in Exon. For a discussion, see Welldon Finn, *Domesday Inquest*, pp. 86–8, 182 n. 1.

[81]'The Domesday Book Account of the Bruce Fief', *Journal of the English Place-Name Society* II (1969–70), pp. 8–17.

[82]Baring, in 'The Exeter Domesday', compared the text of Exon and GDB, and was able to demonstrate the ultimate dependency of the latter on the former. Without the survival of the actual exemplar used by the scribe of GDB for the text of the south-western counties, presumably a fair copy like LDB, we cannot however say whether the GDB scribe himself has made any particular error or has merely copied one from an intermediate MS.

P.H. Sawyer in 1956 when he compared place-name spellings in GDB to those for the same places in Exon (the exemplar at least at one remove).[83] He demonstrated that the 'scribes' of GDB 'were familiar with OE orthography and probably included Englishmen' since some of the Normanized place-name forms of Exon appear to have been changed in GDB to more correct OE spellings.[84] If, as seems likely, these corrections were indeed made during the inscription of GDB and not during that of a copy of Exon which interposed, and if, as argued above, a single scribe was responsible for both editing and writing the Domesday record in GDB, the GDB scribe should thus be thought of either as a native Englishman or at least as someone who had lived in England from an early age.

Later additions of documents and notes to the flyleaves of GDB and LDB are referred to in *Domesday Re-Bound* and relate to the use of the two volumes as an authoritative source of reference in the medieval period and after.[85] Their importance in this respect is also reflected by the several successive bindings of each volume, the most recent being in 1985.[86] It is presumed that Exon was at Exeter in the medieval period; it was certainly there by 1669.[87] It was re-bound at least once in the medieval period, and again in 1816,[88] but it was not recognized as being a direct ancestor, rather than a collateral cousin, of GDB until Baring's pioneering work of 1912.[89] Even then, it was a generation before Exon was restored by Galbraith to its true position in the pedigree of the Domesday record.[90]

Although much work has been done in the last 30 years on the general codicological structure of each of the three MSS which have been here under discussion, there remain more detailed aspects of their physical character still to be investigated. The handwriting in each awaits specific definition and to be compared with that in other surviving contemporary MSS; further study of the relationship between additional leaves and the text they carry may be repaid; and the purpose of all the contemporary marginalia needs explaining. By the time that these subjects have been studied, there will no doubt be others which suggest themselves. With three MSS which are so closely related yet differing in status and immediate purpose, it is unlikely that the exact significance of the contrasts in their individual physical features will be fully appreciated for some years to come, if ever. It is a topic, however, which is worth pursuing if all the available contemporary evidence for the writing of the Domesday record is to be utilized, helping both towards a better criticism of the text and towards a fuller understanding of the Anglo-Norman administration which produced it.

[83] 'The Place-Names of the Domesday Manuscripts', *Bulletin of the John Rylands Library* XXXVIII (1956), pp. 483–506.

[84] *Op. cit.*, p. 495.

[85] *Domesday Re-Bound*, p. 21. In GDB, there are 30 parchment flyleaves (foliated in two series, i–xxii and A–H), gathered in 7 quires, 4 at the front of the volume and 3 at the back, *op. cit.*, Appendix I,A and p. 21. In LDB, there are 24 parchment flyleaves (foliated a–x), made up as 6 quires and 4 singletons, fos. a–i at the front of the volume and j–x at the back, *op. cit.*, Appendix I,B and p. 41.

[86] *Op. cit.*, pp. 18–20, 22, 38–40, 42.

[87] As note 59, above.

[88] Whale, 'History', pp. 246–7.

[89] 'The Exeter Domesday'.

[90] 'Making of Domesday Book', pp. 165–6.

CHAPTER FOUR

The Domesday Satellites

H.B. Clarke

As far as I am aware, the term 'Domesday satellite' has never been rigorously defined. In his last pronouncement on the subject the late V.H. Galbraith, to whom students of Domesday Book owe so much, declared the term 'satellite surveys' to be unfortunate, 'since they are for the most part not formal inquests, but monastic compilations rearranging the text of Domesday and adding thereto relevant facts of later date'.[1] The chief ground for his objection seems to have been the fact that many of the texts in question are updated rearrangements of Domesday material, rather than the outcome of an actual survey or inquest. Galbraith's chapter devoted to the satellites comprises a miscellaneous selection of pre-Domesday, Domesday and post-Domesday texts, with perhaps the implicit assumption that any record that can be related closely to Domesday Book is open to consideration in this respect. The word 'satellite', of course, is linked inescapably in the twentieth-century mind with celestial bodies or man-made objects that gravitate around a larger sphere.[2] The analogy is not exact, but it is permissible in the general sense that the satellite texts are smaller than, and subsidiary to, Great Domesday. In a volume of reassessment such as this it is desirable that clear-cut and valid distinctions be made in the light of past scholarly achievements and for the benefit of future researchers.

By tradition 'Domesday Book' is thought of as the two volumes, known as Great Domesday and Little Domesday, residing in the Public Record Office in London.[3] Arguably Little Domesday is itself a satellite of Great Domesday, in that it is a provincial draft that should have been, but was not, abbreviated in

---

[1]V.H. Galbraith, *Domesday Book: its Place in Administrative History* (Oxford, Clarendon Press, 1974), p. 76.

[2]Compare D.C. Douglas, 'The Domesday Survey', *History*, new series, XXI (1936–7), p. 251: 'Domesday, we now know, is not a record in isolation. It is surrounded, so to speak, by a number of satellite surveys'.

[3]Printed in A. Farley, ed., *Liber Censualis Vocatus Domesday Book* (2 vols., London, Record Commission, 1783), hereafter cited as 'DB'. Good general introductions are available in R.W. Finn, *An Introduction to Domesday Book* (London, Longman, 1963) and in the same author's *Domesday Book: a Guide* (Chichester, Phillimore, 1973). Finn devoted a further work to the evidence of Little Domesday: *Domesday Studies: the Eastern Counties* (London, Longman, 1967).

the standardized format of Great Domesday.[4] Some of its distinguishing characteristics, such as a multiplicity of hands, wordy phraseology and the inclusion of details about livestock, would support the argument. But it would probably be too great a departure from custom to detach Little Domesday from its companion in this way. Nevertheless it should be remembered that there is no generic distinction between Little Domesday and other texts that represent primarily a stage in the production of Great Domesday – the definition of the term 'Domesday satellite' that will be adopted here. The main justification for regarding Little Domesday as an integral part of Domesday Book is that, without it, we should have no complete record of the 1086 survey of the counties of Essex, Norfolk and Suffolk. Furthermore the colophon at the end of the manuscript, declaring that this *descriptio* was made in the year 1086,[5] may be interpreted as contemporary confirmation of Little Domesday's special status in the hierarchy of Domesday manuscripts.[6]

Behind the two volumes of Domesday Book lies a motley collection of satellite texts. Only one of these is in a contemporary manuscript – Exeter Domesday, which is part of a larger volume known as the *Liber Exoniensis*.[7] Galbraith demonstrated brilliantly and lucidly the correct position of this enormous compilation as a provincial draft of the greater part of the south-western circuit (II).[8] Indeed so much significance did he attach to this record that, in a later work, 'Exon Domesday' (an alternative name for Exeter Domesday) was included in a chapter as if it were an integral part of Domesday Book.[9] The statement that 'on these three manuscripts must depend our whole picture of the survey' seems to rule out of account all of the remaining satellites.[10] The

---

[4]As long ago as 1832 Sir Francis Palgrave thought it 'not improbable' that the two volumes of Domesday Book represent different stages in the redaction of the inquest material and that volumes similar to Little Domesday once existed for other parts of the country: *The Rise and Progress of the English Commonwealth* (2 vols., London, John Murray, 1832) II, p. ccccxlvi, n. 6.

[5]DBII 450a: 'Anno millesimo octogesimo sexto, ab incarnatione domini, vegesimo vero regni Willelmi facta est ista descriptio, non solum per hos tres comitatus, sed etiam per alios'.

[6]Table 4.1 is intended to assist the reader in relating the various satellites to Domesday Book and to one another. The table owes its main inspiration to that provided in H.R. Loyn, *The Norman Conquest* (3rd edn, London, Hutchinson, 1982), p. 145, but mine differs significantly from his at several points. That he foresaw the possibility of incorporating the Domesday satellites in such a diagram is clear from the same author's essay 'Domesday Book', in R.A. Brown, ed., *Proceedings of the Battle Conference on Anglo-Norman Studies*, I. 1978 (Ipswich, Boydell Press, 1979), p. 122, n. 7 (at p. 221). Both tables should be contrasted with the genealogy of Domesday Book in J.H. Round, *Feudal England: Historical Studies on the Eleventh and Twelfth Centuries* (London, Allen & Unwin reprint, 1964), p. 123.

[7]Exeter, Dean & Chapter, MS 3500 (here referred to as Exon), fos. 11–12ᵛ, 25–62ᵛ, 83–494ᵛ, printed in H. Ellis, ed., *Libri Censualis Vocati Domesday Book Additamenta* (London, Record Commission, 1816), pp. 11–12, 26–56, 75–457. A detailed description of this manuscript is given in N.R. Ker, *Medieval Manuscripts in British Libraries* (2 vols., Oxford, Clarendon Press, 1969–77) II, pp. 800–7.

[8]V.H. Galbraith, 'The Making of Domesday Book', *EHR* LVII (1942), pp. 161–77; *The Making of Domesday Book* (Oxford, Clarendon Press, 1961), pp. 28–44, 102–22.

[9]Galbraith, *Domesday Book*, pp. 64–72.

[10]*Op. cit.*, p. 64. A subsequent statement (at p. 76) to the effect that 'these subsidiary documents [the Domesday satellites] are the key to the practical role of Domesday over the centuries' suggests that Galbraith's conception of them was quite different from that presented here.

GREAT DOMESDAY

WINCHESTER (Treasury abbreviation)	I	II	III	IV	V	VI	VII
CIRCUITS	1 *Kent* 2 *Sussex* 3 *Surrey* 4 *Hampshire* 5 *Berkshire*	6 *Wiltshire* 7 *Dorset* 8 *Somerset* 9 *Devon* 10 *Cornwall*	11 *Middlesex* 12 *Hertford* 13 *Buckingham* 18 *Cambridge* 20 *Bedford*	14 Oxford 21 *Northampton* 22 *Leicester* 23 Warwick	15 Gloucester 16 *Worcester* 17 Hereford 24 Stafford 25 Shropshire 26 *Cheshire*	19 *Huntingdon* 27 Derby 28 Nottingham 29 Rutland 30 York 31 Lincoln	1 *Essex* 2 *Norfolk* 3 *Suffolk*
(Provincial drafts)		Exeter Domesday *Terrae occupatae* Summaries	*Inquisitio Eliensis*			CLAMORES COUNT ALAN *Inquisitio Eliensis*	LITTLE DOMESDAY INVASIONES SUPER REGEM *Inquisitio Eliensis* The Feudal Book of Abbot Baldwin (?)
COUNTIES (County drafts)		Bath A	*Inquisitio Comitatus Cantabrigiensis* Braybrooke Feodary		Evesham K Evesham Q	YORKSHIRE SUMMARY	
(Records of shrieval, hundredal and manorial administration)	*De hundredis et de hidis* **Haec sunt maneria archiepiscopatus** *Noticia terrarum* P RTD	Bath B Geld accounts		Northamptonshire Geld Roll	Evesham A	Yorkshire Summary ←	
					Ad Begabiriam pertinent xxi hide		

Table 4.1. The Domesday satellites and the making of Domesday Book. Prefatory numbers to counties indicate the sequences in the two volumes of Domesday Book. The names of counties with a consistent hundredal order are printed in italics. Constituent parts of Domesday Book are printed in capital letters.

contemporaneity of the surviving manuscript might justify such an approach, but Exeter Domesday has so many features not characteristic of Great Domesday, or even of Little Domesday, that it is more appropriate to classify it as the biggest and in some ways the most important of the Domesday satellites. One of the major differences is the muddled (Galbraith's own word) nature of its contents, which gave rise to a special appendix in Galbraith's book.[11] The two volumes of Domesday Book do have their imperfections, but muddle on this scale is not among them.

Two other major satellites, the *Inquisitio Comitatus Cantabrigiensis* and the *Inquisitio Eliensis*, are copies dating from the second half of the twelfth century of draft materials for circuits III, VI and VII.[12] With its hundredal arrangement the *Inquisitio Comitatus Cantabrigiensis* formed the mainstay of J.H. Round's hypothesis on the making of Domesday Book.[13] The *Inquisitio Eliensis* is a composite text whose subdivisions are not always made clear in the Victorian edition and which deserves to be re-edited. The two *inquisitiones* survive in manuscripts of private provenance, but their great detail has made it possible to establish a close textual relationship to the two volumes of Domesday Book.[14] It is worth emphasizing the point that a copy of both texts – a full description of the fief of Ely Abbey in six different counties followed by a hundredally arranged description of Cambridgeshire, where most of the monastery's lands lay – is to be found in the *same* Ely manuscript. In other words the monks themselves appear to have attached value to detailed manorial surveys arranged both feudally and geographically. These were two different ways of recording the same information. This administrative duality is a persistent feature of the Domesday satellites and of their post-Domesday successors.[15]

When we move from the well established major satellites to the minor texts that reflect other stages in the making of Domesday Book, we enter even darker recesses of eleventh-century administrative history. In their original form the

[11]*Op. cit.*, pp. 184–8. Before 1816 the leaves were 'in wild confusion' and 'the present order was arrived at gradually': Ker, *Medieval Manuscripts* II, p. 800 and n. 6.

[12]The former survives as a unique copy in London, British Library, MS Cotton Tiberius A vi, fos. 71–98ᵛ, printed in N.E.S.A. Hamilton, ed., *Inquisitio Comitatus Cantabrigiensis . . . subjicitur Inquisitio Eliensis* (London, John Murray, 1876), pp. 1–96 and translated by [A.] J. Otway-Ruthven in *The Victoria History of the County of Cambridge and the Isle of Ely* [hereafter abbreviated to *VCH* followed by the name of the county] I (London, OUP, 1938), pp. 400–27. The earliest version of the latter is in the same manuscript at fos. 36–69, while late twelfth-century versions are preserved in Cambridge, Trinity College, MSS 0.2.1, fos. 191ᵛ–221ᵛ; 0.2.41, pp. 161–274. All three versions are collated in Hamilton's edition, pp. 97–183. The main text ends at p. 167 and the two following sections are known as the Breviate (pp. 168–73) and the *Nomina Villarum* (pp. 174–5).

[13]*Feudal England*, pp. 17–123.

[14]Galbraith, *Making of Domesday Book*, pp. 123–45.

[15]An excellent example is the Lindsey Survey: London, British Library, MS Cotton Claudius C v, fos. 1–27, of which the standard edition is the translation in C.W. Foster and T. Longley, eds., *The Lincolnshire Domesday and the Lindsey Survey* (Gainsborough, Lincoln Record Society, XIX, 1924), pp. 237–60. It is drawn up riding by riding and wapentake by wapentake, but within wapentakes the material is arranged by fiefs. The section dealing with each wapentake is prefaced by a statement of the number of 12 carucate hundreds it contained. The dating limits of this schedule are 1115 x 1118: Round, *Feudal England*, pp. 153–5.

Domesday satellites were produced in 1086 as part of the Domesday inquest. They are therefore to be distinguished clearly from any documents already in existence when that inquest began, soon after the mid-winter council at Gloucester. Such documents relate to the ordinary procedures of county and manorial administration. The Domesday satellites, on the other hand, relate to the extraordinary procedures involved in the making of Domesday Book. One important category of pre-existing documents must have been geld rolls, the earliest of which comes from Northamptonshire and has dating limits of 1072 x 1078.[16] The compiler of this Old English public record seems to have been concerned more with tax assessment than with tax collection; the survey may have been commissioned in order to ascertain why the tax yield from this county had sunk so low.[17] There is a pre-Domesday taxation list for the county of Kent, where the assessments are often higher than those in Exchequer Domesday.[18] Abingdon Abbey has left us a schedule of its lands in Berkshire, arranged by hundreds and reproducing the 'Edwardian' hidage assessments under the heading: 'De hundredis et de hidis ecclesie Abbendonensis in Berchescire sicut scriptura thesauri regis continet per hundreta singula dispositis'.[19] There is a similar list of manors in Gloucestershire and Somerset held by Bath Abbey and headed *De terris Bathae pertinentibus*.[20] The Gloucestershire manors belonging to the church of Worcester are listed in a Latin text whose place-names are written in Anglo-Saxon characters.[21] Its opening words are *Ad Begabiriam pertinent xxi hide* and dating limits of 1066 x 1086 have been

[16]London, Society of Antiquaries, MS 60, fos. 52–54[v]. Printed several times, the best text, with parallel translation, is in A.J. Robertson, ed., *Anglo-Saxon Charters* (2nd edn, Cambridge, CUP, 1956), pp. 230–7. The most recent discussion is in C. Hart, *The Hidation of Northamptonshire* (Leicester, University of Leicester, Department of English Local History Occasional Papers, 2nd series, no. 3, 1970), pp. 16–21. The extant text is a cartulary copy and not in the form of a roll.

[17]Hart, *Hidation of Northamptonshire*, pp. 18–19.

[18]London, Lambeth Palace, MS 1212, fos. 340–344, printed and discussed in R.S. Hoyt, ed., 'A Pre-Domesday Kentish Assessment List', in P.M. Barnes and C.F. Slade, eds., *A Medieval Miscellany for Doris Mary Stenton* (London, Pipe Roll Society Publications, LXXVI [for 1960], 1962), pp. 189–202. An incomplete copy survives in Canterbury, Dean & Chapter, MS Lit. E 28, fos. 5[v]–7, printed with facsimile in D.C. Douglas, ed., *The Domesday Monachorum of Christ Church Canterbury* (London, Royal Historical Society, 1944), pp. 99–104. From its opening words (*Rex tenet Derteford*) this version is called 'RTD' in F.F. Kreisler, 'Domesday Book and the Anglo-Norman Synthesis', in W.C. Jordan, B. McNab and T.F. Ruiz, eds., *Order and Innovation in the Middle Ages: Essays in Honor of Joseph R. Strayer* (Princeton, University Press, 1976), p. 6. The proposed dating limits are c. 1075 x 1086 (p. 10). The same archive also has a complete but partly illegible copy in Register P, fos. 29–33.

[19]London, British Library, MS Cotton Claudius C ix, fo. 187[v], printed in D.C. Douglas, 'Some Early Surveys from the Abbey of Abingdon', *EHR* XLIV (1929), p. 623 and identified in S.[P.J.] Harvey, 'Domesday Book and its Predecessors', *EHR* LXXXVI (1971), pp. 759–60.

[20]Cambridge, Corpus Christi College, MS 111, p. 93, printed in W. Hunt, ed., *Two Chartularies of the Priory of St Peter at Bath* (Frome and London, Somerset Record Society, VII, 1893), pp. 35–6 and in C. and F. Thorn, eds., *Domesday Book: Somerset* (Chichester, Phillimore, 1980), pp. 386–7, where it is called 'Bath B'. For the identification as a pre-Domesday list see Harvey, 'Domesday Book and its Predecessors', pp. 760–1.

[21]London, British Library, MS Cotton Tiberius A xiii, fo. 39, printed in T. Hearne, ed., *Hemingi Chartularium Ecclesiae Wigorniensis* (2 vols., Oxford, 1723) I, pp. 83–4 and translated in J.S. Moore, ed., *Domesday Book: Gloucestershire* (Chichester, Phillimore, 1982), appendix. This schedule is crammed into the upper margin of the folio, at the beginning of the Gloucestershire section.

suggested.[22] The tax known as 'danegeld' was being levied and collected at least periodically during the Conqueror's reign,[23] a fact that must imply that the authorities in English county towns south of the River Tees had local fiscal records as a matter of course.

One of the most remarkable features of the Domesday survey is the astonishing wealth of manorial detail gathered and digested so systematically and so speedily in 1086. This is apparent both in Little Domesday and in the three major satellites just discussed. Commentators on the making of Domesday Book have rightly emphasized the fundamental role played by the manor (*manerium*) as the basic micro-unit of the inquest.[24] Whereas danegeld was collected village by village, the Domesday *descriptio* was ultimately recorded manor by manor. How the manorial statistics were tendered to the Domesday commissioners is largely a matter of speculation: possibly the details were submitted both orally and in written form, depending on the degree to which the use of writing had penetrated the manorial administration of any particular estate. But whatever the method, men were sufficiently conscious of farming practices and resources, and of social grades and distinctions in the English countryside, to have had the facts at their fingertips. This had already been made clear in the early eleventh century by the author of the manorial tract, *Rectitudines Singularum Personarum*, based on a great estate in the West Midlands.[25] It is equally clear from the so-called 'terms of reference' for the Domesday inquest, which are preserved with the *Inquisitio Eliensis*,[26] that the Normans expected such information to be readily available. The earliest surviving survey of a collection of manors seems to be part of a description, in Old English, of the lands of the abbey of Bury St Edmunds in the time of Abbot Leofstan (1045–65).[27] This gives details of food and money rents, and of geld-paying peasant holdings (*manslots*). The abbey's manors were divided into 12 groups, each responsible for one month's 'farm' or food supply.

The Bury St Edmunds survey has some further notes in English that date from the abbacy of Baldwin (1065–1097/8).[28] Their existence refers us to a second category of documents that needs to be distinguished here: records that may be precisely contemporary with the Domesday inquest, yet completely independent of that inquest. Such documents should not be regarded as

[22]H.B. Clarke, 'The Early Surveys of Evesham Abbey: an Investigation into the Problem of Continuity in Anglo-Norman England' (University of Birmingham PhD thesis, 1977), p. 320.

[23]J.A. Green, 'The Last Century of Danegeld', *EHR* XCVI (1981), pp. 241–2 and *passim*.

[24]Galbraith, *Making of Domesday Book*, pp. 37–8; R.W. Finn, *The Domesday Inquest and the Making of Domesday Book* (London, Longman, 1961), pp. 60–73; *Introduction to Domesday Book*, pp. 45–51. Exeter Domesday uses the word *mansio* in the sense of 'manor'.

[25]F. Liebermann, ed., *Die Gesetze der Angelsachsen* (3 vols., Halle, Max Niemeyer, 1903–16) I, pp. 444–53.

[26]Hamilton, *Inquisitio Comitatus Cantabrigiensis*, p. 97.

[27]Oxford, Corpus Christi College, MS 197, fos. 106ᵛ–108, printed and discussed in D.C. Douglas, 'Fragments of an Anglo-Saxon Survey from Bury St Edmunds', *EHR* XLIII (1928), pp. 376–83.

[28]Oxford, Corpus Christi College, MS 197, fos. 108, 109, printed in Douglas, 'Fragments of an Anglo-Saxon Survey', pp. 382–3. These notes are separated by an account in Latin of anniversaries instituted by Abbot Baldwin. The entire sequence is printed and translated in Robertson, *Anglo-Saxon Charters*, pp. 192–201.

Domesday satellites. The most obvious, though still controversial, example is the collection of Latin geld accounts now bound up with Exeter Domesday in the *Liber Exoniensis*.[29] These sections of the manuscript are the documents used in the collection of a 6 shilling geld in 1086. The accounts are arranged hundred by hundred and deal in terms of money received or not received, arrears of payment and wages paid to the collectors. Though associated physically with a provincial draft of Domesday Book for the south-western circuit, these accounts are the ordinary administrative records of a routine fiscal operation. This is why there are so many differences of detail between the geld accounts and Domesday Book.[30] Less straightforward is the compilation produced by the monks of Bury St Edmunds that is very similar in form and scope to the corresponding sections of Little Domesday.[31] It may even have been based on the first draft of this provincial Domesday.[32] The precise origins of the Bury survey remain uncertain and further study seems to be required.

The third category of documents that should be excluded from consideration as Domesday satellites is far more numerous and relates to the period after the completion of Domesday Book. Most Domesday scholars appear to believe that the redaction of Great Domesday had been accomplished either by the late summer of 1086, when William I left England for the last time, or by the time of his death on 9 September 1087. Indeed there may be a connection between the presentation of 'all the writings' to King William[33] and the famous oath of Salisbury.[34] Nevertheless the case for a later date of completion has certainly been argued.[35] Assuming for the moment that the two volumes of Domesday Book had reached their present form by September 1087 at the latest, all post-Domesday documents (other than post-Domesday copies of the true satellites)

[29]Exon, fos. 1–3ᵛ, 7–9ᵛ, 13–16 (Wiltshire); 17–24 (Dorset); 65–71 (Devon); 72–73 (Cornwall); 75–82ᵛ, 526ᵛ–527 (Somerset), printed in Ellis, *Additamenta*, pp. 1–11, 12–26, 59–75, 489–90. The best discussion of these geld accounts is in Galbraith, *Making of Domesday Book*, pp. 87–101, 223–30.

[30]Galbraith, *Making of Domesday Book*, pp. 100–1.

[31]Cambridge, University Library, MS Mm. 4.19, fos. 124–131ᵛ, printed in D.C. Douglas, ed., *Feudal Documents from the Abbey of Bury St Edmunds* (London, British Academy, Records of the Social and Economic History of England and Wales, VIII, 1932), pp. 3–15. An abbreviated version occurs in the same archive, MS Ee. 3.60, fos. 178–181ᵛ, printed in F. Hervey, ed., *The Pinchbeck Register* (2 vols., Brighton, Farncombe, 1925) I, pp. 410–18. The opening section contains an unmistakable allusion to the Domesday survey: 'Hec sunt maneria que habuit sanctus Aedmundus in suo dominio. Et hec sunt terre suorum hominum quas ipsi etiam tenuerunt tempore quo iussu regis Willelmi facta est descriptio tocius Anglie secundum sacramenta que iurauerunt ipsius terre pene uniuersi incole quod unusquisque ueritatem proferret interrogatus de sua propria terra et substancia et de aliorum qui habitabant in uicinitate sua'. See also Harvey, 'Domesday Book and its Predecessors', p. 761.

[32]Galbraith, 'Making of Domesday Book', p. 168. Douglas associated this survey with Abbot Baldwin and dated it 1087 x 1098: *Feudal Documents*, p. xlix. Other writers have denied the association: Galbraith, 'Making of Domesday Book', p. 168, n. 1; *Domesday Book*, p. 77; R. Lennard, *Rural England, 1086–1135: a Study of Social and Agrarian Conditions* (Oxford, Clarendon Press, 1959), p. 359, n. 1.

[33]C. Clark, ed., *The Peterborough Chronicle, 1070–1154* (2nd edn, Oxford, Clarendon Press, 1970), p. 9: '7 ealle tha gewrita waeron gebroht to him syththan'.

[34]*Op. cit.*, p. 9. On the oath see H.A. Cronne, 'The Salisbury Oath', *History*, new series, XIX (1934–5), pp. 248–52.

[35]Douglas, 'Domesday Survey', pp. 254–5.

should naturally be excluded. Among these is the official Breviate of Domesday Book preserved in three thirteenth-century copies, the earliest of which belongs to the second quarter of that century.[36] Private abbreviations survive, too, and from a much earlier date. One example is the 'survey' of the lands of the church of Worcester in Worcestershire, Gloucestershire, Warwickshire and Oxfordshire incorporated in Hemming's cartulary.[37] Post-Domesday schedules and surveys may be classified as follows: county hidage or carucage schedules arranged by hundreds or wapentakes, county hidage or carucage schedules arranged by fiefs, hidage or carucage summaries arranged by fiefs, hidage or carucage schedules of individual fiefs (like Hemming's), lists of confiscated and disputed manors, manorial surveys, lists of subtenants and descriptions of towns.[38] Many of the texts bear some resemblance, or even a strong resemblance, to the corresponding parts of Domesday Book, but they are not Domesday satellites in the sense of representing a stage in the making of Domesday Book.

Having included the major satellites and having excluded pre-Domesday, post-Domesday and contemporary but independent texts, I should like briefly to emphasize two aspects of late Anglo-Saxon and early Anglo-Norman administration before turning to the minor satellites. First, Anglo-Norman England had inherited a regular system of local government based on the shire or county. The process of shiring occurred over a long period of time and had not been completed even south of the Tees by 1086, for what would eventually become Lancashire is in Domesday Book an adjunct of Cheshire described as the land between the Ribble and the Mersey.[39] Nevertheless the historic shires were otherwise well established and had a number of fiscal, judicial and military functions. Furthermore the sheriff (Old English *scirgerefa*), first indicated clearly in King Athelstan's sixth law-code,[40] had evolved as the king's chief representative in the shire.[41] Any instructions regarding the Domesday inquest along the lines of the Ely text would presumably have been sent to him.[42] The county court had an important role to play in the earlier stages of the Domesday inquiry, hence the frequent references to declarations made by 'the county' (*comitatus*). In Worcestershire this body is described on one occasion as

[36]London, Public Record Office, E 36/284; E 164/1; British Library, MS Arundel 153. The most convenient discussion is in Galbraith, *Domesday Book*, pp. 101–11.

[37]London, British Library, MS Cotton Tiberius A xiii, fos. 137ᵛ–141ᵛ, printed in Hearne, *Chartularium* I, pp. 298–313. The heading suggests that the source was a treasury document: 'Descriptio terre episcopatus Wigornensis ecclesie, secundum cartam regis que est in thesauro re[gali]'. Part of the last word has to be supplied, for the manuscript is damaged at this point.

[38]This typology is based on the records of Evesham Abbey and is elaborated in Clarke, 'Early Surveys of Evesham Abbey', pp. 308–48.

[39]DBI 269b–270a.

[40]F.L. Attenborough, ed., *The Laws of the Earliest English Kings* (Cambridge, CUP, 1963), pp. 166–7: thaet aelc gerefa name thaet wedd on his agenre scire . . .'.

[41]W.A. Morris, *The Medieval English Sheriff to 1300* (Manchester, University Press, 1927), pp. 17–39.

[42]The text says that the inquiry was made 'per sacramentum uicecomitis scire et omnium baronum et eorum Francigenarum et tocius centuriatus, presbiteri, prepositi, vi uillani uniuscuiusque uille': Hamilton, *Inquisitio Comitatus Cantabrigiensis*, p. 97.

'the best men of the whole shire'.[43] This inheritance from Carolingian times was, and was to remain, central to the governance of medieval England.[44]

Secondly, the counties themselves were generally subdivided for administrative and judicial purposes into either hundreds or wapentakes.[45] In some counties, for a variety of historical reasons, there were other sub-divisions, such as the 'lathes' of Kent and the 'rapes' of Sussex, which were further subdivided into hundreds and are therefore comparable with the 'ridings' of Lindsey and Yorkshire and their wapentake subdivisions.[46] Hundreds and wapentakes had courts, hence the references in Domesday Book to declarations made by these bodies. The incidence of such references varies sharply from county to county.[47] To judge from the two Ely satellites the hundredal juries were made up in 1086 of four foreigners and four natives: for example, Nicholas of Kennett, William of Chippenham, Hugh of Exning, Warin of Soham (the foreigners), Robert of Fordham, Ordmer of Badlingham, Alan of Burwell and Aelfric of Snailwell (the natives) in Staploe Hundred, Cambridgeshire.[48] Now two of the most striking features of the arrangement of manors within fiefs in both volumes of Domesday Book are that manors in the same hundred or wapentake are grouped together and that there is a consistent order of hundreds or wapentakes. A consistent order of this kind is a characteristic of the majority of Domesday counties and at least one example occurs in every circuit (Table 4.1).[49] This phenomenon is crucial, for it suggests that the Domesday raw materials were drawn up, or at least reviewed, hundred by hundred and wapentake by wapentake. Galbraith was reluctant to give due recognition to the force of this evidence, describing the whole question as unreal and one that should never have been raised in his earlier book and ignoring it altogether in his later book.[50] For a scholar so much at pains to explain how Domesday Book was made, his attitude was surprising enough; it is understandable only against the background of his firm rejection of Round's hypothesis that the 'original returns' of the Domesday inquiry consisted of elaborate hundredal rolls. But any satisfactory explanation of the

[43]DBI 177a: 'Hoc ita fuisse testificantur meliores homines totius comitatus'.
[44]J. Campbell, 'Observations on English Government from the Tenth to the Twelfth Century', *TRHS*, 5th series, XXV (1975), pp. 39–54.
[45]For a simplified map illustrating the geographical distribution of hundreds and wapentakes see D. Hill, *An Atlas of Anglo-Saxon England* (Oxford, Blackwell, 1981), p. 98, no. 175. The North and West Ridings of Yorkshire were subdivided into wapentakes, the East Riding into hundreds.
[46]In Derbyshire, Lincolnshire and Nottinghamshire wapentakes were subdivided into 'hundreds', each assessed at 12 carucates (ploughlands).
[47]Galbraith, *Making of Domesday Book*, pp. 70–4.
[48]Round, *Feudal England*, pp. 102–6. A full list of names is given in A. Rumble, ed., *Domesday Book: Cambridgeshire* (Chichester, Phillimore, 1981), appendix.
[49]P.H. Sawyer, 'The "Original Returns" and Domesday Book', *EHR* LXX (1955), pp. 177–97. For convenience I shall refer to 'hundredal order', but the same principle applies to wapentakes. The analysis demonstrated a consistent order of hundreds or wapentakes in 17 shires (including the lathes of Kent), to which Cornwall and Somerset were added as probabilities on the basis of work by F.H. Baring, now confirmed in Thorn, *Somerset*, p. 374. A further five counties were not analysed: Derbyshire, Oxfordshire, Lincolnshire, Wiltshire and Yorkshire.
[50]*Making of Domesday Book*, p. 160. His statement (*Domesday Book*, p. 84) that the initial proce-dure in circuit I differed markedly from that in circuits II and VII similarly takes no account of the common factor of hundredal order.

making of Domesday Book must take account of hundredal order within shires.[51]

The county of Kent provides us with a number of documents whose precise relationship to one another and to Domesday Book has still not been completely determined. On the basis of three of these Galbraith postulated the existence of a geographically arranged text, which (for obscure reasons) he called 'P'.[52] It recorded the ownership, tax assessment and valuation of each manor and was arranged by lathes, hundreds and villages. The material for each of the five full lathes and two half-lathes was assembled in separate booklets. This was the document that came before the hundredal juries and, once sworn to, was rearranged by fiefs and supplemented by the manorial details. The hypothetical P has now to be related to an important argument advanced independently by two other Domesday scholars, Drs S.P.J. Harvey and F.F. Kreisler. They have emphasized the role of pre-existing taxation records in the earliest stages of the Domesday inquiry.[53] Dr Kreisler views Domesday Book as 'the culmination of Norman administrative procedures developed over a 20-year period in the struggle to organize post-Conquest England.[54] More recently Dr Harvey has suggested that Galbraith's P is best explained in terms of taxation records that were available when the Domesday inquiry began.[55] Not surprisingly Galbraith resisted (verbally) such a notion, for it takes us back towards Round's hundredal rolls.[56] However that may be, what is relevant here is that the Domesday satellites shade off imperceptibly and indeed inevitably into the lost records of contemporary administration. If these three Kentish texts retain the status of Domesday satellites, they may equally represent routine fiscal operations late in the reign of William the Conqueror.

[51]Compare the differences of form and content related to hundreds within the same shire: F.H. Baring, *Domesday Tables* . . . (London, St Catherine Press, 1909), pp. 9–12, 40–1, 133; Finn, *Introduction to Domesday Book*, p. 41.

[52]*Making of Domesday Book*, pp. 146–55; *Domesday Book*, pp. 78–84. The texts in question are as follows: Canterbury, Dean & Chapter, MS Lit. E 28, fos. 2ᵛ–5, printed with facsimile in Douglas, *Domesday Monachorum*, pp. 81–98; London, Public Record Office, E 164/27, fos. 20–28, printed in A. Ballard, ed., *An Eleventh-century Inquisition of St Augustine's, Canterbury* (London, British Academy, Records of the Social and Economic History of England and Wales, IV, part 2, 1920), pp. 1–33; Rochester, Dean & Chapter, MS A.3.5, fos. 209–210, printed in T. Hearne, ed., *Textus Roffensis* (Oxford, 1720), pp. 209–11. A modern facsimile edition of the latter is available in P.H. Sawyer, ed., *Textus Roffensis* (Copenhagen, Early English Manuscripts in Facsimile, VII, XI, 1957–62). The *Domesday Monachorum* version has been compared with the preceding list of ecclesiastical manors in Kent (MS Lit. E 28, fo. 2), which begins with the words *Haec sunt maneria archiepiscopatus* and usually gives the Edwardian fiscal assessments: Harvey, 'Domesday Book and its Predecessors', pp. 757–9. For the lands of St Augustine's Abbey in Kent there is another list in the same cartulary (E 164/27, fos. 14ᵛ–16) arranged by lathes and hundreds, beginning with the words *Noticia terrarum*: Sawyer, 'Original Returns', p. 193.

[53]Harvey, 'Domesday Book and its Predecessors', pp. 753–73; Kreisler, 'Domesday Book', pp. 12–16.

[54]Kreisler, 'Domesday Book', p. 15.

[55]S.P.J. Harvey, 'Recent Domesday Studies', *EHR* XCV (1980), p. 125.

[56]Dr Harvey writes (*op. cit.*, p. 123): 'He then used the defensible but not impregnable grounds that the pre-Domesday texts cited in support of such a framework exist only in post-Domesday manuscript copies, even though the texts portray some pre-Domesday situations'.

The earliest unequivocal Domesday satellite comes from St Peter's Abbey, Bath.[57] This short document is a survey of the seven demesne manors held by the monks in 1086. It is similar to Exeter Domesday's account of these manors in providing details of livestock in addition to the standard information preserved in Exchequer Domesday. At the same time both Bath A and Exeter Domesday contain information not recorded in the other. R. Lennard in his analysis concluded that the former stems from an initial stage in the Domesday inquest, possibly even the return submitted by the abbot to the Domesday commissioners, which was revised before entry into the provincial draft. If this is correct, a process of condensation and regularization may have occurred in the making of Exeter Domesday.[58] The compiler of Bath A appears to have used local knowledge and the survey must represent a type that was common enough by the late eleventh century. For the extraordinary accumulation of data in the provincial drafts presupposes at least a rudimentary level of manorial administration across much of England. A second short text that is apparently based on an initial stage of the Domesday inquest is the so-called Braybrooke Feodary, an account of the fees of Guy de Reinbuedcurt in Cambridgeshire.[59] For each fee is recorded the name of the subtenant and sometimes a sub-subtenant, hidage and ploughland assessments, and a valuation. As and when knights' fees were being established in Norman England, it is likely enough that feodaries were drawn up and the possibility remains that the Braybrooke Feodary coincided with, rather than constituted a part of, the Domesday inquest.

A key text for demonstrating how Domesday Book was made is Evesham A.[60] Its contents, though comparable in some respects with the hypothetical Kentish P, place this text more firmly in the mainstream of Domesday satellites. Professor P.H. Sawyer has shown that Evesham A was abstracted from an early stage in the inquiry, after the tenants-in-chief had submitted their returns, but before the hundredal juries had pronounced on their veracity. Thus the differences between Evesham A and Exchequer Domesday, especially differences in the ordering of information, are due to revision of the raw materials in the course of the hundredal cross-checking or subsequently. Furthermore Evesham A preserves information that may well have entered the lost provincial draft (or drafts) for the circuit containing Worcestershire, but which was omitted from the Winchester abbreviation. If Evesham A was indeed based on returns submitted by tenants-in-chief, as well as on taxation

---

[57]Cambridge, Corpus Christi College, MS 111, pp. 128–129, printed in Hunt, *Two Chartularies*, pp. 67–8 and analysed in R. Lennard, 'A Neglected Domesday Satellite', *EHR* LVIII (1943), pp. 32–41. See also Thorn, *Somerset*, pp. 381–5, where it is named 'Bath A'.

[58]Thorn, *Somerset*, p. 382.

[59]London, British Library, MS Sloane 986, fo. 67, printed and discussed in G.H. Fowler, 'An Early Cambridgeshire Feodary', *EHR* XLVI (1931), pp. 442–3.

[60]London, British Library, MS Cotton Vespasian B xxiv, fos. 6–7ᵛ, printed and discussed in P.H. Sawyer, ed., 'Evesham A, a Domesday Text', in *Miscellany I* (Worcester and London, Worcestershire Historical Society, 1960), pp. 3–36. For subsequent discussion see Galbraith, *Domesday Book*, pp. 84–8; Clarke, 'Early Surveys of Evesham Abbey', pp. 179–90. For a translation accompanied by textual notes see F. and C. Thorn, eds., *Domesday Book: Worcestershire* (Chichester, Phillimore, 1982), appendix IV.

schedules already in existence, it should reveal something of the nature of those returns and thus what sort of information tenants-in-chief were capable of supplying.[61] The standard form of entry is a tax assessment and valuation, with the addition in certain hundreds of the number of demesne and tenant ploughs. The most detailed entries relate to two sections of Worcestershire Domesday: the royal demesne in Came Hundred and the fief of Pershore Abbey. This may imply that some royal agents and tenants-in-chief produced fuller returns than others. The monks of Westminster Abbey subdivided their Worcestershire fief into the following components: feudal demesne, manors partly subinfeudated and manors entirely subinfeudated. Domesday Book, on the other hand, treats the first two components as one, for the parts of settlements containing both feudal demesne and subtenancies must have been brought together during the hundredal inquiry, or after that inquiry had taken place.[62]

The conclusions to be drawn from Evesham A are important. The 'original returns' of the Domesday inquiry supplied by royal officials and tenants-in-chief were varied in nature. Most informants were able to produce a list of manors giving their tax assessments and valuations; beyond this the amount of detail differed between one fief and another, and even within the same fief. Plough figures were submitted for certain Pershore and Westminster manors, for example.[63] To judge from the standard form of entry, tenants-in-chief were asked to declare the number of hides, demesne and tenant ploughs,[64] and a valuation for each manor.[65] Such details would have been sufficient to identify individual manors. County lists of tax assessments, arranged by hundreds, were presumably already available from the machinery of geld collection, making it possible to ensure that no manors were omitted from the inquiry. Assuming that Evesham A had a purpose, the text represents what was committed to writing before the hundredal sessions began in the county court.[66] Much of the material that found its way into the provincial draft must have been added in the course of these quasi-judicial hearings, at which men from all sections of society swore to the truth of the information that had been gathered. Domesday Book is thus an amalgam of written and oral procedures, of feudal *breves* and hundredal verdicts. Exchequer Domesday was undoubtedly the ultimate objective of this elaborate administrative exercise;[67] Evesham A illustrates an early and critical stage in its production.

[61]Since misimpressions lead easily to further misinterpretations, it should be noted that Evesham A is not 'a list of 132 Worcestershire estates belonging to the great abbey of Evesham': Loyn, 'Domesday Book', p. 128. In its full form it would have covered the whole county and the abbey's manors occur as nos. 18–32 in Professor Sawyer's numeration.

[62]DBI 174b–175a; Sawyer, 'Evesham A', pp. 6–7, 10.

[63]The formulaic variations in Shropshire, Leicestershire and Yorkshire tabulated in H.C. Darby, *Domesday England* (Cambridge, CUP, 1977), pp. 347–51 should be viewed in this context and deserve further investigation.

[64]Evesham A's expression *inter homines* may be a reflection of the general instructions that had been issued via the county court.

[65]Compare S.P.J. Harvey, 'Domesday Book and Anglo-Norman Governance', *TRHS*, 5th series, XXV (1975), p. 184.

[66]Compare Sawyer, 'Evesham A', pp. 8–10.

[67]A point always emphasized strongly by Galbraith, as in *Domesday Book*, p. 35.

If Evesham A represents a stage in the making of Domesday Book prior to the hundredal inquiry, the *Inquisitio Comitatus Cantabrigiensis* represents the consummation of that inquiry. This major satellite is similar to Evesham A in being an incomplete twelfth-century copy of a Domesday record of an entire county with the material presented hundred by hundred. The chief difference between them lies in the much greater detail preserved in the Ely text. For each hundred we are given the names of the Domesday jurors followed by manorial descriptions as elaborate as those of Exeter Domesday and Little Domesday. The form and content of the *Inquisitio* suggest that its exemplar was a record contemporary with the court proceedings of the hundredal inquiry.[68] Both Evesham A and the *Inquisitio Comitatus Cantabrigiensis* are survivals of a vital feature of the process by which Domesday Book was made – the use of the ancient machinery of Anglo-Saxon local government to verify the basic facts in the intended feudal survey of early Norman England. A geographical approach and a feudal approach were two ways of investigating the same phenomena: landholders and landholding in a country that had recently experienced the more or less complete replacement of its traditional aristocracy. The Domesday commissioners were fortunate in being able to call upon this relatively sophisticated machinery of public courts for their own purposes. Indeed the existence of such administrative machinery goes far to explain the power and success of the new Anglo-Norman state.

Round made the *Inquisitio Comitatus Cantabrigiensis* the cornerstone of his account of how Domesday Book came into being.[69] Perhaps in an anxiety to undermine Round's concept of original returns in the form of elaborate hundredal rolls, there has been a tendency to regard the *Inquisitio* as something of an aberration and to ignore Evesham A altogether.[70] Yet there were good administrative and legal reasons for checking the facts submitted by landholders and their agents, and this procedure is likely to have been followed in every county.[71] Only on this assumption can we explain the more or less consistent order of hundreds or wapentakes within fiefs in so many counties. It may well have been possible to dispense with such a full geographical record as the *Inquisitio*, but that most counties produced for the purposes of the hundredal inquiry a skeleton survey akin to Evesham A must be virtually certain. It is difficult to imagine how the hundredal cross-checking could otherwise have been undertaken. This is true even of the south-western circuit, where the names of the hundreds were omitted from the provincial draft and from Domesday Book.[72] And the amount of manorial detail available at this stage must have depended on variations in the initial submissions of the tenants-in-chief.

Visually the most striking document in the first cartulary of Evesham Abbey is the account of Gloucestershire arranged by fiefs and known as Evesham K.[73]

[68]Compare Galbraith, *Making of Domesday Book*, pp. 126, 131–2, 135.
[69]*Feudal England*, p. 17.
[70]Galbraith, *Making of Domesday Book*, p. 125.
[71]Galbraith, *Domesday Book*, pp. 43–4.
[72]R.W. Finn, *Domesday Studies: the 'Liber Exoniensis'* (London, Longman, 1964), pp. 37–8.

What strikes the eye is that the scribe systematically wrote part of his material in a larger hand on alternate lines and subsequently completed his text in a smaller hand on the blank lines he had left. Here and there compression in the upper line shows that insufficient space was allocated by the scribe as he wrote the alternate lower lines. This enigmatic arrangement is presumably a direct reflection of the format of the exemplar of this late twelfth-century copy. There can be no doubt that Evesham K is very closely connected with Exchequer Domesday. All 78 landholders listed in the prefatory index to Gloucestershire Domesday are represented.[74] Every place-name in Evesham K has its equivalent in Domesday Book, generally with close agreement in spelling. But, apart from the inclusion of two borough surveys of *c.* 1100,[75] the most conspicuous feature of the content of Evesham K is the considerable number of variations in the sequence of fiefs and of manors within them, as compared with Domesday Book.[76] One possibility is that Evesham K belongs to a stage in the making of Domesday Book between the hundredal inquiry and the preparation of a provincial draft for circuit V. On the assumption that the hundredal sessions took place in the county town, there may have been a point at which county officials drew up a hidage schedule similar to Evesham K, arranged by fiefs but with hundredal cross-references.

Differences in the sequence of manors within fiefs as between Evesham K and Great Domesday are not serious and usually amount to simple displacements and reversals. When two or more manors in the same hundred are out of phase, they still remain together in Evesham K. This suggests that the hundredal inquiry had already taken place. Differences in the sequence of fiefs and manors imply that the manorial descriptions were written up on separate leaves or bifolia and in quires, just as in Exeter Domesday. There 'the guiding rule for making it seems to have been to provide at least one quire for each holder, the minimum size of quire being probably a single bifolium'.[77] In other words the description of the lands of each tenant-in-chief was being handled physically as a separate unit. The manorial details later omitted from the exchequer abbreviation occupied much space, making the provincial drafts extremely bulky documents when bound. It is also clear from Exeter Domesday and Little Domesday that more leisurely phraseology was employed by provincial scribes. Judging by the inversions of pairs of fiefs, the

[73]London, British Library, MS Cotton Vespasian B xxiv, fos. 57–62. For an analysis and numbered edition of the main text and the associated surveys of Gloucester and Winchcomb see Clarke, 'Early Surveys of Evesham Abbey', pp. 246–70, 553–68. Despite the Edwardian arrangement of the royal demesne, Evesham K should not have been described as a pre-Domesday text: Harvey, 'Domesday Book and its Predecessors', p. 763. Nor should the following text, Evesham M (MS Cotton Vespasian B xxiv, fos. 62–63ᵛ), a post-Domesday county hidage schedule arranged by fiefs.

[74]DBI 162b. Gloucestershire in 1086 had an unusually large number of tenants-in-chief.

[75]London, British Library, MS Cotton Vespasian B xxiv, fos. 57 (Gloucester), 59 (Winchcomb). The last printed Latin edition of both texts is in A.S. Ellis, 'On the Landholders of Gloucestershire named in Domesday Book', *Transactions of the Bristol and Gloucestershire Archaeological Society* IV (1880), pp. 91–3. Both are translated in Moore, *Gloucestershire*, appendix.

[76]The differences in the sequence of fiefs are tabulated in Clarke, 'Early Surveys of Evesham Abbey', p. 251.

[77]Ker, *Medieval Manuscripts* II, p. 806.

reverse sequences and the thorough jumbling of others, it would appear that a preliminary attempt was made to arrange the unbound leaves and quires for Gloucestershire and that the sequence of fiefs and manors was subsequently disturbed by accident or by design. The most plausible inference, therefore, is that Evesham K represents an outline draft by officials of the shire in preparation for the provincial draft that had yet to be assembled, possibly at Worcester.[78] Some editorial revision must have occurred during the process that led from Evesham K to Great Domesday; a comparison between the latter and Exeter Domesday yields plenty of evidence of such revision.

After the hundredal inquiry had taken place in each county court, the raw materials of the inquest must have comprised a miscellaneous collection of documents: tax schedules similar to the Kentish P; submissions from individual tenants-in-chief, such as Bath A; preliminary lists prepared for the hundredal inquiry, as suggested by Evesham A; finally the mass of documentation accumulated during the court sessions and simultaneously out of court. In order to proceed further on a rational basis, it would have been essential to construct a schedule of fiefs and manors akin to Evesham K. Even in Cambridgeshire county officials would have arranged their material by fiefs, at least in the form of an outline draft. And it must be considered more likely than not that county drafts dispatched to circuit headquarters included the manorial details as well. All of this may correspond to the initial phase of activity reported by Bishop Robert of Hereford.[79] The phrase *in agris singularum prouinciarum*, together with the emphasis on manorial appurtenances, suggests that here *provincia* is being used in its sense of 'county' or 'shire'.[80] Certainly the account given in the Peterborough Chronicle places the operation unmistakably in the context of the individual shire,[81] which we must regard as the primary geographical arena of the Domesday survey.

Evesham K poses questions relating to a stage in the making of Domesday Book about which little is known. How did county officials working in (say) Bodmin, Dorchester, Ilchester and Wilton link up with circuit officials in Exeter? Before we reach a conclusion on this point attention should be drawn to a fragmentary equivalent of Evesham K for Worcestershire, now known as

[78]Worcester is more likely than Gloucester to have been the place where the provincial draft for circuit V was produced, being more central. The Worcester monk, Hemming, recorded the only surviving list of circuit commissioners (*legati*), namely, Bishop Remigius of Lincoln, Henry de Ferrers, Walter Giffard and Adam FitzHubert: Hearne, *Chartularium* I, p. 288.

[79]W. Stubbs, ed., *Select Charters and Other Illustrations of English Constitutional History* . . . (9th edn by H.W.C. Davis, Oxford, Clarendon Press, 1913), p. 95: '. . . hoc anno totius Anglie facta est descriptio in agris singularum prouinciarum, in possessionibus singulorum procerum, in agris eorum, in mansionibus, in hominibus tam seruis quam liberis, tam in tuguria tantum habitantibus quam in domos et agros possidentibus, in carrucis, in equis et ceteris animalibus, in seruitio et censu totius terre omnium'. The importance of Robert of Losinga's account was first highlighted in W.H. Stevenson, 'A Contemporary Description of the Domesday Survey', *EHR* XXII (1907), pp. 72–84.

[80]R.E. Latham, *Revised Medieval Latin Word-list from British and Irish Sources* (London, OUP, 1965), p. 380.

[81]Clark, *Peterborough Chronicle*, pp. 8–9: 'Sende tha ofer eall Englaland into aelcere scire his men 7 lett agan ut hu fela hundred hyda waeron innon thaere scire, oththe hwet se cyng himsylf haefde landes 7 orfes innan tham lande, oththe hwilce gerihtae he ahte to habbanne to xii monthum of thaere scire'.

Evesham Q.[82] The first 28 items are part of a once longer list of tenants-in-chief, manors and tax assessments. As in the case of Evesham K the sequence of fiefs is quite different from that in Great Domesday, as is the order of manors within the fief of Sheriff Urse. This implies that Evesham Q, though closely related to Domesday Book, was not derived from Great Domesday or from any Domesday record with the same order of fiefs and manors. The striking similarity to Evesham K suggests that Evesham Q goes back to an outline draft of Worcestershire Domesday. The nature of these satellites gives strength to the argument that the prime concern of the hundredal juries was with land-holders and landholding and that the wealth of manorial detail was added behind the scenes by stewards, bailiffs or village reeves.[83] Neither Evesham K nor Evesham Q shows any sign of having been abstracted from a more detailed source, from which we may infer that they were drawn up as working documents left behind in, or returned to, the county towns once they had been superseded by the provincial draft. That the lost provincial draft could have followed the order provided by these Evesham satellites is indicated by differences between Exeter Domesday and Great Domesday. Most relate to the arrangement of the royal demesne and to the order of fiefs and of manors within fiefs.[84] These differences are precisely those existing between Evesham K and Great Domesday.[85]

The second geographical arena of the Domesday survey was the circuit made up of a number of counties. Even now much uncertainty attaches to the composition of the Domesday circuits.[86] The reason for this is not hard to seek. It is to be attributed to the diversity of the county drafts which, despite instructions and supervision from the central administration, could not overcome the diversity of local tradition in the administration of intensely localized societies.[87] County drafts must have been the written records that lie behind Exeter Domesday, 'for the information has already been carefully digested and the description of each manor presents facts in invariable order and with unvarying formulas'.[88] Once the county draft had been submitted to circuit

---

[82]London, British Library, MS Harley 3763, fo. 82, printed and translated respectively in Round, *Feudal England*, p. 146; *VCH Worcestershire* I (London, Archibald Constable, 1901), pp. 330-1. For an analysis and numbered edition of the main text and the associated survey of Droitwich see Clarke, 'Early Surveys of Evesham Abbey', pp. 298-305, 584-5. See also Thorn, *Worcestershire*, appendix IV.

[83]Galbraith, *Making of Domesday Book*, pp. 117, 121-2, 143-4, 148-50; *Domesday Book*, pp. 42-4.

[84]Galbraith, *Making of Domesday Book*, p. 105. Other discrepancies are listed in H.C. Darby and R.W. Finn, eds., *The Domesday Geography of South-west England* (Cambridge, CUP, 1967), pp. 396-428; C. and F. Thorn, eds., *Domesday Book: Cornwall* (Chichester, Phillimore, 1979), appendixes E, L; Thorn, *Somerset*, pp. 310-32, 334-46.

[85]I hope to publish more detailed analyses of Evesham K and Evesham Q elsewhere. A complete edition of the two Evesham cartularies is being prepared for the Worcestershire Historical Society.

[86]Maps that have a bearing on this question are to be found in Darby, *Domesday England*, pp. 97, 139, 177, 212; 'ploughlands' are also considered circuit by circuit (pp. 95-120).

[87]Compare Finn, *Introduction to Domesday Book*, pp. 38-40.

[88]Galbraith, *Making of Domesday Book*, p. 108.

headquarters, there was probably little chance that any gaps in the record could be filled, except perhaps with respect to the county in which the head-quarters was situated (Devon in circuit II). This would explain many of the imperfections of Exeter Domesday.[89]

While the provincial return was being compiled, the second body of com-missioners referred to by Bishop Robert was conducting its investigations.[90] There can be little doubt that these *inquisitores* were concerned mainly with claims and disputes that had been discovered in the course of the survey of each county. The terminology varies from circuit to circuit, reflecting this relatively late stage in the Domesday inquest. The commissioners in circuit II dealt with what they called *terrae occupatae*, those in circuit VI with *clamores* and those in circuit VII with *invasiones super regem*.[91] Except for three counties in the northern circuit, these details were not included in the much abbreviated exchequer text, though the latter contains many hints of tenurial disputes. The surviving lists are Domesday satellites in the sense advanced here: they represent a stage in the complex process by which Domesday Book was made. The same applies to the summaries of individual fiefs scattered among the major texts.[92] There is no mention of such claims, disputes or summaries in the Ely terms of reference and we may presume that questions of seisin either were already present when the survey was first mooted or arose during the initial stages in the shire courts. The varied incidence and nature of these quasi-judicial appendages, in contrast to the relative uniformity of the manorial descriptions within fiefs, suggest what we might reasonably expect to have been the case – that the contents of Domesday Book and of its satellite texts were partly foreseen and planned, partly unforeseen and unplanned. The question of towns should be viewed in the same light.

[89]Finn, '*Liber Exoniensis*', pp. 28–9.

[90]Stubbs, *Select Charters*, p. 95: 'Alii inquisitores post alios, et ignoti ad ignotas mittebantur prouincias, ut alii aliorum descriptionem reprehenderent et regi eos reos constituerent'. Compare Finn, *Introduction to Domesday Book*, pp. 59–67. The emphasis on sending outsiders to counties unknown to them may be interpreted as a contrast with the earlier county-based inquiry.

[91]Exon, fos. 495–525 (Devon, Cornwall and Somerset), printed in Ellis, *Additamenta*, pp. 457–89; DBI 208a–b (Huntingdonshire), 373a–374a (Yorkshire), 375a–377b (Lincolnshire); II 99a–103b (Essex), 273b–280a (Norfolk), 447b–449b (Suffolk). While the Huntingdonshire claims are arranged by landholders, those of Lincolnshire and Yorkshire are grouped by hundreds or wapentakes. This may account for Galbraith's over-sharp distinction between *clamores* on the one hand and *terrae occupatae* and *invasiones super regem* on the other: *Making of Domesday Book*, pp. 176–7. Similar material for Ely Abbey was incorporated in the *Inquisitio Eliensis*: Hamilton, *Inquisitio Comitatus Cantabrigiensis*, pp. 127–30 (Essex), 137–53 (Norfolk and Suffolk), 175–89 (Cambridgeshire, Essex, Hertfordshire, Norfolk and Suffolk). For a discussion, accompanied by numerous examples, see R.W. Finn, 'The *Inquisitio Eliensis* Reconsidered', *EHR* LXXV (1960), pp. 398–405; *Domesday Inquest*, pp. 92–111.

[92]Exon, fos. 173 (Glastonbury Abbey, its knights and English thegns in Somerset), 527ᵛ–528ᵛ (Glastonbury Abbey in circuit II and the church of St Petroc in Cornwall), 530ᵛ–531 (several lay tenants-in-chief in circuit II), printed in Ellis, *Additamenta*, pp. 160–1, 490–2; DBI, 381a (Count Alan of Brittany in Yorkshire). In the latter the carucage assessments are interlined above the names of the settlements. Again similar material was incorporated in the *Inquisitio Eliensis*: Hamilton, *Inquisitio Comitatus Cantabrigiensis*, pp. 121–3 (Ely Abbey), 123–4 (three lay tenants-in-chief in Cambridgeshire). For a discussion see *VCH Wiltshire* II (London, OUP, 1955), pp. 218–21; Finn, '*Inquisitio Eliensis*', pp. 394–7; '*Liber Exoniensis*', pp. 124–9; R.W. Finn, *The Making and Limitations of the Yorkshire Domesday* (York, St Anthony's Press, Borthwick Papers, no. 41, 1972), pp. 26–9.

The third geographical arena of the Domesday survey was in Winchester, the seat of the treasury. This brings us to yet another satellite arranged geographically and located, surprisingly enough, in Great Domesday itself. The last folios of the volume bear a schedule of carucates in Yorkshire.[93] This summary of the county was drawn up by ridings, hundreds or wapentakes, and 'vills'. It records the number of carucates in each settlement, while the name of the tenant-in-chief is interlined systematically above the place-name. The Yorkshire Summary, therefore, is the geographical counterpart of the feudally arranged Evesham K, which also employs the technique of interlineation in order to refer to the hundred in which each manor lay. In fact the Yorkshire Summary lends support to the hypothesis that Evesham K was derived from an outline draft of Gloucestershire Domesday, for the task of converting from geographical to feudal ordering and vice versa could have been accomplished accurately and speedily with the aid of interlinear schedules. The Yorkshire Summary may have been derived ultimately from the normal processes of fiscal administration, for it begins with a statement of danegeld assessments (in carucates) for the various districts that made up the city of York. This would explain the apparent geographical order in which the settlements occur:[94] the men who rode so purposefully from place to place were not the Domesday commissioners, but the geld collectors whose schedule had been 'borrowed' for other purposes. Furthermore places outside the historic county do not appear in the Summary.[95] This geographically arranged Domesday satellite is remarkable chiefly because it was incorporated in the abbreviation compiled from the circuit draft and because its interlinear format reveals one half of a hitherto unappreciated administrative technique – the use of what we might describe as 'conversion tables'.

The minor Domesday satellites exhibit a good deal of variety, as might be expected of the primary, county-based phase of the inquest. Although each shire, through its sheriff, presumably received an identical set of instructions for the conduct of the great survey, the response was far from being identical. It is doubtful whether we shall ever be able to reconstruct with certainty the exact procedure followed in any particular circuit. What is certain is that we should not oversimplify by presupposing uniformity of practice. This is why the concept of 'original returns' sent to Winchester was always inappropriate, for it suggested a homogeneous body of documents that formed the basis of Great Domesday. The Galbraith thesis, now more or less universally accepted, envisages returns to Winchester in the shape of provincial or circuit drafts. These,

[93]DBI 379a–381a, 381b–382a, translated by W. Farrer in *VCH Yorkshire* II (London, Constable, 1912), pp. 296–327. The Yorkshire Summary follows Lincolnshire Domesday and the claims section, while fo. 381a bears the carucage schedule of the North Riding fief of Count Alan, together with a summary of all the lands of the count and his men. The arrangement is less strictly geographical than that of the main Summary: H.C. Darby and I.S. Maxwell, eds., *The Domesday Geography of Northern England* (Cambridge, CUP, 1962), p. 460. For a discussion see Darby and Maxwell, *op. cit.*, pp. 458–94; Finn, *Yorkshire Domesday*, pp. 16–22 and *passim*. The Yorkshire Summary needs to be compared with a section of the royal demesne in Yorkshire Domesday itself: DBI 300a–302a; Harvey, 'Domesday Book and its Predecessors', pp. 762–3.
[94]Darby and Maxwell, *Domesday Geography of Northern England*, pp. 459, 489.
[95]*Op. cit.*, p. 461.

too, may have been far from uniform, judging from the two surviving examples and allowing for the possibility that Exeter Domesday was super-seded by a more polished draft arranged strictly by counties, like Little Domesday. And if the circuit drafts are indeed to be regarded as the true original returns, we have to admit that behind each one must have lain a vast mass of preliminary material, together with the day-to-day records of shrieval, hundredal and manorial administration. The originality of the original returns has more to do with their unique place in English administrative history than with their position in the chronology of the making of Domesday Book.

The concept of Domesday Book as a geld book has been firmly put aside but, if Great Domesday was always intended by its initiators as the end-product of the whole exercise, it can hardly be regarded alternatively as the blueprint for a feudal society modelled on that of Philip I's France. The primary unit within which the material is arranged is the shire, the nucleus of local government at the king's command and to which the fief is subsidiary. The more 'feudal' arrangement of the material in Exeter Domesday was not adhered to in Great Domesday and the *Inquisitio Eliensis* is a privately made abstraction from the returns of three circuits.[96] The Oxfordshire fief of William FitzOsbern is pure anachronism, for he had been killed in battle in 1071,[97] while the oft-repeated phrase *tempore regis Edwardi* exemplifies the strongly retrospective character of Domesday Book. To reconstruct the feudal geography of Domesday England, or any part of it outside the boundaries of a single county, requires an immense effort of reorganization.[98] Modern historians of individual fiefs still confine themselves inappropriately and unnecessarily to the county format.[99] Further-more two of the standard attributes of a feudal society – the seigneurial castle and the knightly subtenant – are either neglected or undifferentiated in the Domesday texts. According to Professor H.C. Darby 'castles are named, or implied, in Domesday Book in connexion with 48 places, of which 27 were boroughs'.[100] The total number of unnamed 'knights' (*milites*) in the two volumes of Domesday Book, including six stated to have been English, is only 115.[101] Of course most of the lay tenants-in-chief had presumably trained as knights, as had their subtenants who may have numbered several thousand,[102]

[96] Some of the complexities that lay behind this process are discussed in Sawyer, 'Original Returns', pp. 186–90.

[97] DBI 161a.

[98] For example, P. Byrne, 'The Aristocracy in the West Midland and Welsh Border Regions of England in the Late Eleventh Century' (University College, Dublin, MA thesis, 1972); Clarke, 'Early Surveys of Evesham Abbey', pp. 372–417.

[99] For example, J.A. Raftis, *The Estates of Ramsey Abbey: a Study in Economic Growth and Organi-zation* (Toronto, Pontifical Institute of Mediaeval Studies, 1957), p. 20; F.R.H. Du Boulay, *The Lordship of Canterbury: an Essay on Medieval Society* (London, Nelson, 1966), pp. 43–6; E. King, *Peterborough Abbey, 1086–1310: a Study in the Land Market* (Cambridge, CUP, 1973), p. 14. Failure to escape from the county format can have disastrous results: R.W. Finn, *Domesday Studies: the Norman Conquest and its Effects on the Economy, 1066–86* (London, Longman, 1971); H.B. Clarke, 'Domesday Slavery (adjusted for Slaves)', *Midland History* I, no. 4 (1972), pp. 43–4.

[100] *Domesday Book*, pp. 313–14. See also the map and list at pp. 316–17.

[101] *Op. cit.*, p. 337. The relation between this figure and a sample of 'nearly 500' needs to be explained: S.[P.J.] Harvey, 'The Knight and the Knight's Fee in England', *Past and Present*, no. 49 (1970), pp. 14–18.

[102] Darby, *Domesday Book*, p. 89.

but whose precise identity is often unknown or uncertain. At best our view of the feudal superstructure of Domesday England is decidedly hazy and not a word was written about military quotas, despite the appearance of Archbishop Lanfranc's knights and the 'men' (*homines*) of the abbot of Peterborough.[103] What Domesday Book, together with its major and minor satellites, does reveal is a subtle blend of change and continuity that has usually been obscured by the excessive polarization of historical opinion.

APPENDIX:

The Manuscripts of the Domesday Satellites

The Domesday satellites, in the sense advocated in the foregoing discussion, are scattered among the folios of the two volumes of Domesday Book and in manuscript repositories at Cambridge, Exeter and London. After the relevant parts of Domesday Book itself (nos. 1–4) the independent satellites are here listed in strict archival order. The texts classified as records of shrieval, hundredal and manorial administration in Table 4.1 have not been included. A degree of uncertainty attaches to nos. 8 and 9 and perhaps also to no. 18, which may be contemporary with the Domesday survey rather than integral elements of it. The main text of the *Inquisitio Eliensis* incorporates claims and summaries, while other lands claimed by the monks of Ely in five counties come after the section known as the *Nomina Villarum*.[1] I hope to publish complete editions of nos. 16 and 17 elsewhere.

Among the large number of surviving schedules and surveys, it is always possible that other Domesday satellites in the strict sense will be discovered by close textual analysis. I am preparing for publication a discussion and provisional list under the title 'Pre-Domesday and Post-Domesday English Surveys, 900–1200: a Proposed Typology'. During this period of English history the prime characteristic shared by most types of 'survey', used here in a non-technical sense, is that the individual items are described or identified in terms of hides, carucates or (in Kent) sulungs. Apart from a complete list, one of the prerequisites for further progress in understanding these texts is that each one should be accorded a clear and unambiguous name. As far as I am aware, only the Evesham Abbey series has been treated in this way. In this case the two cartularies that preserve the surveys were taken in chronological order and a capital letter was assigned to each text in order of occurrence in the manuscripts, omitting the letter 'I' lest it should be confused with the Roman

---

[103]DBI 4a–b, 221b–222a. These lists should be compared with the section of Exeter Domesday detailing the knights of Queen Matilda in Dorset: Exon, fos. 31–32, printed in Ellis, *Additamenta*, pp. 31–3.

[1]See above, pp. 53, n. 12; 66, nn. 91–2. The last part of the *Inquisitio Eliensis* (Hamilton, *op. cit.*, pp. 184–9) occurs only in no. 6.

numeral when cited alone. As it happens, the first and last surveys in this series have been identified as Domesday satellites, along with Evesham K. This may be the appropriate place and time, therefore, to invite students of the various English scriptoria to name comparable texts as logically and systematically as possible.

1   DBI 208a-b (Huntingdonshire), 373a-374a (Yorkshire), 375a-377b (Lincolnshire). *Clamores* in circuit VI.

2   DBI 379a-381a, 381b-382a. Yorkshire Summary.

3   DBI 381a. Summary of the fief of Count Alan in Yorkshire.

4   DBII 99a-103b (Essex), 273b-280a (Norfolk), 447b-449b (Suffolk). *Invasiones super regem* in circuit VII.

5   Cambridge, Corpus Christi College, MS 111, pp. 128-129, printed in Hunt, *Two Chartularies*, pp. 67-8. Bath A.

6   Cambridge, Trinity College, MS O.2.1, fos. 191ᵛ-221ᵛ, printed in Hamilton, *Inquisitio Comitatus Cantabrigiensis*, pp. 97-189. *Inquisitio Eliensis*. See also nos. 7, 13.

7   Cambridge, Trinity College, MS O.2.41, pp. 161-274, printed in Hamilton, *op. cit.*, pp. 97-183. *Inquisitio Eliensis*. See also nos. 6, 13.

8   Cambridge, University Library, MS Ee. 3.60, fos. 178-181ᵛ, printed in Hervey, *Pinchbeck Register* I, pp. 410-18. The Feudal Book of Abbot Baldwin. See also no. 9.

9   Cambridge, University Library, MS Mm. 4.19, fos. 124-131ᵛ, printed in Douglas, *Feudal Documents*, pp. 3-15. The Feudal Book of Abbot Baldwin. See also no. 8.

10   Exeter, Dean & Chapter, MS 3500, fos. 11-12ᵛ, 25-62ᵛ, 83-494ᵛ, printed in Ellis, *Additamenta*, pp. 11-12, 26-56, 75-457. Exeter Domesday or Exon Domesday.

11   Exeter, Dean & Chapter, MS 3500, fos. 173 (Glastonbury Abbey, its knights and English thegns in Somerset), 527ᵛ-528ᵛ (Glastonbury Abbey in circuit II and the church of St Petroc in Cornwall), 530ᵛ-531 (several lay tenants-in-chief in circuit II), printed in Ellis, *op. cit.*, pp. 160-1, 490-2. Summaries.

12   Exeter, Dean & Chapter, MS 3500, fos. 495—525 (Devon, Cornwall and Somerset), printed in Ellis, *op. cit.*, pp. 457-89. *Terrae occupatae* in circuit II.

13   London, British Library, MS Cotton Tiberius A vi, fos. 36-69, printed in Hamilton, *op. cit.*, pp. 97-183. *Inquisitio Eliensis*. See also nos. 6, 7.

14   London, British Library, MS Cotton Tiberius A vi, fos. 71-98ᵛ, printed in Hamilton, *op. cit.*, pp. 1-96. *Inquisitio Comitatus Cantabrigiensis*.

15   London, British Library, MS Cotton Vespasian B xxiv, fos. 6-7ᵛ, printed in Sawyer, 'Evesham A, a Domesday Text', pp. 22-36. Evesham A.

16   London, British Library, MS Cotton Vespasian B xxiv, fos. 57-62, edited in Clarke, 'Early Surveys of Evesham Abbey', pp. 553-68. Evesham K.

17   London, British Library, MS Harley 3763, fo. 82, edited in Clarke, *op. cit.*, pp. 584-5. Evesham Q.

18   London, British Library, MS Sloane 986, fo. 67, printed in Fowler, 'An Early Cambridgeshire Feodary', p. 443. Braybrooke Feodary.

CHAPTER FIVE

1066–1086:
A Tenurial Revolution?

Peter Sawyer

Students of English feudal history are fortunate to have Domesday Book as their starting point; despite the great changes that occurred later the roots of the feudal relationships of medieval England can be traced in it. One of the main purposes of the enquiry was, indeed, to discover 'what or how much everybody had who was occupying land in England, in land or cattle and how much it was worth'.[1] Enquiry was also made into the names of pre-Conquest tenants and that information is given in most entries, but not in all. Domesday Book's evidence about landholding before and after the Conquest suggests that there was a dramatic change in tenurial structure in the 20 years after 1066. Some extensive estates did remain more or less intact in the hands of new owners but, according to Domesday Book, most pre-Conquest manors were held by free men and women of no more than local importance almost all of whom were replaced by a small group of William's supporters, some of whom held vast estates. A few English landowners survived and in 1086 they or their heirs held at least part of their former property but most manors changed hands. Many of the fiefs of 1086 consisted of manors that had formerly been held by numerous individuals. In Hampshire, for example, Hugh de Port's fief had been held by at least 40 different people before the Conquest.[2] The general impression given by Domesday Book is, therefore, that a pre-Conquest 'squirearchy' was largely replaced by, or subordinated to, a new aristocracy. Sir Frank Stenton's assertion that 'there can be no question that the redistribution of land after the Norman Conquest amounted to a tenurial revolution of

In the notes to this chapter the following abbreviations for counties will be used:

Bd Bedfordshire; Bk Buckinghamshire; Brk Berkshire; C Cambridgeshire; Co Cornwall; D Devon; Db Derbyshire; Do Dorset; E Essex; Gl Gloucestershire; Ha Hampshire; Hrt Hertfordshire; Hu Huntingdonshire; K Kent; L Lincolnshire; Lei Leicestershire; Mx Middlesex; Nf Norfolk; Nt Nottinghamshire; Nth Northamptonshire; O Oxfordshire; R Rutland; Sa Shropshire; Sf Suffolk; So Somerset; Sr Surrey; Sx Sussex; W Wiltshire; Wa Warwickshire; Y Yorkshire

[1] *The Anglo-Saxon Chronicle, s.a.* 1085, trans. D. Whitelock *et al.* (London, Eyre & Spottiswoode, 1961), p. 161.
[2] DB I 44b–46b.

the most far-reaching kind' seems to be well grounded in the evidence of Domesday Book.[3]

There are, however, indications that that evidence may be somewhat misleading. Some of the pre-Conquest tenants named in Domesday Book can be shown to have been not owners but sub-tenants of lords who are not named, and there are reasons to suspect that this was true of many others. The full extent of pre-Conquest lordships is thus concealed. What is more, there are hints that at least some of the un-named lords were the *antecessores* from whom William's tenants-in-chief derived their legal title. It is remarkable that, despite the many changes that occurred during William's reign, as land was sold, exchanged, given away or forfeited, so many identifiable pre-Conquest estates remained more or less intact to form the basis of fiefs in 1086. It will be argued here that Domesday Book conceals many other large pre-Conquest lordships that similarly survived the Conquest to form feudal honours and that, as a result, the scale of the tenurial revolution after the Conquest has been exaggerated and the character of the transition from Anglo-Saxon to Anglo-Norman England has been misinterpreted.

The first and most obvious problem to be faced in any attempt to reconstruct pre-Conquest lordships is the identification of the tenants named in Domesday Book. Most are only given a single name and, apart from the few instances of a name appearing only once, it is normally impossible to determine how many individuals are represented by one name. As Round remarked, 'in the absence of a distinctive name or of a definite succession, the identification of English thegns is apt to be rash work'.[4]

The identification of individuals depends on the provision of such additional details as the name of the father, or a son, a nick-name or a title. Thus, among the 450 entries in which the tenant or his lord is called Aelfric there are 22 in Bedfordshire, Buckinghamshire and Cambridgeshire in which he is called the son of Goding.[5] It is not possible to say whether the same man appears else-where without that detail or in some other guise. Domesday Book was certainly not consistent. Titles such as *comes* or *stalre* or other details that make identi-fication possible were not always given. Some omissions can be detected with the help of Domesday satellites or duplicate entries. Thus the *Inquisitio Comitatus Cantabrigiensis* shows that the Ulf named in the Cambridgeshire Domesday as the tenant of Fen Drayton was in fact Ulf *Fenesce*, who is named as a tenant in Derbyshire, Huntingdonshire and Lincolnshire.[6] Similarly, Exeter Domesday shows that the Brihtric who held Leigh in Churchstow, Devon, was in fact the son of Aelfgar and therefore one of the greatest landowners.[7] He is only described as the son of Aelfgar in two counties. In Worcestershire where he held 2 hides from the bishop, and in Gloucestershire where Queen Matilda

[3]F.M. Stenton, *Preparatory to Anglo-Saxon England*, ed. D.M. Stenton (Oxford, Clarendon Press, 1970), p. 325.

[4]*VCH So* I (1906), p. 418.

[5]Olof von Feilitzen, *The Pre-Conquest Personal Names of Domesday Book* (Uppsala, Nomina Germanica 3, 1937), pp. 176–80.

[6]N.E.S.A. Hamilton, *Inquisitio Comitatus Cantabrigiensis* (London, John Murray, 1876), p. 91; DB I 197b; cf. von Feilitzen, *Personal Names*, p. 401.

[7]Exon, fo. 397; DB I 112b.

obtained his great manor of Tewkesbury and other property held by him and his men, worth in all over £300.[8] Almost all Matilda's property in Cornwall, Devon and Dorset had been held by a Brihtric and there is no good reason to doubt that he was the same man.[9] Brihtric son of Aelfgar held a few manors that appear in other fiefs, some as gifts of the queen,[10] and it is therefore possible that other references to Brihtric, especially in the west, were to the same man, but that cannot be proved. We are on safer ground in assuming that most of the manors held in turn by Brihtric and Matilda had belonged to one pre-Conquest estate. Similarly, as all explicit references to Ulf *Fenisc* occur in connection with Gilbert de Ghent's fief, it seems more reasonable to assume that the Ulf who was Gilbert's predecessor in six other counties was the same man than that Gilbert had several predecessors called Ulf.[11] There are many other examples. In Geoffrey de Mandeville's fief most references to Asgar are presumably to Asgar the staller and in Count Alan's fief Eadgifu the Fair often appears simply as Eadgifu.[12]

The most natural explanation for these, and similar, cases is that William often granted all the lands of one English landowner to one person. This would normally have been done by writs addressed to the relevant shire courts or by some form of delivery effected by royal agents. The new owner's title depended on such a grant and he was, in theory, supposed to have the same rights as his *antecessor*. This was normally the tenant on the eve of the Conquest but there are exceptions. Some, like Earl Aelfgar, died several years before 1066, while others were post-Conquest owners, such as Hugh de Beauchamp's *antecessor* Ralf Tallebosc. It is, however, made clear in some entries that Ralf in his turn traced his title back to a pre-Conquest owner.[13] The significance of pre-Conquest ownership is demonstrated by the particular attention given to property that an *antecessor* acquired after the Conquest,[14] and there are many references to tenants-in-chief claiming lands that had been held by their *antecessores* in the time of King Edward. Thus Gilbert de Ghent and Henry de Ferrers claimed land in the Isle of Axholme that had been held by their *antecessores*, Ulf *Fenisc* and Siward *Barn*, that had been acquired, along with the rest of Axholme, by Geoffrey de Wirce. The men of the West Riding of Lindsey testified in favour of these claims.[15] In Derbyshire Henry de Ferrers had to face a similar claim from Geoffrey Alselin who considered that Henry's manor of Scropton should be in his fief as it had belonged to his *antecessor*, Toki

---

[8]DB I 163b–64a, 173a.

[9]DB I 75b, 101ab, 120ab. Queen Matilda also had land in Bk which had belonged to Earl Aelfgar, who was presumably Brihtric's father, DB I 152b.

[10]Tyneham Do, Sampford Peverell D, and Wickwar Gl were given by the queen, DB I 83a, 113a, 170a; William de Eu held one of the manors that had belonged to Brihtric son of Aelfgar, in Gl, DB I 166b. See also *VCH Do* III (1968), p. 31.

[11]See note 28 below.

[12]See notes 26 and 31 below.

[13]*VCH Bd* I (1904), pp. 200–1.

[14]For example at *Eddintone* K, Chessington Sr, in Wantage Hundred Brk, and at Tiscot Hrt, DB I 6a, 36b, 60b, 137b; also at Kelvedon Hatch, Lees and Manhall E, and in Nf, DB II 14b–15a, 59a, 62b, 187b.

[15]DB I 376b.

son of Auti.[16] It is no less revealing that in the same county Gilbert de Ghent held a manor that the Domesday jurors said had not belonged to Ulf *Fenisc* in Edward's reign.[17] Similarly, Geoffrey de Mandeville is described as holding land in Surrey *injuste quia ad terram Asgari non pertinet*, while in Suffolk the description of his manor of Thorington ends *non est de honore Ansgari*.[18] At the other end of the country, the same term was used in Exeter Domesday to describe lands that had not belonged to the *antecessores* of the Count of Mortain.[19]

Post-Conquest tenants clearly had a claim to property that had belonged to their *antecessores*, apart from manors that had been granted to someone else or that had been disposed of. It is sometimes possible to show how part of an estate was detached from the rest. Thus, Geoffrey de Wirce acquired the lands of Leofwine and his son Leofric, apparently by marriage,[20] but Domesday Book shows that he exchanged one of Leofwine's manors, Thurcaston in Leicestershire, with the king; in 1086 it was held by Hugh de Grandmesnil.[21] There were also some changes on the eve of the Conquest. For example, Aethelric son of Maergeat granted Doddington Pigot, Lincolnshire, to Westminster Abbey. It duly appears in the abbey's fief while the rest of his property was held by Robert de Vesci.[22] Such evidence is exceptional and in the absence of additional details to aid identification, we can normally only hope to recognize the property of an *antecessor* that was retained by his main successor or, if it was divided, by his successors. A good example of a division is provided by the fiefs of Robert d'Oilli and Miles Crispin, both of whom claimed Wigot of Wallingford and a man called Brihtric as their *antecessores*.[23] This division was probably made when Miles married Robert's daughter.[24]

Several pre-Conquest estates that can be recognized in this way were very large. Apart from members of the royal family and the earls,[25] many landowners held land in several counties. Asgar the staller had land in at least ten,[26] Wulfweard *Wita* in eleven,[27] Ulf *Fenisc* in nine,[28] Alstan of Boscombe in eight,[29]

---

[16]DB I 274b. For Toki and Geoffrey see DB I 336a, 369b–70a and F.M. Stenton in C.W. Foster and T. Longley, *The Lincolnshire Domesday and the Lindsey Survey* (Lincoln Record Society 19, 1924), p. xxx.

[17]DB I 277b.

[18]DB I 36a, DB II 412b. Geoffrey also held land in Creeting Sf *sed non pertinuit ad feudum ansgari*, DB II 411a. See also DB I 167a *sed non fuit Alestani*, that is of Boscombe, the *antecessor* of William de Eu.

[19]Exon, fos. 210–23.   [20]Stenton, *Preparatory*, p. 329.
[21]DB I 232a, 235b.   [22]DB I 346a, 363a, 377a.
[23]Miles – DB I 71a, 149b–50b, 159ab, 169b; Robert – DB I 62a, 137b, 149ab, 158ab.
[24]*VCH Bd* I, p. 202.

[25]Ann Williams, 'Land and power in the eleventh-century: the estates of Harold Godwinesson', in R. Allen Brown, ed., *Proceedings of the Battle Conference III 1980* (Woodbridge, Boydell and Brewer, 198), pp. 171–87, 230–34.

[26]DB I 62a Brk, 129b Mx, 139b Hrt, 149b Bk, 159b–60a O, 197a C, 227ab Nth, 243b Wa; DB II 57b–63a E, 411ab Sf. He also had men in Bd (DB I 209b) and Nf (DB II 149b) and probably owned land in Sr, see below p. 84.

[27]DB I 1b, 9a K, 62b Brk, 66a W, 82a Do, 87a So, 129a–30a Mx, 153a Bk, 160a O, 169a Gl 212a Bd (*Wluuardus leuet*), 337a L.

[28]DB I 149b Brk, 159b O, 197ab C, 207a Hu, 215a Bd, 227b Nth, 227b Db, 290b Nt, 354b–56a L. Burley on the Hill R, (DB I 293b) is duplicated DB I 355b.

and Wigot of Wallingford in at least seven.[30] Others were less extensive but were nonetheless substantial. Eadgifu the Fair's property, for example, lay mainly in Cambridgeshire but she had significant interests in neighbouring counties and in Buckinghamshire.[31] Others, like Eadric of Laxfield in Suffolk[32] or Wihtgar son of Aelfric, lord of Clare in Essex[33] had important estates largely limited to one or two counties.

The extent of an estate is, of course, no measure of its value. Some land-owners who only had property in one of two counties were far wealthier than others whose estates were more widely scattered. Thus Cheping, a Hampshire thegn, had property there and in Berkshire worth about £140[34] and Toki, William de Warenne's *antecessor* in Cambridgeshire and Norfolk, had lands worth over £130.[35] In contrast, Aethelric son of Maergeat's estate, including what he gave to Westminster Abbey, was worth less than £65 even though it extended into four counties[36] while Eadnoth the staller's, in seven counties, was worth even less.[37]

There were many other valuable estates in pre-Conquest England but, according to Domesday Book, most tenants had relatively little land and almost all post-Conquest fiefs included manors that had been held by many such small-scale landowners. In Wiltshire, for example, Ernulf de Hesdin had 19 named predecessors, only three of whom had property worth more than £4.[38] It can sometimes be shown that apparently independent predecessors of a Norman lord were kinsmen. Domesday Book rarely draws attention to such relationships and many instances must remain undetected. In Lincolnshire, for example, the fact that two of Robert Dispensator's *antecessores*, Aki and Wiglac, were sons of the third, Siward, is only revealed by the list of pre-Conquest landowners at the beginning of the county survey.[39] The number of completely independent pre-Conquest tenants is therefore smaller than Domesday Book suggests. There were, nevertheless, many of them but it is unlikely that they were all *antecessores* from whom the Norman owners traced their title. The transfer of land to an individual Norman from dozens of predecessors would have posed great administrative problems and led to many

---

[29]DB I 47a Ha, 61a Brk, 71b W, 80b–82a Do, 96b So, 138b Hrt, 166b–67a Gl, 211b–12a Bd.

[30]DB I 28b Sx, 50b Ha, 61b–2a Brk, 71a W, 149b–50a Bk, 158a–59b O, 169b Gl. He probably also held land in Mx and Wa (DB I 129a, 239a), cf. von Feilitzen, *Personal Names*, p. 404. In *VCH W* II (1955), pp. 67–8 R.R. Darlington claimed that he held land in 11 shires but that total appears to include places that Wigot acquired after the conquest in Sr and Hrt (DB I 36b, 137b).

[31]DB I 134a, 137a Hrt, 146b, 152a Bk, 193b–95b C: DB II 7b, 35ab E, 284b–85a Nf, 430b–31a Sf.

[32]von Feilitzen, *Personal Names*, pp. 233–36.

[33]von Feilitzen, *Personal Names*, p. 414.

[34]DB I 38b, 39b, 46b–47a, 51a, 52a Ha, 62b Brk.

[35]DB I 196ab C; DB II 157b–69b Nf.

[36]DB I 225a Nth, 234a Lei, 242b Wa, 346a, 363a L.

[37]DB I 58b, 60a Brk, 68b–69a W, 80a Do, 91b, 98a (= Exon, fo. 447, *Alnodus stalro*) So, 104b D, 166b Gl, 237a Lei.

[38]DB I 69b–70a.

[39]*Achi filius Siuuardi et Wilac frater ejus*, DB I 337a, cf. 363b. For other examples see DB I 277a, where Leofric and Leofnoth were apparently brothers, and *VCH Nth* I (1902), p. 293 for the relationship between the *antecessores* of Gunfrid de Cioches.

more disputes about ownership than are reported. Most disputes mentioned in Domesday Book were not, in fact, about the ownership of manors but about small parcels of land or appurtenances such as soke-rights, mills, fisheries, woods and even churches. It is significant that the name of the pre-Conquest tenant was not an essential item of information. In Oxfordshire only one of Robert d'Oilli's predecessors, Wigot, is named[40] and the Count of Evreux's fief names none.[41] In Leicestershire the former tenants of Hugh de Grandmesnil's manors are named in only 12 entries and omitted in 57.[42] Most counties have entries that simply state that a manor had been held by one or more un-named people. The statement that the manor of Marston in Bedfordshire had been held by 21 sokemen is unusual only in the large number of people involved.[43] Such groups cannot have been *antecessores* in the sense that Ulf *Fenisc* was Gilbert de Ghent's. It is more likely that they were sub-tenants of a lord who is not named.

It is sometimes possible to demonstrate that the people named as pre-Conquest tenants were not the owners from whom title was traced. This can be seen most clearly in those counties for which Domesday supplies a separate section of *clamores*. The longest of these is for Lincolnshire and it is reported there that Robert of Stafford claimed against Count Alan some land in Billingborough that had been held by Carle, Robert's *antecessor*. This was said to be unjust because Carle held this land from Ralf the staller, whose lands passed to Count Alan. In the text of the Lincolnshire Domesday Billingborough is said to have been held by Carle with no mention of Ralf's superior interest.[44] Robert made a similar claim against Count Alan in respect of land that Carle had held in Stoke Rochford, but there the text of the survey named Ralf the staller as the former owner.[45] It appears that Carle was Ralf's tenant in both places and that Domesday is inconsistent, naming him in one entry and his lord in another. In the Yorkshire *clamores* Ralf Paganel claimed land in Nun Monkton that had belonged to his *antecessor* Merleswein but in the survey Nun Monkton is said to have been held by five thegns with no mention of Merleswein.[46] In the Huntingdonshire *clamores* Summerled is described as having held his land from Thorulf, who gave it to him, and afterwards from Thorulf's sons, who had sake and soke over him. There is no mention of Thorulf in the Huntingdonshire survey but Summerled appears as the former tenant of Waresley.[47] In the same *clamores* Aelgeat is described as having $1\frac{1}{2}$ hides from Earl Tosti, and later from Earl Waltheof. The only Aelgeat in the Huntingdonshire survey was the former tenant of $1\frac{1}{2}$ hides in Hail Weston.[48] There is no mention there of either Tosti or Waltheof, although the latter's interest may be deduced from the fact that his widow, Judith, claimed this land. In all these entries, and others, the *clamores* reveal superior interests that are concealed by the text of Domesday Book.

[40] DB I 158ab.
[41] DB I 157a.
[42] DB I 232a–33a.
[43] DB I 214a.
[44] DB I 348a, 377b.
[45] DB I 348b, 377a.
[46] DB I 329a, 374a.
[47] DB I 206b, 208a.
[48] DB I 206b, 208a.

There are hints of concealed sub-tenancies within the text of the survey itself. Bygrave in Hertfordshire, for example, is said to have been held by Leodmaer, Archbishop Stigand's man, but on that manor there were two soke-men who could not sell without Stigand's permission, suggesting that Leodmaer was not just Stigand's man, but his tenant.[49] There are also many references to tenants who were either not free to leave their lord or could only do so with their lord's permission. The lord is named in many entries, but not in all. Another indication of concealed lordship is provided by the Lincolnshire Domesday which lists a number of pre-Conquest landowners who were especially privileged and had sake, soke, toll and team throughout the county. At least two of these do not appear as landowners in the county survey.[50] The similar list of privileged landowners in Derbyshire and Nottinghamshire includes Aelfgifu *comitissa* who did not have land in either county, according to Domesday.[51]

There is no doubt that there were many sub-tenants on the eve of the Conquest. There are explicit references to tenants holding of or under someone else. Brihtric son of Aelfgar had a number of un-named thegns as tenants at Tewkesbury *in sua potestate*.[52] In Leicestershire the whole fief of Earl Aubrey is said to have been held by Harding and his men but, as none of his men is named, we do not know which manors Harding kept in demesne.[53] Similarly, in Warwickshire all Geoffrey de Wirce's fief is described as having belonged to Leofwine although Wulfric is named as the former tenant of one of his manors, Appleford.[54] He was presumably Leofwine's tenant, as he was Geoffrey's later. As already mentioned, Domesday Book can sometimes be shown to have omitted reference to sub-tenants. The fact that Ralf the staller had Carle as tenant at Stoke Rochford is only revealed by the *clamores*[55] and these also show that Tonne had at least parts of Baumber and Edlington, presumably as the sub-tenant of Ulf *Fenisc* who is named as the owner of both places.[56] The Exeter Domesday also shows that Domesday Book fails to name some sub-tenants, for example at Wedfield in Devon.[57]

In some counties, for example Lincolnshire and Wiltshire, Domesday mentions no sub-tenants at all, but it is hardly likely that they did not exist. The explanation must be that Domesday either failed to mention them or that some of the people who are named were themselves sub-tenants. When sub-tenancies are mentioned, their nature is rarely specified. There are references to land being held at farm or on a lease, generally for three lives or less, but most entries only state that A held *de* or *sub* B. There are, however, many references to two particular forms of superiority that served as the basis for post-Conquest claims; commendation and soke. It will be convenient to consider commendation first. Domesday Book shows that the lands held by the men and women who were commended to a pre-Conquest lord were often acquired by that lord's successor. Thus, in Middlesex Geoffrey de Mandeville obtained not

[49]DB I 135a.
[51]DB I 280b.
[52]DB I 163b.
[54]DB I 243b.
[56]DB I 354b, 375b.

[50]Harold the staller and Fyach, DB I 337a.
[53]DB I 231b.
[55]See note 45 above.
[57]Exon, fo. 211b.

only all the land of Asgar the staller but also all that Asgar's men had held.[58] Similarly, the Bishop of Coutances obtained most of the land that had been held in Buckinghamshire by the men of his *antecessor* in that county, Burgraed,[59] while in Northamptonshire he claimed from Countess Judith land that had been held by Burgraed's men and from William Peverel he claimed rights over Burgraed's sokemen.[60] Such examples suggest that pre-Conquest England had fiefs very much like those of 1086. This possibility was vigorously denied by Round on the ground that the lands of a lord and his men did not always pass 'as an indivisible whole' into a post-Conquest fief.[61] He cited the example of Aelfric son of Goding, an important Buckinghamshire landowner. His demesne estates were acquired by Walter Gifford but those of his men were dispersed among several fiefs. Walter only obtained seven but the Count of Mortain had as many, and others were held by Miles Crispin, Countess Judith and Swaerting.[62] In Round's judgement such examples, and there are many others, demonstrated the weakness of the bond between lord and man in pre-Conquest England. This is a questionable conclusion.

In the first place it is somewhat misleading to put greater weight on the examples of dispersal than on those where the lands of a lord and his men remained undivided. If Aelfric son of Goding's hold over his men was weak, Asgar the staller's appears to have been strong, at least in Middlesex.

There are other examples of undivided transfers and many where the dispersed lands were only a tiny part of the whole. In Cambridgeshire, for example, Count Alan held all but one of the demesne manors of Eadgifu the Fair, the exception was held by the king, and almost £150 worth of land that had been held by more than 120 of her men and women, with a total assessment of over 165 hides.[63] This outweighs the 10 entries that show about seven hides that had been held by 15 of Eadgifu's men and women dispersed among five other fiefs.[64] In considering the strength of pre-Conquest lordships such cases merit attention. It may also be remarked that disruption after the Conquest hardly proves that the bonds of lordship were weak before it. The lands held by a lord's men must sometimes have been dispersed by exactly the same kinds of exchange and transfer that also affected demesne manors.

Further proof of the weakness of pre-Conquest lordship has been sought in the freedom enjoyed by many tenants to seek new lords. It is, however, doubtful whether Domesday's references to freedom should be taken so literally. The ideal of loyalty to a lord was familiar in pre-Conquest England and, as Maitland remarked, 'we cannot believe that either party to the contract (of commendation) could dissolve it just when the other party had some need to enforce it'.[65] After the Battle of Hastings many people must have found it urgently necessary to find new lords but in normal circumstances such shifts of loyalty would only have been necessary, or even politic, when a lord fell out of favour and was exiled or killed. The literal interpretation of Domesday's refer-

---

[58]DB I 129b.
[60]DB I 225b, 229a.
[62]DB I 146a–48a, 150b, 152b, 153a.
[64]DB I 196b, 198a–200a, 201ab.
[65]F.W. Maitland, *Domesday Book and Beyond* (Cambridge, CUP, 1897), p. 73.

[59]DB I 145ab, 146b, 151b.
[61]*VCH Bk* I (1905), pp. 218–9.
[63]DB I 189b, 193b–95b.

ences to freedom would imply that pre-Conquest England enjoyed social anarchy. One entry raises the problem in an acute form. Feckenham in Worcestershire was held from Earl Edwin by five thegns who could go with the land where they would and had under them four knights who were as free as themselves.[66]

The suspicion that freedom in Domesday Book had a special meaning is encouraged by the fact that many people who clearly enjoyed the greatest degree of freedom, the bishops, earls and leading thegns, are normally never described as free. In Middlesex, for example, where many entries state whether the pre-Conquest tenant was free to sell or grant his land, this formula is never used for Archbishop Stigand, Bishop William of London, for the earls, for Godgifu or for Earl Ralf's son Harold, or for such important *antecessores* as the king's housecarl Ulf, Wigot of Wallingford, Eadmaer *atule*, Asgar the staller or Wulfweard *Wita*. The implication is that the people described as free in fact had some limitation on their freedom.

One limitation that is frequently mentioned concerned the right to transfer land. Many men and women were free to choose a new lord but not to give him any claim over land that they held. In Essex, for example, Geoffrey de Mandeville had a manor called Shelley that had been held by *Levedai* (Leofdaeg) but it is said not to have been of Asgar's fief because he was only Asgar's man.[67] Another of Geoffrey's manors, Abbess Roding, belonged to Barking Abbey before the Conquest and 'he who held this land was only the man of Geoffrey's *antecessor* and had no power to put this land in the possession of anyone but the abbey'.[68]

Simple commendation, that is the acknowledgement of a lord without transferring any right over land, must have created a relatively weak bond but this implies that the lordship over the land that was not transferred was relatively strong. The dispersal of the lands of the men of Aelfric son of Goding, cited by Round to prove the weakness of lordship, could alternatively have been the result of strong land-lordship. Men who were free to commend themselves must often have chosen their own land-lord but for various reasons they might turn elsewhere and if the land-lord was powerful or influential he would normally retain his rights. This could produce the kind of situation described at Weston Underwood in Buckinghamshire where the Bishop of Coutances held a manor that had been held by 11 thegns, 10 of them the men of the Bishop's *antecessor* Burgraed, while the other was the man of an unidentified *Alric*.[69]

The rights that could not be legally transferred by simple commendation are variously described. They generally included soke and sometimes custom. Thus in the Bishop of London's manor of Copford in Essex a free man held a virgate of land and he could go whither he would, that is he could put himself

---

[66]DB I 180b.   [67]DB II 57b.

[68]DB II 57b. Maitland, *Domesday Book and Beyond*, p. 72, assumed that the tenant was un-named and commended to Leofhild, Geoffrey's *antecessor*. A more satisfactory interpretation is that Leofhild was the tenant and was herself commended to Geoffrey's *antecessor* Asgar.

[69]DB I 145b. *Alric* may well be Aelfric son of Goding. Another part of Weston, in the Count of Mortain's fief, had been held by two men of Burgraed and one of Aelfric son of Goding, DB I 146b. Wulfric, a man of Earl Waltheof, had a small holding in the same place, DB I 152b.

under another lord, but the soke remained in the bishop's manor.[70] This may be contrasted with two similarly small holdings at Chignall where Saewine the priest and *Etfin* each held 15 acres of land and were so free that they could sell the land with sake and soke to whom they would.[71] References to custom are less common, but they clearly imply a more extensive form of lordship than soke alone. Thus at Barton Bendish in Norfolk Aethelgyth had four men for all custom and four for soke only, while at Feltwell in the same county Ely Abbey had had 34 sokemen with all custom and six freemen by soke and commendation only.[72] The fullest rights that were normally held over freemen seem to have been represented by the combination of all three; soke, commendation and custom. Freemen at Herringswell, Suffolk, were free to sell or give their land but the sake and soke, commendation and all customs would remain to St Edmund.[73] A similar situation is described in different words at Harbury, Warwickshire, which was held by two men who were free to sell *sed non discedere cum terra*.[74] This apparently meant that the tenants were free to transfer their rights and obligations to someone else, but not to put it under another lord. This must also have been the meaning of the many references to lands that could not be separated from a church or from a particular manor even though the tenants were free.

References to simple commendation or that imply it are outnumbered by those in which the tenant is said to have been free to commend himself with his land to any lord he chose. These appear to confirm the weakness of pre-Conquest lordship for it is nowhere suggested that this freedom was limited to one transfer, the implication being that the bond could be broken at any time. Here too Domesday's terminology may be misleading. In Wiltshire, for example, Toti bought a hide of land from Malmesbury Abbey for three lives and within that term he could go with that land to what lord he pleased.[75] Any lord to whom Toti commended himself would presumably expect not only Toti's personal support but also some form of service and renders from the land, but the abbey retained its reversionary right, thus limiting both Toti's freedom and his lord's claims.

This case is unusual but there are many others in which Domesday explicitly states that although the tenant was free to go with his land, the soke remained; that is, the superior right of the lord of the soke, generally an important individual or institution, was not affected by the commendation.[76]

The Norman conquerors put much greater weight on commendation than on soke. There are many instances of a Norman assuming the ownership of land that had been simply commended to his *antecessor*. Richard son of Gilbert, for example, held a great deal of land in Essex that had belonged to men who had commended themselves, without their land, to his *antecessor* Wihtgar.[77] The newcomers were unlikely to treat the soke-rights over land that could be commended with greater respect. This high-handed attitude naturally weakened

[70]DB II 10b.
[71]DB II 59a.
[72]DB II 250b, 213ab.
[73]DB II 358b.
[74]DB I 239b.
[75]DB I 72a.
[76]For example, Earl Harold's soke at Hitchin and Eadgifu's in C, DB I 132b, 194a.
[77]DB II 101b–2a.

the sokes that were not held by men of equal power and influence.

The significance of sokes as lordships has been obscured by the assumption that they were a novelty introduced in the ninth century by Scandinavian invaders. They were in fact much older lordships and were apparently based on regalian rights.[78] In the eleventh century most were still held by the king and the earls or, as a result of royal gifts, by churches. References to the soke lying in a hundred or being held jointly by king and earl underline the official character of soke.[79] The centre of a soke was normally the demesne, the land that was held by and exploited directly for the lord himself. From the other land that lay within a soke a lord could expect some relatively small services and renders but, more important, he could claim possession of land that was forfeited within his soke. Thus, when Robert Dispensator claimed two Lincolnshire manors that had been held by one of his *antecessores* Wiglac, who had forfeited his lands, he failed because those manors lay within the sokes of Earl Harold and Ulf *Fenisc* and their right to forfeitures had passed to their successors, Earl Hugh and Gilbert de Ghent, who duly appear as the owners in 1086.[80] Wiglac can therefore be regarded as the tenant of both Harold and Ulf. They and their successors were very influential men, well able to protect their interests. Others were less successful, including many churches who lost not only their soke-rights but even demesne lands that they had leased to laymen.[81]

The sokes that survived best were the king's. Royal sokes were to be found in most parts of eleventh-century England but the most important and extensive seem to have been in the dynastic heartland of Wessex. On the eve of the Conquest there were many royal estates there together with a large number of thegns holding manors that lay within the sokes of these estates.[82] These thegns are described as holding land from the king. Most of them were free to commend themselves and many may have done so, but Domesday gives no information about commendation in those counties. There were also many non-royal estates in Wessex, mostly held by churches and privileged laymen, which had in effect been created by the alienation or usurpation of royal rights. Some were centuries old, but most seem to have been formed in the tenth and eleventh centuries. Outside Wessex non-royal estates were more extensive and numerous.

The post-Conquest landowners acquired sokes as well as commended men from their *antecessores* and the clash between these two forms of lordship underlies many of the disputes reported in Domesday Book. It was the issue when William de Chernet claimed a tiny Hampshire manor from a certain Picot on the grounds that it belonged to his manor of Chardford and that he had inherited it from his *antecessor, per hereditatem sui antecessoris*.[83] In support of his

---

[78]G.W.S. Barrow, *The Kingdom of the Scots* (London, Edward Arnold, 1973), pp. 7–68; William E. Kapelle, *The Norman Conquest of the North* (London, Croom Helm, 1979), pp. 50–85.

[79]There are many references of this kind in DB II, e.g. 225b, 230a, 238b, 241b, 247b, etc.

[80]DB I 349a, 375a (Claythorpe), 355a, 375b (Scremby).

[81]Most churches suffered in this way. The best documented example is Worcester Cathedral, *Hemingi Chartularium Ecclesiae Wigorniensis*, ed. T. Hearne (Oxford, 1723), esp. pp. 248–81.

[82]P.H. Sawyer, 'The Royal *Tun* in Pre-Conquest England', in Patrick Wormald *et al.*, eds, *Ideal and Reality in Frankish and Anglo-Saxon Society* (Oxford, Blackwell, 1983), pp. 273–99.

[83]DB I 44b.

claim he brought the witness of the better and old men of the county and hundred but Picot countered with the witness of the villeins and of the common people, *de vili plebe*, and of bailiffs, who were willing to maintain by oath or by the judgement of God, that is by the ordeal, that Vitalis, who held this land, was a free man and could go with his land where he wished. William's witnesses refused to accept any law but that of King Edward until King William settled the point. Unfortunately we do not know what, if anything, the king decided, but the dispute is a nice illustration of the conflict between the two types of lordship, soke-right and commendation. Many other disputes were clearly about the same issue but few are described in such revealing detail.[84]

There is a marked tendency for the freedom of pre-Conquest tenants to be emphasized in such disputes. In Bedfordshire Hugh Beauchamp claimed Tillbrook from William de Warenne as part of the property of his *antecessor* Ralf Tallebosc, who had been granted it by King William.[85] It must be this claim that explains the unusually elaborate description of the status of the 20 soke-men who held it before the Conquest. These men, who still held it in 1086, 'belonged in such a way to the king's soke and sake that they could assign and sell their land to whom they wished and put themselves under another lord without the leave of him under whom they were'. It appears that Ralf had been granted, in effect, the royal soke but that William claimed by commendation. The Count of Mortain's fief as described in the Exeter Domesday is particularly revealing.[86] His main *antecessores* were Eadmaer and Ordulf but he also acquired a number of other manors that are said to have been added to the honours of Eadmaer and Ordulf, including some that had been held by men commended to them. The previous tenants of all these 'added' manors are described as holding freely or *pariter* (these terms are here equivalent) but with one exception they are not used in any other entry in the count's fief. One of the most illuminating entries describes Modbury where Wado held one hide *pariter* (in the Exchequer Domesday this is changed to *libere*) and he could go to what lord he liked. Wado also held a virgate in Modbury of Ordulf, 'and with that virgate he could not be independent of Ordulf, but with the aforesaid hide he could . . . And this hide the count wrongfully holds along with Ordulf's honour'.[87] The freedom of such men as Vitalis in Hampshire, Wado in Devon or the 20 sokemen at Tillbrook was perhaps emphasized because it reinforced or justified claims that were challenged. This explanation cannot, however, apply to the thousands of entries in which the pre-Conquest tenant is simply described as free or holding land freely. Their freedom was perhaps recorded regularly because it served the interests of royal government; more could be demanded from free tenants, and their successors, than from the unfree who were expected to serve their lords.

The inconsistencies of Domesday Book greatly complicates the study of pre-Conquest lordships. Commendation is only mentioned regularly in the eight

[84]For example at Badlesmere K and *Estone* (= Little Staughton) Bd, DB I 10a, 12b, 211b.
[85]DB I 211b
[86]Exon, fos. 210–23; see also below, p. 84.
[87]Exon, fo. 221a.

counties of circuits III and VII.[88] Sub-tenants occur sporadically in some counties, but in many there is none. There are, for example, neither commended men nor sub-tenants in the Lincolnshire Domesday although both figure prominently in the neighbouring county of Cambridge. There are also differences between fiefs which suggest that the information about pre-Conquest tenants was often supplied by the landowners or their agents. Some seem to have taken care to name the legal *antecessores* and do not name any sub-tenants. Thus, most of Ralf Paganel's property had belonged to Merleswein but as it was scattered from Yorkshire to Devon he is unlikely to have kept it all in his own hands.[89] In some fiefs the names of the tenants who actually held the land seem to be given, possibly to define the property in question rather than to prove title, which was in any case rarely challenged. The contrast between the Wiltshire fiefs of Ernulf de Hesdin with 19 named predecessors and of William de Eu, 14 of whose 17 manors had belonged to Alstan of Boscombe, is as likely to reflect the different treatment of these fiefs as a real difference between them.[90] We cannot, however, assume that fiefs were internally consistent; as already noted Count Alan's fief in Lincolnshire followed no regular rule.[91]

It is clearly impossible to reconstruct pre-Conquest lordships from the evidence of Domesday. There is enough to show that it is misleading but not enough to make it possible to determine how many sub-tenants or superior lords are concealed. There are, however, several indications that a very large number of the men and women described as holding manors freely before the Conquest were in fact sub-tenants. The distribution of manors that were held by one individual among several fiefs may sometimes have been due to exchanges, sales or other forms of transfer, but some are more satisfactorily explained on the assumption that the named tenant was holding from two or more lords whose property passed to different successors. A good example is afforded by the Lincolnshire tenant called Code. This was a rare name and in Domesday only occurs in Lincolnshire;[92] the references are therefore probably to one man. He held two manors that passed to Ivo Taillebois, two others that were later held by Rainer de Brimou, whose only other antecessor was Jalf, and jointly with Rolf he held a double manor that later belonged to Alfred of Lincoln.[93] As all Code's manors lay quite close together it seems reasonable to assume that he was the tenant of three different lords, one of whom may have been Jalf.

Another indication of concealed lordships is provided by the statements that before the Conquest particular manors did not belong to the *antecessores* of the men who later held them. The point is sometimes that the *antecessor* acquired the land after the Conquest, while his successor was only supposed to be entitled to his pre-Conquest possessions.[94] That explanation does not seem to

[88]Mx, Hrt, Bk, C, Bd in circuit III, E, Nf, Sf in circuit VII.

[89]DB I 96b So, 113b D, 168a Gl, 325b–26a Y, 362b–63a L. Merleswein had other property in So and Co, DB I 86a, 95a, 121b–24b.

[90]DB I 69b–70a, 71b.   [91]See above p. 76 and notes 44–5.

[92]von Feilitzen, *Personal Names*, p. 306.   [93]DB I 350a, 357b, 364a.

[94]For example, Chessington Sr did not belong to Wigot when William came to England and TRE Ulf *Fenisc* did not hold Shipley Db, DB I 36b, 277b.

apply to Geoffrey de Mandeville's fief in Surrey.[95] It is there stated that two of his manors did not belong to Asgar, which suggests that other Surrey manors did although Asgar is not named. A more striking example is provided by the Count of Mortain's Devon fief in Exeter Domesday.[96] Twenty-eight manors in this fief are said to have been added to the honours of his *antecessores* Eadmaer and Ordulf. The clear implication is that his other manors did belong to these honours; there would otherwise be little point in insisting that these 28 did not. It appears that the count had obtained the estates of two pre-Conquest lords who between them had 18 demesne manors and twice as many that were considered to belong to their honours. The count, or his men, also took over another 28 manors that did not belong to these lordships. At least seven of these were held by men who were commended to Eadmaer or Ordulf; a good example of a Norman claiming lordship over land on the basis of simple commendation.

Eadmaer, whose by-name is variously given as *ator* or *atule*, was also the antecessor of the Count of Mortain in Buckinghamshire, Hertfordshire, Middlesex and Somerset, and perhaps also in Cornwall and Dorset where one of the count's predecessor's is named simply Eadmaer.[97] It is probably significant that Eadmaer's manors included some of the most valuable that the count owned. One of them was Berkhamstead which became the *caput* of the honour of Mortain.[98] It is possible, even likely, that some of the count's other manors were held by people who were in some way dependant on Eadmaer. In Buckinghamshire, for example, Eadmaer preceded the count at Bledlow which was assessed at 30 hides and valued at £20 in 1066. The only comparable manor among the 38 entries in the count's fief in that county is Wing, which had been held by Edward *cilt*, a man of Earl Harold, and which, although only assessed at five hides, had land for 40 ploughs and was worth £32 in 1066.[99] These were the only manors in the county that the count retained in demesne. It is tempting to speculate that in Buckinghamshire all the other manors of the count were dependent on these two before the Conquest as they were afterwards.

There are some indications that the structure of at least a few post-Conquest lordships was largely determined by the pre-Conquest pattern of demesne and tenancies. One of the best examples is Gilbert de Ghent's fief. He had 20 demesne manors and 17 of these had been held by his *antecessor* Ulf.[100] The Essex Domesday has several clear examples of the same tendency. Thus all Aubrey de Vere's demesne manors, including the *caput* of his honour, Castle Hedingham, had all been held by his *antecessor* Wulfwine,[101] and all Geoffrey de Mandeville's demesne manors, with two minor exceptions, had been held by Asgar the staller, including the sites of the Mandeville castles at Pleshey and

[95]DB I 36a.
[96]Exon, fos. 210–23. See above p. 82.
[97]DB I 79b–80 Do, 90b Camerton So, exchanged by the count (Exon, fo. 170 has *Edmeratorius*), 136b Hrt, 122a, 125a Co, 129b Mx, 146a Bk. Most of Eadmaer's manors were kept in demesne by the count.
[98]*VCH Hrt* I (1902), pp. 280–1.
[99]DB I 146ab.
[100]See above note 28.
[101]DB II 76a–78a.

Saffron Walden.[102] A similar situation can be observed in other fiefs.[103]

These indications of continuity between the days of Edward and William suggest that the conventional interpretation of the effect of the Conquest on land-ownership needs some revision. The Conquest was undoubtedly followed by a great deal of disruption and in time there were fundamental changes; the sokes declined in importance, the number of thegns directly dependant on the king was reduced and the land-owning aristocracy was almost entirely replaced. After the confusion of the first years the transfer of lordships and land seems to have been conducted in a fairly regular manner. Many of William's supporters were granted the whole or large parts of the property of one or more English lords. In conformity with William's wish that the laws and customs of the land should be maintained, apart from alterations 'made for the benefit of the whole people of the English',[104] the new men held their land as their *antecessores* had done. Some kept the demesnes, or part of them, in their own hands and several centres of Old English lordships continued to serve as capitals of feudal honours. The new men not only claimed the demesnes of their predecessors but also the lands that they had on lease from churches, or as pledges, together with soke-rights and lands that had been held by their tenants and their men. The forms of these sub-tenancies varied and will probably never be fully understood. Some held land on lease or at farm, others were commended with their land. Many held soke-land, some from more than one lord. The full extent of the pre-Conquest estates and their structure is forever concealed by Domesday Book, whose compilers were more interested in contemporary circumstances than in the situation *Tempore Regis Eadwardi*. We cannot complain that the makers of Domesday Book did not collect the information we need to answer the questions that interest us. We should rather be grateful for the evidence they have provided; it is enough to suggest that the changes in tenurial structure after the Norman Conquest were less than revolutionary.

---

[102]DB II 57b–63a. Pleshey comprised the Domesday manors of Great Waltham and High Easter, see *VCH E* I (1903), pp. 343, 505, 509.

[103]For example Ralf Bainard and his *antecessor* Aethelgyth, DB II 68b–71a, 247b–53b, 413b–15b, and see D. Whitelock, *Anglo-Saxon Wills* (Cambridge, CUP, 1930), pp. 190, 192–7, 205–6. Ranulf Peverel retained as demesne several manors of his *antecessor* Siward of Maldon, DB II 71b–76a, 416a–18a, but his chief manor, Hatfield Peverel, had been held by Aethelmaer, who may, of course, have been Siward's kinsman (DB II 72a) and several of his demesne manors had been held by others.

[104]A.J. Robertson, *The Laws of the Kings of England from Edmund to Henry I* (Cambridge, CUP, 1925), p. 240, clause 7.

CHAPTER SIX

Taxation and the
Ploughland in Domesday Book

Sally P.J. Harvey

To those who directed, drafted and derived administrative benefit from the Domesday survey, what was the significance of the 'ploughland'? Scholars have suggested many approaches to this contentious issue. The present paper attempts a critical review of some current interpretations and argues for a single, fiscal, explanation.

The meaning of the recurrent formula in Domesday Book 'there is land for x ploughs' (*terra est x carrucis*) seems, at first glance, straightforward enough: a statement of the extent of the arable land. Yet, long ago, Vinogradoff felt obliged to dismiss 'this simple inference',[1] and Stenton, whilst considering that the item probably provided 'an estimate of the number of plough teams that could be employed upon [an estate]', still acknowledged that 'few of the questions which arise in the study of Domesday terminology are more difficult than the interpretation to be put upon this estimate'.[2] The so-called ploughland or teamland of Domesday Book has continued to pose a vexed problem, as the obvious definition does not accord with much of the evidence. Yet the question of the ploughland is not only of interest to specialists in Domesday Book, it is also of importance to English economic history, in so far as studies of the economy, and of cultivation and its development, take the evidence of Domesday Book as a major departure point.

In the last two decades several scholars have revived the topic without producing a satisfactory solution. Due to the ploughland's 'doubtful nature', the five regional Domesday Geographies have been unable to put the ploughland figures to use either independently or in correlations; although H.C. Darby's concluding volume on Domesday England contains the clearest discussion of the problem and the best collection of evidence, he does not subscribe to any existing theory of the ploughland's nature or offer one of his own.[3] On these grounds his work is criticized by J.S. Moore, who returns to the view that the

---

[1] Paul Vinogradoff, *English Society in the Eleventh Century* (Oxford, OUP, 1908), p. 157.

[2] F.M. Stenton, 'Introduction' in C.W. Foster and T. Longley, eds., *The Lincolnshire Domesday and the Lindsey Survey* (Lincoln Record Society 19, 1924), p. xv.

[3] e.g. H.C. Darby, *The Domesday Geography of Eastern England* (Cambridge, CUP, 2nd edn., 1957), p. 42; H.C. Darby, *Domesday England* (Cambridge, CUP, 1977), pp. 95–136, 347–51.

formula represents an estimate of the arable capacity in 1086.[4] Yet Moore's restatement does not take account of the original obstacles to this interpretation, as R.W. Finn has pointed out.[5] On the other hand, C. Hart has recently become an advocate of a very different interpretation, which is that of an old fiscal rating, indeed not old, but ancient, of over two-centuries standing when Domesday Book was made.[6] Finn concluded his critique of the problem discouragingly. The difficulties of the matter had been 'comprehensively indicated' by Maitland and thoroughly discussed by Darby and his team and it was 'indeed doubtful if . . . there was much more to say about the teamland'.[7]

A counsel of despair should not, however, be too readily accepted by historians. A large body of evidence exists, and the intentions of such an administrative effort should be in some way perceptible. First, it should be said that the translation 'teamland' used by some historians rather than 'ploughland' reflects no basic difference in meaning but simply emphasizes that the weighty side of the working capital represented in a medieval plough is the team of oxen which pull it and their maintenance throughout the year, rather than the plough itself. It is in fact an 8-oxen team that Domesday Book records when it records a plough. There were, of course, differences in the size of the working team, depending on the soil, and the state of clearing, but after thorough debate it has been conclusively demonstrated that in Domesday Book the data on ploughs refer to a standard nominal team of 8 oxen and not to a variable one.[8] It is thus salutary to keep in mind possible differences in size between recorded plough-teams and those actually functioning on the ground.

What are the merits of the literal interpretation of arable capacity that it should still gain new followers, and what its demerits that even those adherents despair of useful definition? The primary argument in favour of the view of arable capacity is of course the phrase itself: *terra est x carrucis* is the recurrent formula in many counties of Domesday Book I (though it does not appear in every county). Where the abbreviated Domesday Book I for the south-western counties has the usual formula *terra est x carrucis*, the detailed Exeter Domesday originally used the phrase *possunt arare x carucae*. A neat correlation does its best to uphold the literal interpretation. Starting with the county of Middlesex, on manor after manor the ploughlands equal the total of ploughs in demesne, plus the ploughs held by the tenantry. Where they do not, the equation is even more instructive. Then the ploughlands equal the total for three items: the ploughs of the demesne and the tenantry and the additional ploughs that the holding could support. To take an arbitrary instance: 'there is land for 25 ploughs. In demesne 18 hides and 3 ploughs; the villeins have 17 ploughs and still another 5

[4]J.S. Moore, 'The Domesday Teamland: A Reconsideration', *TRHS* 5th ser., XIV (1964), pp. 109–30.
[5]R.W. Finn, 'The Teamland of the Domesday Inquest', *EHR* LXXXIII (1968), pp. 95–101.
[6]C. Hart, *The Hidation of Northamptonshire* (Leicester, Leicester University Press, 1970), esp. pp. 24–32.
[7]Finn, 'Teamland', p. 101.
[8]J.H. Round, *Feudal England* (London, Allen & Unwin, 1964), pp. 40–1; H.P.R. Finberg, 'The Domesday Plough-Team', *EHR* LXVI (1951), pp. 67–71; cf. R. Lennard, 'Domesday Plough-Teams: The South-Western Evidence', *EHR* LX (1945), pp. 217–33.

ploughs could be there'.[9] The next two counties, Hertfordshire and Buckinghamshire, would confirm the interpretation of arable capacity; but, farther afield, the equation becomes unstuck. Indeed, further investigation shows that of the 33 Domesday counties, in only five will the straightforward interpretation of arable land fit neatly. They prove to be the five counties of a single circuit of inquiry, now called Circuit III. Validity for five out of 33 counties is not good foundation for a general theory, even though we cannot ignore that in those five the ploughland denotes the available potential arable land.

A single character cannot be given to the ploughland throughout the rest of the country. An analysis begun in the north with the counties of Nottingham and Derby produces a consistent and obvious relationship often of 1 : 1 between ploughlands and existing fiscal assessments, and no relation to the ploughs working there. A Derbyshire entry runs: 'Siward had 7 carucates of land for the geld and $\frac{1}{6}$ of a carucate. There is land for 7 ploughs and $\frac{1}{6}$ plough'.[10] In Yorkshire too, a consistent ratio between fiscal carucates and ploughlands often persists, which makes more impact because it occurs on lands which in 1086 lay waste, carrying no ploughs at all. It was the evidence of these northern counties which led some scholars, Round, Baring and now Hart, to reject the possibility that the ploughland referred to the arable land of 1086 and to argue that it was an *old* fiscal assessment.[11] Alternatively, such evidence led Maitland to infer that the ploughland recorded the arable of 1066, that is, before the Conqueror's reprisals had struck.[12] But, neither the theory of former or present arable capacity, nor of old fiscal asessment, can help to interpret ploughlands elsewhere of yet another character, unrelated either to ploughs or to fiscal assessments. The variance is easily explicable in the situation where the ploughlands are greater than the ploughs: on the arable capacity theory there is simply room for expansion. In such cases, Domesday Book, giving 'X' ploughlands and 'Y' ploughs, has not bothered to record the tautologous fact that the number of possible ploughs is 'X' minus 'Y'. We can see that some tautologous information of precisely that nature *was* omitted from Domesday Book I in the course of abbreviation. In the Inquiry of the County of Cambridge for Kirtling 'there is land for 21 ploughs, the villeins have 16 ploughs; there are 4 ploughs in demesne and there could be a fifth', whereas in the abbreviated version in Domesday Book I the last item is omitted.[13] However, this example is supplied by one of the five counties of Circuit III, the circuit in which the possible ploughs and the existing ploughs do correspond to the ploughlands, so it is of little general help, except to remind us that if the

[9]DB I 130a.

[10]DB I 275a.

[11]J.H. Round, 'The Hidation of Northamptonshire', *EHR* XV (1900), pp. 78–86; F. Baring, 'The Hidation of Northamptonshire in 1086', *EHR* XVII (1902), pp. 76–83, 470–9; C. Hart, 'The Hidation of Huntingdonshire', *Proceedings of the Cambridge Antiquarian Society* LXI (1968), pp. 55–6; Hart, *Hidation of Northamptonshire*, pp. 24–32.

[12]F.W. Maitland, *Domesday Book and Beyond* (London, Fontana-Collins, 1960), pp. 484–8; A. Ballard, *The Domesday Inquest* (London, Methuen, 1906), p. 43.

[13]N.E.S.A. Hamilton, ed., *Inquisitio Comitatus Cantabrigiensis* (London, John Murray, 1876), p. 11; DB I 202a.

ploughland had merely represented just such a standard addition throughout the country it would, most certainly, not have appeared in Domesday Book at all, as it would have been a mere waste of space.

It is not so easy to be satisfied with the explanation of room for expansion where a correlation is seldom to be found between ploughlands and ploughs and where an excess of ploughs over ploughlands as well as of ploughlands over ploughs both occur. Devon provides some striking examples. At Otterton 'there is land for 25 ploughs. In demesne are 6 ploughs and 50 villeins and 20 smallholders with 40 ploughs'. Devon also produces several examples on the lines of Hartland which runs 'there is land for 110 ploughs. In demesne are 15 ploughs and 30 slaves and 60 villeins and 45 smallholders with 30 ploughs'.[14] The first type of entry is the more awkward. Yet, based on the Yorkshire evidence, come two different explanations of the discrepancy between ploughs and ploughlands. Thus T.A.M. Bishop, taking the ploughlands to be arable, views the discrepancies as signs of recent movement of peoples with their teams from relatively unprofitable upland areas to better sites left partially vacant and waste by the passage of armies; he argues that such a population shift would result in some villages with teams which were in excess of recent reclamation and cultivation, and in other settlements with ploughlands but no teams or population.[15] The answer supplied by W.E. Wightman lies in changed manorial organization: the discrepancies represent reciprocal arrangements on two or more units under the same lordship.[16] Whilst both suggestions might well have been true in some cases – we do know of several cases of neighbouring ploughs working on adjacent manors in Domesday Book – it is difficult to see this argument on its own solving the whole ploughland problem:[17] it does not, for instance, explain the presence of many adjacent and artifical-looking ploughlands in the northern counties which obviously lie worthless and uncultivated even by neighbouring ploughs. Nor, on the strength of the first theory, do the cases with more ploughs than ploughlands make sense in the context of the perennial difficulties of the medieval economy. One of the crucial factors which held back development in agriculture was lack of winter feed for stock. The smallest acreages of natural hay-producing meadow land were at a premium as no grass was sown and no winter roots planted at this time. Northern England regularly resorted to such expedients as holly for winter feed.[18] The evidence of Domesday Book itself shows both the value and the scarcity of meadow land. Plough beasts could not be killed off each winter or permitted to become debilitated when their power was needed most; and they it was who constituted the heaviest call on winter feed. Although there is an instance in Herefordshire where we are expressly told that

---

[14]DB I 104a, 100b.

[15]T.A.M. Bishop, 'The Norman Settlement of Yorkshire', *Studies in Medieval History presented to F.M. Powicke*, ed. R.W. Hunt, W.A. Pantin and R.W. Southern (Oxford, Clarendon Press, 1948), pp. 1–14; also I.S. Maxwell in H.C. Darby and I.S. Maxwell, eds., *The Domesday Geography of Northern England* (Cambridge, CUP, 1962), pp. 217–21.

[16]W.E. Wightman, *The Lacy Family in England and Normandy 1066–1194* (Oxford, OUP, 1968), pp. 43–54.

[17]e.g. DB I 304b–307a, 320b.

[18]J. Radley, 'Holly as Winter Feed', *Agricultural History Review* IX (1961), pp. 89–93.

'the villeins have more ploughs than arable land',[19] it is not possible to subscribe to any theory (and it is all variants of the arable capacity theory which suffer here) which assumes that many peasants were, even for one winter, supporting more ploughteams than they had land to use them on.

All in all, the character of the ploughland, present or past, must be recognized as variable. It is indeed Darby's conclusion that the item presents a bewildering array of evidence. The character of the evidence varies chiefly by circuit of counties of inquiry, but also by county, and even (for the three inconsistent counties analysed in Darby's tables) by landholder.[20] This variation means that the problem does not lend itself to resolution by detailed local studies alone, and any solution must be adequate to embrace the variations.

The question of the original date of the ploughland information has become an integral part of the dispute about its meaning. If there are insuperable obstacles to interpreting the ploughland as a unit of arable of 1086, it by-passes some of them to suggest that it belonged to 1066. Three of Maitland's arguments for this date and theory have been effectively outlined and argued down in Moore's paper.[21] The most specific of Maitland's points is that the formula in Leicestershire 'in King Edward's day x ploughs were there' (*tempore regis Edwardi erant x carucae*) occurs as an alternative to 'there is land for x ploughs', showing, Maitland thought, that the two phrases were equivalent and interchangeable.[22] Yet, it could equally be argued that, as the ploughland occurs in Domesday Book I in stereotyped formula in most counties, the somewhat different 'in King Edward's day were x ploughs' means something somewhat different, probably intended as a substitute, the nearest that could be provided in the circumstances, but not the exact equivalent. (It could indeed be argued that this early Leicestershire variant is nothing but a scribal mistake somewhere in the process of collecting information. The variation takes place according to landholder and the similarity between the highly abbreviated 'tra.e.' for *terra est* and 't.r.e.' for *tempore regis Edwardi* seems close enough for a misunderstanding to be a possibility.) Vinogradoff has already pointed out that where ploughlands exceeded ploughteams in number, there often occurred stable or rising estate values.[23] On Maitland's interpretation of declining teams and cultivation in such cases, it is difficult to see why values should rise.

The other line of argument for an early date, but this time as fiscal assessment, was constructed by Round, and has since been defended by Finn and by Hart and accepted by Darby. The proponents of this theory have come to their interpretation largely through analysis of the detailed Northamptonshire evidence, which consists of the assessment in hides in Domesday Book for King Edward's day and 'now', a county geld roll for some interim date, and also a survey of the early twelfth century. Round's view that the ploughland is an old

---

[19]DB I 181b.
[20]Darby, *Domesday Geography of Eastern England*, pp. 42–3; Darby, *Domesday England*, pp. 348–9.
[21]Moore, 'Teamland', pp. 112–13.
[22]Maitland, *Domesday Book and Beyond*, pp. 484–6.
[23]*English Society*, p. 159.

fiscal assessment seems to depend on two points.[24] First, in Northamptonshire the ploughland is obviously an artificial, not an arable unit. In the south-west of the county the ploughlands bear a regular ratio to the hides of 5 : 2, which obtains remarkably even in fractions such as those at Grafton Regis with 2 ploughlands : $\frac{4}{5}$ hide and Evenley with 4 : 1 $\frac{3}{5}$.[25] In the south of the county the ratio is 2 : 1. The second point followed from the successive alterations in the hidation of Northamptonshire in the two decades before DB, which all gave reductions in assessment. From this, Round concluded that as the county's ploughland assessment is larger than any of the assessments in hides of the three previous dates, it must also be earlier than all the other assessments. The assumption that the ploughlands must be old because they are large in number is not self-evident. They could also be large because they are new. Two rating reductions in two decades had followed the ravaging of the county, but these known reductions surely render it unlikely that yet another should be conceded when we have data indicating the revival of agriculture in the county (see below p. 97). On the other hand, the re-imposition of a higher rate is in tune with the context of the high taxation of the 1080s. The observed facts in Round's arguments are all valid. The Northamptonshire ploughlands *are* obviously artificial units bearing in different hundreds a regular and observed ratio to the hides therein; they *are* larger in number than the current hides. But the assumptions made in order to reach the accompanying theory have no supporting evidence. Hart takes his assumptions even further back in time, to the Danish settlement. He asserts: 'It is becoming increasingly clear that, for many shires of the Danelaw, the ploughland figures of DB preserve a record of the taxation imposed by the Danish earls soon after the settlement of 877'. However, we are not yet given the evidence which justifies such clarity, only another assumption: 'That this generalization applies in the case of Huntingdonshire is suggested by the duodecimal character of its Domesday ploughland assessments'.[26] But duodecimal units of plough were created anew right through the medieval period, with no directly 'Danish' associations whatever.[27] Having made a chronological leap backwards of two centuries, Hart then goes on to use his assumption as a basis for a deduction which is itself argument against his own dating: 'it could be argued from the fact that these assessments (the ploughlands) are usually equal to the number of ploughs employed on an estate at the time of Domesday that there was no great advance in the exploitation of arable land within the county between the period of Danish settlement and the Norman Conquest'. The very closeness of the two figures ought to have caused Hart to reconsider his interpretation of the ploughland as a ninth-century fiscal rating.

The bulk of the evidence on the point of date is obvious and straightforward. It will therefore need more than assumptions to unseat it. In general,

[24]Round, 'Hidation of Northamptonshire', pp. 78–86.

[25]DB I 224a, 226b.

[26]Hart 'Huntingdonshire', pp. 55–6. Hart also uses this postulate as evidence for dating the crown's acquisition of certain lands, *Hidation of Northamptonshire*, pp. 28–32.

[27]e.g. A. Tomkinson, 'The Carucage of 1220 in an Oxfordshire Hundred', *Bulletin of the Institute of Historical Research* XLI (1968), pp. 212–16.

Domesday Book affords data for two, sometimes three dates: at the time of King Edward, aiming ideally at the last day of his rule – the day on which he was alive and dead; at the time when the estate changed hands, though for many counties this information was not recorded; and, at the time of the Domesday Inquiry, that is 'now', 1085–6. The information for King Edward's day is phrased in the past tense, usually in the perfect, sometimes in the imperfect tense. The information for 1085–6 is in the present tense, as is the data on ploughlands, the only exception to this being the Leicestershire alternative 'in King Edward's time there was land for x ploughs'. Thus the bulk of the Domesday Book's ploughlands ought not to be assigned to a nebulous past in order to avoid awkwardnesses.

The argument which will be advanced in this article is that the ploughland figures are, first and foremost, contemporary fiscal assessments of 1086–7. As such, they will naturally often reflect agricultural or simply arable capacity. This is not an argument which should startle. Although as a general explanation of the ploughland it seems not to have been forwarded before, some studies of particular counties have been drawn to this conclusion on a local basis – as, for instance, by Stenton on Leicestershire. The idea of a fiscal unit based on ploughs was a familiar one in England. This is shown by the use in DB of a fiscal 'carucate' (Latin *caruca*: plough) made up of 8 'bovates', (Latin, *bos, bovis*: ox), in native speech 'oxgang', in Yorkshire, Derbyshire, Nottinghamshire and Rutland. Although its precise origin and date is debated, the carucate is generally assumed to be Anglo-Danish in origin.[28] In Kent the pre-existing fiscal unit was the sulung (Latin *sulcare*: to plough, furrow; Anglo-Saxon *suhl*: a plough) made up of 4 yokes (iugum). An instructive earlier parallel for the overall principle argued here exists in the Roman fiscal unit of Diocletian's time, the *iugum* or yoke. To quote A.H.M. Jones. 'the *iugum* was the unit of assessment and corresponded to the varying quantity of land according to its use and quality. In one schedule, established by Diocletian for Syria and still in use there in the late fifth century, one *iugum* might consist of 20 *iugera* of first-class arable land, or 40 *iugera* of second-class arable land, or 60 *iugera* of third-class arable land, or five *iugera* of vineyard, or 220 *perticae* of old olive trees or 450 *perticae* of mountain olive trees.[29] The result was always reckoned in yokes for uniformity's sake. To return to DB: like the early rating in hides (originally reckoned to be the land for one household), the ploughland assessment might also have taken account of the man-power and tenantry on an estate. Alternatively, in devastated areas and in regions where few developed resources existed, new assessment could only utilize what guidance there was: often the existing hides or carucates were adjusted in an approximately suitable ratio. According to several chroniclers it was a major objective of the Domesday inquiry to widen the fiscal base. But no such new base has been identified in the data. This paper argues that evidence of the attempt is the Domesday plough-

---

[28]R. Lennard, 'The Origin of the Fiscal Carucate', *Economic History Review* XIV (1944), pp. 51–63 and references therein.

[29]A.H.M. Jones, 'Census Records of the Later Roman Empire', *Journal of Roman Studies* XLIII (1953), pp. 49–64; 'Capitatio et Iugatio', *Journal of Roman Studies* XLVII (1957), pp. 88–94; *The Later Roman Empire (282–604)* (Oxford, Blackwell, 1964), I, pp. 448–69.

land, calculated in different ways varying with the regional character of the administration, of the agriculture, and of the obstacles to such a task.

We turn first to the most primary form of calculation, the ploughland based directly on arable realities. Several of the arguments for and against this as a complete interpretation of the ploughlands have been mentioned already. Now, rather differently, it is argued that the ploughland is a fiscal unit which, in some areas, took the working ploughs and their prospective scope as the bases for its formula. Primarily and most clearly this is true of the Circuit III of Domesday: Middlesex, Hertfordshire, Bedfordshire, Buckinghamshire and Cambridgeshire, where, as we have seen, in entry after entry the ploughlands are the same in number as the total of ploughs there, plus the scope for possible ploughs. 'Geoffrey holds Thornton from Roger. It answers for 8 hides. There is land for 10 ploughs: in demesne are 3 and a fourth could be there. There, 12 villeins with 5 smallholders have 5 ploughs and a 6th could be there'.[30] That the ploughlands here are based on the actual arable is indisputable.

The quality of the arable as well as the extent seems to be a major criterion in the south-eastern counties. In the south-eastern circuit in DB the ploughlands often follow the number of ploughs, but by no means regularly so. A.H.R. Baker has studied the evolution of holdings on the Kentish manor of Gillingham. By mapping the soils of the manor, the sizes of holdings and the rent per acre from a mid-fifteenth century survey, he demonstrates a correlation between the quality of the soil and the size of the fiscal division, the yoke, and concludes that the variations in rental values reflected not the sizes but the soil qualities of the assessed area, thus also providing an explanation for the previous puzzle that the Kentish yoke can be shown to consist of anything between 25 and 250 acres.[31] This leads to a second criterion on which the ploughland might be calculated, that is, not merely on arable but on total agricultural capacity. Though the arable was important in determining the size of the units on any given manor, the units themselves also comprised the appurtenant marsh, or woodlands, or whatever local resources were widely available. Such resources, as at Gillingham, were part and parcel of each fiscal division. Close study of the rural economies and of the values of estates in DB can show how misleading are figures for ploughs alone as a guide to agricultural prosperity. The meres and heavy clays of Holderness which were, under medieval techniques, likely to produce low yields of most crops nevertheless sustained dense settlement, partly by fishing and fowling.[32] In Berkshire, lands in the Chilterns which feature relatively few ploughs had nevertheless a high value derived, in all likelihood, from sheep farming.[33] Here it should be added that the ploughlands for Berkshire (2,057) number nearly 300 more than

[30]DB î 151b.

[31]A.H.R. Baker, 'The Kentish *iugum*: its relationship to soils at Gillingham', *EHR* LXXXI (1966), pp. 74–9.

[32]D.J. Siddle, 'The Rural Economy of Medieval Holderness', *Agricultural History Review* XV (1967), pp. 40–5.

[33]P.H. Sawyer, review of H.C. Darby and Eila M. Campbell, eds., *The Domesday Geography of South-East England* (Cambridge, CUP, 1962) and Darby and Maxwell, eds., *Domesday Geography of Northern England*, in *Economic History Review*, 2nd series, XVI (1963–64), pp. 155–7.

ploughteams, and nearly 300 less than the high value in pounds;[34] as such they constitute a considerable fiscal increase from the current hidage of 1,300 odd, yet not an unreasonable one.

The assessment of the wealth and poverty of extra-arable resources was particularly important in the south-west circuit of counties. Poor arable prospects in some parts, along with the importance of raising livestock on extensive rough pasture and supplementary sources of livelihood such as mining, made assessment of wealth and its taxation complex. When considering revenue raised from livestock, mention must be made here of several practical possibilities not usually raised in connection with the ploughland and the variation in its numbers from the Domesday ploughs. Since DB II shows a different, and lower, proportion of non-working animals to ploughteams in eastern England, compared with the evidence of the south-west in the Exeter Domesday, it may well be that some areas, particularly the south-west, bred oxen for sale to other regions. Thus numbers of oxen may well be recorded which were not intended for arable production, but for sale.[35] Other apparently surplus working oxen might, especially on distant royal manors, be heavily engaged in the carriage of goods for long distances to royal palaces and castles. Thirdly, some arable field rotations might demand more effort in ploughing than others. In marginal soils variants of the infield/outfield system were employed. These required considerably more clearing and rough ploughing as fields in only intermittent use were brought back into cultivation, without an accompanying increase in the sown arable, or in prosperity. In each of these situations the surplus profit would not be as high as if the oxen were used for conventional two or three field arable production. Thus, the extra oxen would be viable: but not an appropriate basis for assessment. Since in the arable circuit, Circuit III, 'meadow for x .teams' was recorded in addition to the arable, the ploughland figure in pastoral regions might include the information that there was sufficient grass to raise x teams. In Shropshire notable examples of the discrepancy between ploughlands and ploughs occur in areas in which much of the wealth lay in livestock rather than arable. Some discrepancies are attributable to 'the intense economic dislocation following the Norman Conquest',[36] but they are also associated with areas subsequently famous for cattle and sheep-raising, such as the region of Lydbury North with much natural meadow. As a result of the process of conquest there are certainly signs in the economy generally of a decline in arable and a raising of the levels of livestock,[37] which a new fiscal assessment would do well to account for.

There is certain evidence that in the less populated regions, the working population also sometimes contributed more to the ploughland assessment than the ploughs themselves. The 110 ploughlands of Hartland, Devon, are much more closely allied to the population of 60 villeins and 45 smallholders, as

[34]Figures in Maitland's tables in *Domesday Book and Beyond*, pp. 464–5.
[35]S.P.J. Harvey, 'Cattle', in 'Domesday England', in *The Agrarian History of England and Wales* II (Cambridge, CUP, forthcoming).
[36]V.A. Saunders in H.C. Darby and I.B. Terrett, eds., *The Domesday Geography of Midland England* (Cambridge, CUP, 1971), pp. 116, 122–3.
[37]Harvey, 'Cattle'.

well as 30 slaves, than to the 45 ploughs or the 9 geld-paying hides there.[38] The levy on plough or person was a feature of one of the taxes of Aethelred II's reign. 'From every plough shall be given a penny or the value of a penny' and 'everyone who has a household shall see to it that each of his dependents gives a penny. If anyone is without money, his lord shall give it for him.'[39] The manpower and the free tenantry of an estate was an ingredient that no fiscal assessment could afford to ignore. Indeed so essential was it that its role in eleventh-century assessments tended to be assumed. It is recognized that 'warland', as contrasted with 'inland', was the land which answered for fiscal purposes as is the principle that 'warland' was usually tenanted land, villein land, whilst 'inland' was the demesne or what was originally allowed to be demesne, and so exempt.[40] Of the importance of the cultivators as a major criterion in the assessment of the ploughlands, a survival from the Burton Abbey estates offers clues. (And, as frequently the case, an understanding of the intent makes comprehensible some oddities in the Domesday text.) The oddity is the large number of free tenantry, rent-payers (*censarii*) in two Burton surveys (*c.*1114 and 1126) and their almost complete absence on the estate in DB. J.F.R. Walmsley's study of Burton Abbey poses the problems. 'One of the disturbing features about the *censarii* on the Burton Abbey lands is that, for the most part, they were tenants of warland, which the surveys tell us paid geld to the king, and therefore should have been of some interest to the Domesday commissioners'. Walmsley's search for the missing *censarii* has revealed an illuminating equation. On seven Burton manors, the number of the ploughs of the villeins in DB, plus the size of the holdings of the *censarii* in the Burton surveys, equal, or nearly so, the number of ploughlands given in Domesday Book. At Wetmore are 7 ploughlands, the villeins have 2 ploughs and the rent-payers of Survey B have $4\frac{7}{8}$ ploughlands. At Applebury there are 5 ploughlands, the villeins in DB have 1 plough, and the rent-payers of Survey B have 4 ploughlands. In other words these rent-paying tenants are in several cases represented in DB only by the ploughlands they hold. This equation does not even hold good for every Burton manor however. In one or two places variations in the DB formula make such comparison impossible; in two other cases, Stretton and Leigh, it seems that the ploughlands represent the land of the rent-payers alone without even including the land of the villeins.[41] One may compare the discovery of additional assets here amongst the free tenantry, with examples from the east midlands where the ploughland uncovers the exempt demesne by instances such as 'nine hides for the geld, land for nine ploughs, and in demesne land for two ploughs besides the aforesaid hides'. As the corollary to DB's assertion that the demesne is exempt in that the villeins and free tenants bear the geld, any

[38]DB I 100b.

[39]A.J. Robertson, *The Laws of the Kings of England from Edmund to Henry I* (Cambridge, CUP, 1925), p. 109, VII Aethelred 1. 2 and 1.3.

[40]e.g. D.C. Douglas, *The Social Structure of Medieval East Anglia* (Oxford, Clarendon Press, 1927); D. Cromarty, 'The Fields of Saffron Walden in 1400', *Essex Record Society Publications* 43 (1966), pp. 1 ff.; Vinogradoff, *English Society*, p. 211.

[41]J.F.R. Walmsley, 'The *Censarii* of Burton Abbey and the Domesday Population' *North Staffordshire Journal of Field Studies* VII (1968), pp. 74–5.

fiscal inquiry must be concerned with the lands of free tenants.

Of course, the element of man-power was present in the old hide assessment, in the concept of land sufficient for a family or household. In the Middle Ages as in the late Roman period, the successful combination of land, man-power and traction power was the *sine qua non* of agricultural production. It is of interest to compare again with the eleventh century the principles of the Roman *iuga/capita* assessment. 'The inhabitants, persons and livestock, were either enumerated individually or converted into *capita*, a levy on man-power and its products. Tenants tied to their farms, *coloni*, were entered on the census of their landlords; free tenants were apparently entered independently from their village centres. The two totals, of *iuga* and *capita*, were separately recorded, then often added to form the grand total of assessment'.[42] Not dissimilar was the approach of the Domesday inquiry. The complex make-up of DB II, the unabbreviated volume for East Anglia and Essex, reflects both that greater preponderance of free tenants in the region and the different local tax-collecting structures.[43] The free tenants of eastern England were so numerous that they could not be, as it seems some were in the western counties, an almost forgotten element.

A fourth major base on which the ploughland figures were constructed was that of the old fiscal assessment, probably through force of circumstances in regions chiefly subjected to deliberate laying waste for political purposes in the previous two decades, in the north and in the borderlands. In Yorkshire, many estates which were wasted entirely nevertheless supply two items, the former carucates and the ploughlands. Commonly the ratio was 2 : 1 especially in wasted areas. One example shows a group of five waste holdings which totalled $23\frac{1}{2}$ carucates, estimated to have 12 ploughlands. There are other regions where ratios are clearly defined. The light soils and more easily wasted agriculture of the Yorkshire Wolds have half the number of new ploughlands to old carucates. On the other hand, the heavy clay soils of Holderness, productive chiefly at the time of wealth from fishing, fowling and turbary, have still a 1 : 1 ratio of ploughland to carucate.[44] Where they were able, the compilers of Domesday based their assessment on agricultural capacity. Where there were but few criteria on which to gauge the capacity they had to use what existing guidelines there were, though lands might be temporarily waste. The evidence of Domesday itself shows how quickly some estates could pick up in value, so even wasted lands could not be allowed to go officially scot-free indefinitely.

The ploughland numbers do not often coincide with the current values of estates, however, the values seem to be brought into its estimation when either the old fiscal assessment or the ploughs offer indicators which are widely aberrant from the values. We have seen that this was true quite generally in Berkshire. It is also quite frequently true, in regions where the old assessment plays a part in the ploughland figure, that the ratio between them is 1 : 1 when the value has remained constant since King Edward's day. If we take for

[42] Jones, 'Capitatio et Iugatio', pp. 88–9.
[43] S.P.J. Harvey, 'Domesday Book and its Predecessors', *EHR* LXXXVI (1971), pp. 753–73.
[44] Siddle, 'Medieval Holderness', pp. 40–5. For previous interpretations of this phenomenon see Vinogradoff, *English Society*, pp. 165–7.

example the entry for Keisby used by Darby to illustrate the impossibility of saying 'what the Lincolnshire "ploughland" really implied': 'Offram had 4 bovates for the geld. There is land for 4 oxen. It is waste except for 3 villeins with 6 oxen. There are 4 acres of meadow and 2 acres of small wood. In King Edward's day and now, it is worth 10s'.[45] It is not possible to reconstruct agriculture here exactly, but we can see that despite the uncultivated land the value has remained the same, and that the new assessment is thus the same as the old. Elsewhere in Lincolnshire, which in 1086 boasted a large amount of grazing, it is noticeable that ploughlands often follow values. A whole column of a single folio produces the following figures: 6 ploughlands, £6; 1 ploughland, £1; 5 ploughlands, £5; 2 ploughlands, £1.10s; 2 ploughlands, £2; 2 ploughlands, £1.10s; 3 ploughlands, £2; 5 ploughlands, £3; 1 ploughland £2.[46]

How does the ploughland, seen as a fiscal revision, fit in with the most telling evidence for the continual fiscal revision of the eleventh century from Northamptonshire? Baring showed how much Northamptonshire's hidage had been reduced immediately before the Norman Conquest following the activities of the northern insurgents of 1065. The geld roll indicated how this and later reductions had brought the tax-paying rating of Northamptonshire down from the order of the County Hidage which was 3,200 to the 1,250 hides recorded in 1085–6 in DB, and these reductions took place on a *pro rata* scale.[47] This lowest figure seems likely to have been allocated some years before DB as, by the time of the record, the values show that the agriculture of the county had revived quite considerably. The total DB value of the county in 1086 was about £1,850 whilst the existing assessment was 1,250 hides, thus well above the recurrent average of £1 per hide observable through much of DB; moreover the teams recorded were twice the number of hides.[48] This revival of agricultural and arable activity is accurately reflected in the ploughland. The examples already cited from the south-west of Northamptonshire, where the hide: ploughland ratio was 1 : $2\frac{1}{2}$, show Grafton Regis's valuation had risen from 3s. to 26s. ($\frac{4}{5}$ hide : 2 ploughlands) and Evenley's value from £2 to £4 ($1\frac{3}{5}$ hides : 4 ploughlands). Seen as a new fiscal rating, the total of 2,900 ploughlands for the county (Maitland's), stands half-way between the 2,500 teams at work in Northamptonshire in 1086 and the 3,200 hide rating prevailing up to the mid-1060s.

That the ploughland of DB is a fiscal calculation for the future rather than a record, fiscal or real, of the past is also strongly indicated in the colonization of the Welsh borderlands. Places which had never been cultivated within memory, and which had never paid geld, now had their potential estimated in ploughlands, often calculated by doubling the existing data. A list of 11 holdings entirely without assets, totalling 18 hides, is concluded: 'in these manors there is land for 36 ploughs but it was and is waste. It has never paid

[45]Darby, *Domesday Geography of Eastern England*, pp. 42–3.

[46]DB I 356a.

[47]F. Baring, 'The Pre-Domesday Hidation of Northamptonshire', *EHR* XVII (1902), pp. 470–9.

[48]Maitland, *Domesday Book and Beyond*, pp. 464–5, 535; Vinogradoff, *English Society*, Appendix vii, pp. 506–7.

geld; it belongs in the March of Wales'. Other land not assessed in hides has its potential arable assessed by ploughlands. 'In the fief which Robert holds of the king, Ross and Reveniou, are 12 leagues of land in length and 4 leagues wide. There is only land for 20 ploughs. It is estimated at £12. All the other land is in woodland and marsh and cannot be ploughed.' Other uncultivated land merely has the old assessment doubled. One waste holding in Herefordshire boasts only a deer trap, yet with 3 hides that pay geld, it is recorded to have 'land for 6 ploughs'. On one dramatically large example we are actually told that the ploughlands pay geld. 'In the Valley of *Stradelie* 56 hides, 112 ploughs could plough there and they pay geld'.[49] Other Marcher examples of doubling are based on the working ploughs; in quick succession in Shropshire in and near Much Wenlock.

Between them all they have 17 ploughs; and another 17 could be there.
In demesne is 1 plough and 6 villeins and 6 smallholders and a radman with 5 ploughs, and still another 6 ploughs could be there.
In demesne are 2 ploughs and 6 villeins and 4 smallholders with 4 ploughs. There 4 slaves and still another 6 ploughs could be there.[50]

It is notable that such doubling of either ploughs or hides frequently occurs in districts where cattle and sheep raising were likely to provide agricultural wealth.

Occasionally in other circuits of inquiry, DB lets slip how reliant the ploughland calculation is on existing hides. In Hampshire, at Andover, where 'no one has said how many hides there are', the ploughland figure also remains blank, though the number of ploughs appear, showing again that the arable alone was not the criterion for the ploughland.[51] One type of calculation uses the existing number of hides as a departure point, then assesses in ploughlands land which had previously escaped. One of several instances in Dorset runs: 'land for 6 ploughs, besides this it has in demesne land for two ploughs which never paid geld'.[52] Or, 'in the time of King Edward it used to pay geld for 22 hides; there is land for 35 ploughs. Besides this there is land there for 14 ploughs in demesne which never paid geld'.[53] Or the demesne might be taken into the present assessment with a note of the hides originally exempt: 'There is land for 10 ploughs. Of this 4 hides are in demesne'.[54] Some fiscal demesne or inland continues to be conceded: a Warwickshire entry has 'land for 1 plough of *inland*', and 'there are 5 hides besides *inland*; there is land for 17 ploughs', though such instances are rare and the assessment in ploughlands usually embraces the demesne.[55] The exemption of the greater ecclesiastical tenures from geld obligations survives in DB for the abbot of Ramsey where in Hurstingstone hundred, 'the ploughs of the demesne are exempt from the king's geld; the

[49] DB I 186b, 187a, 269a.
[50] DB I 252b.
[51] DB I 39b. On one Sussex folio land which had 'never' paid geld consistently appears without the ploughland item at all, DB I 19a.
[52] DB I 75b.   [53] DB I 77b.
[54] DB I 79a.   [55] DB I 242b.

villeins and sokemen pay tax on the recorded hides', demonstrating the tendency for the demesne to off-load responsibility onto the tenanted land.[56] For the smaller landholders the principle of exempt demesne seems to have been conceded afresh in Henry I's Charter, after the exactions of the first two Normans.[57] DB even manages to uncover previously unhidated land on the royal fisc which probably survives because it has been sanctioned. At Lincoln, 'in addition to the 8 carucates, the king and earl have *inland* 231 acres of ploughland and 100 acres of meadow'.[58]

Why should two assessments, the hidage or carucage, and the ploughlands be both present in DB at the same time? First of all not all counties in DB do record the current hides or current carucates; Wiltshire, Dorset, Somerset, Devon, Huntingdonshire, Derbyshire, Nottinghamshire and Rutland only record assessments for the time of King Edward, phrased in the past tense. Even in the south-eastern circuit of inquiry, where two sets of figures are consistently recorded for King Edward's day and 'now', the recent reassessment was both less revealing than the Domesday inquiry and unable to put an end to large-scale evasion. DB records that on one large holding of the bishop of Bayeux there were, in King Edward's day, 34 hides, but that no geld had been paid on it since Odo of Bayeux had held it. In addition to these hides, there is land for two ploughs which has never paid geld.[59] The Kentish evidence of a slightly pre-Domesday fiscal list has shown that the DB 1085-6 rating in hides was a very recent one,[60] and yet a totalling of its figures shows how little it succeeded in spreading the basis of assessments and extending its net, rather the reverse. In Surrey the total fell from 1,850 hides in King Edward's day to 706 hides; from 2,588 to 1,572 hides in Hampshire; from 2,473 to 1,338 in Berkshire; from 3,472 to 2,241 in Sussex.[61] On the other hand, the ploughlands represent a general doubling with approximately 60,000 recorded, compared with 32,000 hides; yet the distribution was not unreasonable. In Surrey for instance, its Edwardian hidage was quite steep at 1,800 plus, whilst the 1086 hides were absurdly low at 700, for the value of estates in 1085 was over £1,500. The often observed relationship of £1 per hide in much of DB makes the assessment in ploughlands of 1,200 understandable. This is also true of Berkshire. With the current hidage only 1,300 odd, and the total value of the county nearly £2,400, the ploughlands figure of just over 2,000 represents a well-merited step-up in assessment. In Middlesex, though the ploughland figure totals over 200 lower than the hides, it rests about 100 above the number of working teams and 100 below the total value of the shire in 1086. The few counties in which the ploughlands represent a fall in assessment seem to have good reason – for instance, Yorkshire, where the assessment was almost halved had suffered severely from several devastations, and Wiltshire, saddled with

[56]DB I 203a.
[57]W. Stubbs, *Select Charters* (Oxford, Clarendon Press, 9th edn., 1921), p. 119.
[58]DB I 336a.   [59]DB I 31a.
[60]R.S. Hoyt, 'A Pre-Domesday Kentish Assessment List', in Patricia M. Barnes and C.F. Slade, eds., *A Medieval Miscellany for Doris Mary Stenton* (London, Pipe Roll Society, 1962), pp. 189-202.
[61]Figures in Maitland, *Domesday Book and Beyond*, pp. 464-5.

an enormous rating of over 4,000 hides.

More than one chronicler had the view that the Domesday inquiry had a primary interest in the ploughland and its fiscal application. Henry of Huntingdon chronicles William's efforts: he

> 'sent his justices through every shire, that is to say every province of England, and caused inquiry to be made by sworn inquest how many hides, that is to say amount of land sufficient for one plough in the year there were in each village and what livestock.' (*quot hidae id est iugera uni aratro sufficienter per annum*)[62]

Robert Losinga, bishop of Hereford's earlier description also puts ploughlands first. The survey was made 'in respect of ploughlands and habitations, of men both bond and free, both those who dwelt in cottages and those who had their homes and their share in the fields, and in respect of ploughs and horses and other animals; and in respect of services and payments due from men in the whole land. Other investigators followed the first and men were sent into provinces which they did not know and where they themselves were unknown, in order that they might be given the opportunity of checking the first survey, and, if necessary, of denouncing its authors as guilty to the king. And the land was vexed with much violence arising from the collection of the royal taxes'.[63] Similarly, Orderic Vitalis puts the estimation of ploughed lands first and foremost in his general description of the Domesday enquiry, and chronicles immediate fiscal consequences. His has long been treated as a garbled account in which he has muddled most of the facts.[64] Now, in Orderic's account ploughlands are given a major role in the revision of the 'description' of England carried out by Rannulf Flambard. Rannulf Flambard, for whom indications exist that he was the mastermind behind the Domesday survey,

> had all the ploughlands, which are called hides in English, measured by the rope and registered, setting aside the larger measurement which the generous English had apportioned by order of King Edward, and, in the course of building up the royal revenues, he reduced the size of the ploughlands belonging to the peasants. By this shortening of land long since acquired and held, and by the piling up of unaccustomed taxation, he shamefully oppressed the humble and common people of the kingdom, impoverished them by taking away their goods, and reduced them to extreme poverty from a state of great plenty.[65]

---

[62]T. Arnold, ed., Henry of Huntingdon *Historia Anglorum* (London, Rolls Series, 1879), pp. 207–8.

[63]Based on the translation in D.C. Douglas, *English Historical Documents* II (London, Eyre Methuen, 2nd edn., 1981), no. 198 (p. 912).

[64]R.W. Southern, 'Rannulf Flambard and Early Anglo-Norman Administration', *TRHS* 4th series, XVI (1933), pp. 107, 109.

[65]*The Ecclesiastical History of Orderic Vitalis*, ed. M.M. Chibnall IV (Oxford, Clarendon Press, 1974), p. 172.

There no longer remains any difficulty about this passage. What Orderic is describing is the cutting down of the size of the fiscal unit, not the length of furrow![66] The term 'ploughland' (*terra unius carrucae* or sometimes *terra unius aratri*) occurs in his chronicle several times, and it is instructive that the usage of the ploughland in Normandy in the twelfth century is of a notional 60 acres of land, often including pasture and woodland as well as arable, whereas the hide in England comprised a notional 120 acres and the carucate the order of 100 acres.[67] There are hints of the currency of both these characteristics of the Norman ploughland in DB. One Devon entry slips in 'there is land for 41 ploughs with all its appurtenances.[68] Fifteen of the hides at Chedworth, Glos. are 'woodland, field and meadow', and at Abbots Langley there is one hide of 'woodland and field'; and of another Gloucestershire hide DB says 'in this hide when it is ploughed there are only 64 acres of land'.[69] We have seen that the ploughlands amounted to almost double the assessment in hides as we know them in DB, and also the Welsh Marches produced many examples of a doubling of ploughlands to hides. It was in the Welsh Marches, near Shrewsbury, that Orderic had lived as a boy until 1085, his father being a priest in the household of Roger of Montgomery and his mother an Englishwoman.[70]

When did the notion of ploughland come to England? The study of Gillingham made by Baker offers the possibility of the continuity of the Roman principle, for there is considerable evidence of Roman settlement in Gillingham and neighbouring districts.[71] And, it is in Kent that the yoke, the *iugum*, continues to be used as an agrarian fiscal unit as part of the *sulung*. Some continuity is known in Roman successor kingdoms. In Gaul the Roman fiscal machinery and the land tax was still grinding slowly through its motions at the end of the sixth century. Some attempts were made at revision in *descriptiones, libri descriptionum*, but they were not entirely successful and could provoke exemptions or riots. Ferdinand Lot has argued the descent and continuity of line from the late Roman *iugum*, to the *manse*, a Gallic tenurial and fiscal unit equivalent to the hide, finally to tenurial units of agriculture in modern France.[72]

However interesting it would be to try to pick up odd links of a lost chain which might stretch between late Roman and early medieval England, the search is not essential to the argument here. The concept of using a ploughing

---

[66]S.P.J. Harvey, 'Domesday Book and Anglo-Norman Governance', *TRHS* 5th series, XXV (1975), pp. 187–9, 192; F. Pollock, 'A Brief Survey of Domesday', *EHR* XI (1896), p. 213.

[67]*Ecclesiastical History of Orderic Vitalis*, ed. Chibnall II (Oxford, 1969), pp. 33, 37, 55, 127.

[68]DB I 100a.

[69]DB I 164a, 135b, 165a. There is also a controversial but interesting entry which concerns a grant in Wales which reads: *in eodem feudo dedit Willelmus comes Radulfi de Limesi L carucatas terrae sicut fit in Normannia*, DB I 162a. This has been translated as '50 carucates of land as it is measured in Normannia'. It seems likely that the clause refers not to the actual carucates but to the method of the grant, and thus would not add to the thesis here. It may be, however, that it is meant that the type of measurement is all part of the way land was granted in Normandy.

[70]*Ecclesiastical History of Orderic Vitalis*, ed. Chibnall IV, pp. xxii–xxiv.

[71]A.H.R. Baker, 'Open Fields and Partible Inheritance on a Kent Manor', *Economic History Review* 2nd series, XVII (1964), p. 22.

[72]F. Lot, 'Le iugum, le manse, et les exploitations agricoles de la France moderne', *Mélanges offert à Henri Pirenne* (Bruxelles, 1926), I, pp. 307–26.

unit as a fiscal criterion is such a basic one in settled societies that it might well have arisen independently; in any case to prove continuity of concept would neither strengthen nor weaken the definition argued here of the Domesday ploughland. In western civilization alone, societies ranging from Ptolemaic Egypt to early modern Scotland supply examples. Several types of survey survive, predominantly fiscal in purpose, from Ptolemaic Egypt including some arranged by landholders which give details of cultivators, of crops which the land did and might produce, and of the extent of uncultivated land.[73] In Scotland 'carucates' and 'ploughgates' were used in the late medieval and sixteenth centuries as units on which military service was assessed and public burdens apportioned;[74] yet, the raising of livestock constituted an important element in the agricultural sector and, with infield–outfield methods, arable cultivation was far from simple to assess in this way.

It seems that, however different the conceptual origins, the fiscal workings of the hide and the ploughland were not dissimilar. At the time of the Tribal Hidage and the early hide, when populations were small and highly mobile, manpower and the land for a household was the key element. By the eleventh century, land as well as labour could be in short supply. By then, both hide and carucate might take account of households and tenants, though the basic unit was the arable plot, plus attendant resources. Similarly, H.P.R. Finberg saw the early hide also as an estimate of potentialities, and concluded 'the hide, then, is a unit of assessment, applied to the land. It is laid on the estate as a whole, with behind it some rough and ready notion of actual or potential value, without enquiring whether the value is derived mainly from pasture or plough-land'. Pasture was often appreciated to be more profitable than tillage; and Finberg cited the Isle of Ely, a centre of fenland pasture, which was early assessed at a huge 600 hides.[75]

The carucage of 1198 created no new fiscal concept; it was merely an up-dated modification. The introductory short-hand description of this 1198 tax was that it was taken from each carucate of land or hide (*de unaquaque carucate terrae sive hyda*).[76] Roger of Hoveden elaborates on the method of collection. Information was gathered by counties on the ploughed lands under culti-vation, or possibly, plough-teams (*carucarum wainagia*) in each vill, both in demesne and in villeinage. The amount was testified by the stewards of barons, lords and bailiffs, the reeve and four men of each township, whether free or villein, and two knights from each hundred. This at least was the theory. But Roger himself says how the free fiefs of churches were exempted, as were all escheated baronies in the king's hands; and, reminiscent of Henry I's con-cession, how all sergeanties were exempted. But this exemption did not

[73]D.J. Crawford, *Kerkeosiris: an Egyptian Village in the Ptolemaic Period* (Cambridge, CUP, 1971), pp. 5–38.

[74]A. McKerral, 'Ancient Denominations of Agricultural Land in Scotland: a summary of recorded opinions with some notes, observations and references', *Proceedings of the Society of Anti-quaries of Scotland* LXXVIII (1943–44), pp. 48–53.

[75]H.P.R. Finberg, *The Agrarian History of England and Wales*, I part II (Cambridge, CUP, 1972), pp. 413–14.

[76]Stubbs, *Select Charters*, pp. 249–50.

prevent many of the lands being recorded with their plough-lands (*carrucatarum terrae*) and values. In 1198 the instructions were to calculate the ploughlands on the basis of 100 acres; so, in many cases, there might well result a discrepancy between the number of working ploughs and the calculated extent of the ploughlands. Or, in practice, local information on working ploughs probably prevailed whatever the ambitious intention of the government, and the chronicler, Ralph Coggeshall, recorded the tax as one levied on each working plough (*caruca arans*).[77] The very instructions as to the size of the ploughland illustrate the attempt to impose uniformity but also hint at the difficulties attendant on such an endeavour. This method recalls the principle relied on in the estimation of the Domesday ploughland.

A coherent assembly of the evidence accumulated suggests the following picture. In or following the military crises of 1084–5, William started a reappraisal of fiscal liability in the south-east. It seems to have been unsuccessful. It was certainly short-lived: further abbreviations of DB by the Exchequer omitted it altogether and preserved the 1066 rating in them. William had in 1084 already extorted a huge geld of 6s on the hide which was not completely collected, so there was little possibility of increasing the levy on the existing rating. Moreover, on that rating many of the wealthiest lands lay untapped and exempt. It seems likely that the abortive attempt at reappraisal formed a motive for the searching enquiry into assets and possibilities (and by inference into exemptions and their validity) called Domesday Book, with the ploughland representing a completely new assessment. Hence, the chroniclers' concern over Domesday's fiscal context.

[77]Stubbs, *Select Charters*, p. 267.

CHAPTER SEVEN

Secular Minster Churches in Domesday Book

John Blair

Of the thousands of churches listed in Domesday Book, a large minority are treated rather more fully than the rest. It is now widely accepted that many or most of these entries record a distinct class of church: the college or 'minster' of secular priests. They have received less attention than they deserve, for the simple reason that they are extremely badly recorded. Far more numerous than the cathedrals and Benedictine abbeys, they left no comparable legacy of literary or narrative texts: their place in the life of Domesday England can only be perceived through reconstruction and inference. The aim of this paper is to take a few steps towards such a perception.[1]

Central to the problem are two issues, distinct but related: the nature of secular minsters as religious communities, and their place in the English parochial system. Recent work, concentrating on the second issue, shows that minsters played a crucial pastoral role in the earlier days of English Christianity. During the seventh and eighth centuries, kings and bishops founded them as primary foci for local religious organization. They were staffed by communities of priests who served big *parochiae* covering perhaps 5 to 15 modern parishes, and from whom the inhabitants of rural England first received the Church's ministry. Between the eighth and twelfth centuries thousands of little churches, founded by private lords and served by single priests, sprang up in the *parochiae*, assumed the pastoral functions of the minsters, and became the raw material of the fully-fledged parochial system.[2]

---

[1] As the most substantial work in this field remains unpublished, I wish to emphasize my debt to the doctoral theses of D.H. Gifford, P.H. Hase and M.J. Franklin, details of which are given in note 2 below. For comments on earlier drafts, I am indebted to Dr Clive Brown, the Revd H.E.J. Cowdrey, Dr J.H. Denton, Dr Michael Franklin, Dr Richard Gem, Dr D.H. Gifford, Dr Brian Golding, Miss Barbara Harvey, Dr P.H. Hase, Dr Brian Kemp, Mrs Jane Murray, Dr B.L. Olson, Mr O. Padel, Dr David Rollason, Dr Julia Smith, Dr Alan Thacker and Mr Christopher Whittick. I am also extremely grateful to Miss P. Lloyd for typing several revisions of this paper.

[2] A valuable survey of recent work on minster *parochiae* is provided by C.N.L. Brooke, 'Rural Ecclesiastical Institutions in England: the Search for their Origins', *Settimane di Studio del Centro Italiano di Studi sull'Alto Medioevo*, XXVIII, 2 (Spoleto, 1982), pp. 685–711. See also: D.H. Gifford, 'The Parish in Domesday Book' (unpublished London PhD, 1952) [cited hereafter as 'Gifford']; P.H. Hase, 'The Development of the Parish in Hampshire' (unpublished Cambridge PhD, 1975) [cited hereafter as 'Hase'], pp. 1–2, 211–16; W.J. Blair, 'Land-holding, Church and Settlement in Surrey before 1300' (unpublished Oxford DPhil., 1982) [cited hereafter as 'Blair'],

By 1086 this encroachment had deprived the minsters of much of their original *raison d'être*. Consequently, historians have tended to observe their fragmenting *parochiae* and conclude that their day was over. In 1952, Dr Gifford claimed that 'the old minster perished largely in the Danish invasions and its final demise from the mid-tenth century was hastened by Dunstan's revival of monastic life and by the rapid growth of small, private churches served by a single priest. There was no longer room in the English ecclesiastical system for the groups of clerks who ministered to the countryside'.[3] R.V. Lennard's survey of 1959 concluded that they 'usually prove on examination to be either in a state of decay or to be undergoing some process of transformation', and described several minsters which had ostensibly lost both their community life and their ministry by 1086.[4]

In two respects, such interpretations do less than justice to the 'special' churches of Domesday Book. First, there are spheres, apparent from later sources though not from Domesday, in which the vested rights of minsters continued to influence parochial arrangements beyond the twelfth century. Secondly, there is evidence that secular colleges fitted easily into the religious world of eleventh-century England, and enjoyed patronage both from the last Anglo-Saxon generations and from the first Norman ones. Hence Domesday Book records a wide range of collegiate churches, of which many were old minsters but some were relatively new and non-parochial. With this complex situation it seems best to examine religious and parochial functions in relation to each other, and to take Domesday Book as the starting-point. So first we must establish criteria for recognizing the 'superior' churches of 1086, and for assessing the value and completeness of the Domesday data.

I

Mynster is simply the vernacular form of *monasterium*. In some tenth- and eleventh-century contexts the modern usage was the normal one, but the word could on occasion mean anything from the greatest cathedral or abbey to the smallest village church. A law of 1014 ranks churches in four categories, of which all but the humblest, the 'field-churches', are called 'minsters'.[5] We need to consider all the Domesday churches which, for whatever reason, are described with more than a simple *est ibi aecclesia* or *est ibi presbyter*. Excluded are

ch. IV; M.J. Franklin, 'Minsters and Parishes: Northamptonshire Studies' (unpublished Cambridge PhD, 1982) [cited hereafter as 'Franklin']; D.C. Douglas, *The Domesday Monachorum of Christ Church Canterbury* (London, Royal Historical Society, 1944); B.R. Kemp, 'The Mother Church of Thatcham', *Berkshire Archaeological Journal.* LXIII (1967-8), pp. 15-22; B.R. Kemp, 'The Churches of Berkeley Hernesse', *Transactions Bristol and Gloucestershire Archaeological Society* LXXXVII (1968), pp. 96-110.
[3]Gifford, p. 33.
[4]R.V. Lennard, *Rural England* (Oxford, OUP, 1959), pp. 396-404.
[5]VIII Aethr. 5; *Councils & Synods, with Other Documents relating to the English Church: vol. I: AD 871-1204*, eds. D. Whitelock, M. Brett and C.N.L. Brooke (Oxford, OUP, 1981), Part i [cited hereafter as 'C & S'], pp. 389-90.

those longer entries for little urban churches which are there merely to distinguish them from their neighbours; included, on the other hand, are others which mention identifiable minster lands but not the minsters themselves.

Six criteria, only the first of which gives *explicit* evidence for collegiate life, can be identified as marking superior status:[6]

(i) References to groups of *clerici*, *presbyteri* or *canonici*, where there is a fair presumption that they were resident.[7] Some are named explicitly as colleges of canons ('canonici S. Trinitatis de Thuinam tenent in ipsa villa v hidas');[8] others simply appear among the inhabitants ('ibi vii villani et iiii bordarii et iiii presbyteri et unus radman').[9] Pairs of priests often occur and are accepted here, though the status of some such cases is doubtful.

(ii) Endowments of at least one hide or carucate.[10] As the Domesday glebes of ordinary manorial churches (recorded in East Anglia and Middlesex) were much smaller,[11] such generous provision suggests a church of unusual status.

(iii) Tenure of the church or its land separately from the parent manor, especially if the tenant is a royal clerk or other named ecclesiastic.

(iv) Separate valuations of churches and surveys of their assets. ('De his xx hidis habet Reinbaldus presbyter de rege i hidam et dimidiam in elemosina, et aecclesiam ipsius manerii cum viii cotariis et una caruca et xv acris prati; valet l sol.')[12]

(v) Miscellaneous marks of status, including named dedications, eleemosinary exemptions from geld, and (very occasionally) references to church-scot or rights over neighbouring churches or chapels.

(vi) Just under half of the greater Domesday churches are attached to royal demesne, and about a fifth to bishops' manors. Royal or episcopal ownership has not in itself been used as a ground for inclusion, but has been held in favour of some doubtful cases.

Figure 7.1 plots 311 entries chosen on these criteria, with the cathedrals (both regular and secular) and the Benedictine abbeys. Only churches whose importance can be deduced from Great, Little, or Exon Domesdays (including the Geld Rolls), or from the Domesday Monachorum, are included; some ambiguous entries are accepted in the light of other sources, but not simple *est ibi aecclesia* entries where minster status is known only from external evidence.

How complete is this record? It is notorious that the Domesday listing of ordinary churches is incomplete and haphazard. Between and within the commissioners' seven circuits, there are major differences both in the quality of the data and in the form of its presentation.[13] Nonetheless, there are some grounds

[6]Cf. F. Barlow, *The English Church 1000–1066* (2nd impression, London, Longman, 1966), pp. 187–92.
[7]This excludes, for instance, most of the manors held by the Bishop of Hereford's clerks.
[8]DB I 44a (Christchurch).
[9]DB I 254b (Wroxeter).
[10]Dr Hase suggests to me that churches valued at 20s. (as representing the value of 1 hide) should also be included. These cases are not considered here.
[11]Lennard, *Rural England*, pp. 306–15; cf. Blair, pp. 304–10.
[12]DB I 56b (Cookham, Berks.).
[13]These problems are considered by Gifford, pp. 91–154, and by R. Morris, *The Church in British Archaeology* (CBA Research Report XLVII, 1983), pp. 68–71.

Key Map

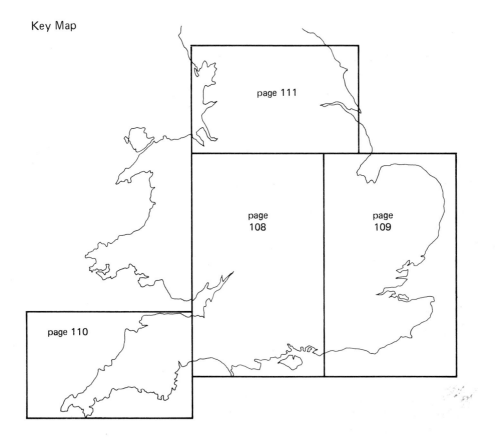

Figure 7.1 Map plotting the Domesday Book data for 'superior' churches in 1086. The thin broken lines indicate the boundary of the 'Circuit D' area and the Welsh border. The map only shows cases where the internal evidence of Domesday Book demonstrates or implies minster status.

Yale ▲   ▲ Farndon   ▲ Acton   Southwell ◉   ○
                                                                                            Newark
                               ▼ Ashbourne   Nottingham ○
                                                                              ○ Orston
                               ▲   ◆ ◆ Derby
     Ellesmere   Melton
  Baschurch   Norbury ▲   ◉ Stafford   Repton ◆   Mowbray   Grantham ○
        ■   ⊞ Burton
Shrewsbury ◉◉   Sheriffhales ○   ◉ Penkridge   Oakham ○
Wigmore ◉◉◉   ◉ Lichfield   Ridlington ○
Westbury ▲   ◉▼ Wrockwardine   Hambleton
           Wroxeter ◉   Tettenhall ◉
   ○ Condover ⊞ Wenlock   ◆ Wolverhampton
           ◉ Morville   ◉   ▲ Kingsbury
Lydbury ◉   ▲ Monks Kirby
North   Corfham   ⊞ Coventry
           ◉ Stottesdon   ▲ Halesowen   ▲ Stoneleigh
◆ Stanton Lacy   ▲ Long
◉ Bromfield   Chaddesley   Itchington
▲ Burford   ▲ Corbett
                                                Pattishall ▼
      Ombersley ▲ ◆ Droitwich
  ○ Leominster   Upton   N.Crawley ○
     ◆ Bromyard   ⊞ Worcester ◉
Avenbury ▲   ◆ Cleeve
     ▲ Stoke Edith   ▼ Prior   ◉ Buckingham
    Pershore ⊞   Leighton
◉◉ Ripple   ⊞ Evesham   Buzzard ◉
Hereford ◉   ■ Ledbury   ▼ Tredington   Wing ■
   ▲ Fownhope ◆ Tewkesbury   ▼ Blockley
○ Llanwarne Winchcombe ⊞ ◉ Stanway   ◉ Aylesbury
Bishops Cleeve ▼ ○ Prestbury   Stow-on-   ◉ Haddenham
Gloucester ⊞   ▼ Cheltenham   the-Wold ◉
        Bisley   Eynsham ◉   ◉ Oxford
        ▲   ● Bibury   ● Bampton   Abingdon ⊞
   Cirencester ◉   Highworth ◉ Faringdon ◉
○ Berkeley   Cricklade ◉   ◉ W. Hanney   ◉ Cholsey   Cookham ○
   Malmesbury ⊞ Shrivenham ◉   Wantage   ◉ Compton   Bray ◉
        Chippenham Ashbury ▼   Sparsholt Blewbury ◉ Streatley ◉
Bristol ◉ Marshfield Calne ◉ Avebury ▼ Lambourn   ◉ Reading
Bedminster ■ Bitton Corsham ■ Wootton ◉ Ramsbury ▲ Thatcham Bucklebury ◉
Yatton ▼ Keynsham ⊞ ◉ Bath Rivers ▼ Marlborough ◉ Aldermaston
○ Congresbury Melksham ⊞ Bromham Bishops ◉ Bedwyn ◉ Highclere ▼
        Kilmersdon ○ Potterne ◉ Cannings Pewsey ◉ Kingsclere ■
Cannington ○ Wells ⬡ Frome ■ Rushall ◉ Collingbourne Hurstbourne ◉ Basingstoke
  ▼ Stogumber   Upavon ◉ Kingston ○ Tarrant ○ Odiham ◉
◉ N. Petherton Westbury Netheravon ◉ Whitchurch ◉ Overton ○ Farnham ◉
⊞ Athelney Heytesbury ■ Winterbourne Wherwell
◉ N. Curry Brixton Stoke ▼ Amesbury ⊞ Stoke Bishops
Taunton ◉ Muchelney Deverill Nether Wallop ▼ Charity Sutton ▼
Ilminster ▲ Ilchester ⊞ Gillingham Wilton ◉ Houghton ◉ Winchester ⊞
  ■ Sherbourne Britford ◉ ◉ Alderbury Kings Sombourne Hinton Iping
Crewkerne ◉ Milborne ◉ Shaftesbury Downton Mottisfont ◉ Ampner ■ E. and W.
Whitchurch Port ⊞   Romsey ○ ◉ Meon Elsted
Axminster ▼ Canonicorum Cerne ⊞ Milton Cranborne ⊞ Bishops Stoughton ▼
  ▼ Bridport Puddletown ○ Bere Horton ⊞ Waltham Aldingbourne
Burton Bradstock ▼ ⊞ Dorchester Regis Wimborne ◉ Southampton ○ Bosham ◉ ⬡
Abbotsbury ○ ◉ Winfrith Christchurch ◉ Chichester Walberton
   Fleet ○ E.Chaldon Wareham ◉ ○ Swainston Boxgrove

Boothby Graffoe ▼
Wellingore ▼

Threekingham ○

Long ○
Sutton

Crowland ⊞

Stamford ▼   Thorney ⊞

Peterborough ⊞

Ramsey ⊞   Chatteris ⊞

Ely ⊞

Huntingdon ◆

Swavesey ⊞

Great Paxton ▼

St Neots ⊞

Bourn ◆   Little Shelford ○

Bedford ◉   Meldreth ○

Melford ▼

Stoke ◉
-by
-Clare   Sudbury   Hadleigh ▼

Colchester ◆

St Benet Holme ⊞

Langley ○

Morley ▼
St.Botulph

Thetford ⊗   Wissett ◆

Hoxne ○   Blythburgh ▼

Eye ▼

Stowmarket ○

Thorney ▼

Ipswich ◉

Hitchin
Houghton ○   Weston ▲
Luton ◉
Welwyn ▼
Sawbridgeworth ▼   Hatfield ▼
Broadoak
St Albans ⊞

Waltham
◉
Boreham ○

Writtle ▼

St Martin
-le-Grand
Harrow ▼
Colham ▼
Hayes ▼
Staines   Barking ⊞
Westminster ⊞   St Paul's ⊗
Southwark ○
Windsor ▼   Lambeth ◉   Dartford ○
Bermondsey
Chertsey ⊞   Rochester ⊞

S. Benfleet ◉
Horndon-on-the-Hill
Milton ○

Woking ○
Leatherhead ○
Stoke ○
Godalming ◉

Newington ◉
Maidstone ○   Teynham ○

Charing ○

Wye ○
Lyminge ○

Lympne ◉

Canterbury
⊞ ▲
Eastry ◆

Wingham ○

Dover ◉

Folkestone ○

S. Malling
◉
Amberley ▲
Arundel ◉   Lewes ◉
Bexhill ▲

Lyminster ○

Battle ⊞

Eastbourne
◉

0   10   20 Miles
|—|—|—|—|
0   10   20   30 Km

OTHER 'SUPERIOR' CHURCHES

- ▲ Two or more priests or canons
- ◉ Land over 2 hides
- ▼ Land of 1-2 hides
- ○ Other indications (dedication, separate tenant, separate value, etc.)

CATHEDRALS AND REGULAR HOUSES

- ⊞ Cathedral with monastic chapter
- ⊗ Cathedral with secular chapter
- ⊞ Benedictine monastery or nunnery

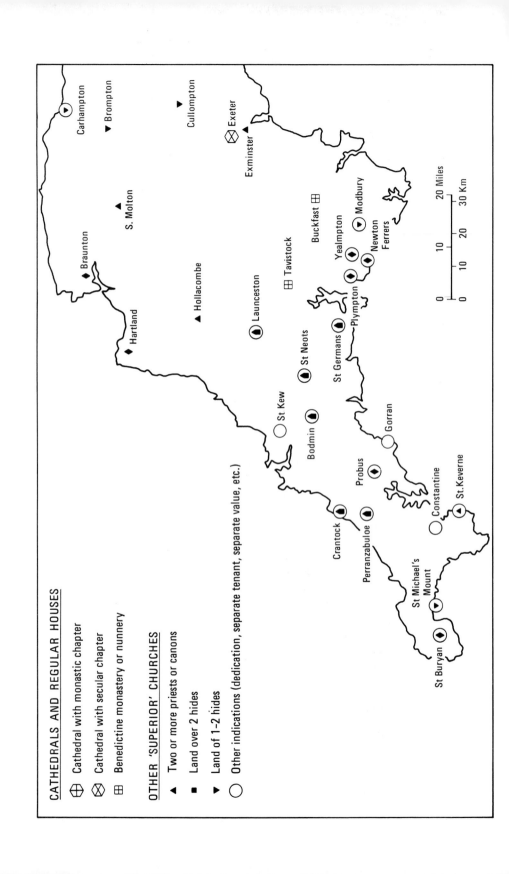

CATHEDRALS AND REGULAR HOUSES

⊕ Cathedral with monastic chapter

⊗ Cathedral with secular chapter

⊞ Benedictine monastery or nunnery

OTHER 'SUPERIOR' CHURCHES

▲ Two or more priests or canons

■ Land over 2 hides

▶ Land of 1-2 hides

◯ Other indications (dedication, separate tenant, separate value, etc.)

Carhampton

▼ Brompton

Cullompton ▶

⊗ Exeter

Exminster ◆

▲ S. Molton

◆ Braunton

Buckfast ⊞

▶ Modbury

Yealmpton

Newton
Ferrers

◆ Hartland

▲ Hollacombe

⊞ Tavistock

Plympton

◉ Launceston

St Neots ◉

St Germans ◉

◯ St Kew

Gorran ◯

Bodmin ◉

Probus ◆

Constantine ◯

◀ St.Keverne

Crantock ◉

Perranzabuloe ◉

St Michael's
Mount

St Buryan ◉

0   10   20 Miles

0   10   20   30 Km

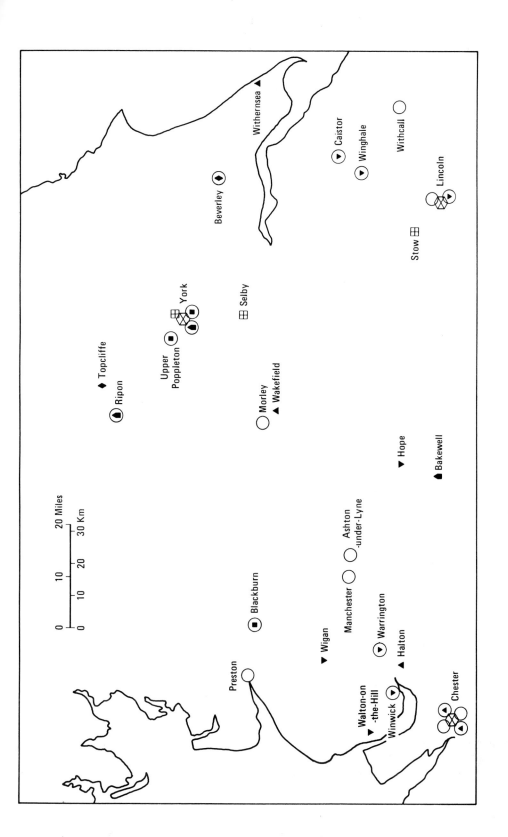

0 10 10 20 30 Km
0 10 20 Miles

Preston ○

Blackburn ■

▼ Wigan

Manchester ○
Ashton
-under-Lyne ○

Warrington ⊙
Walton-on
-the-Hill ⊙
Winwick ▼ ▲ Halton

Chester ▲ ⊙ ⊙ ⊗ ⊙ ▲ ⊙

Topcliffe ◆
Ripon ◐

Upper
Poppleton ⊙
York ⊞ ⊗ ■ ◐ ▲

⊞ Selby

Morley ○
▲ Wakefield

▼ Hope

▲ Bakewell

Withernsea ▲

Beverley ◆

Caistor ⊙
Winghale ⊙
Withcall ○
Lincoln ⊙ ⊗ ⊙
Stow ⊞

for thinking that the recording of greater churches is distinctly better than the recording of churches in general.

A 'superior' church which was still important or wealthy in 1086 must always have had a better chance of notice, in one way or another, than an ordinary manorial church. Circuits using the *est ibi aecclesia* formula often mention large endowments; those using *est ibi presbyter* mention groups of priests. In either case, a valuable church in the hands of its own tenant is less likely to escape notice. Even if it does, the land and the clerical farmer may be recognized for what they are with the help of outside sources. Sometimes (as in the south-western counties) *only* the 'superior' churches appear; but we will rarely find the lesser churches recorded and the minsters ignored.[14] When royal demesne churches are listed more fully than others, or are the only ones listed, this selection will probably still include a high proportion of the minsters.[15]

Undoubtedly a good many were ignored, or their endowments subsumed in the entries for larger holdings. Royal minsters still in royal hands were treated more summarily than those which had been granted out: to find the church of the coronations at Kingston-on-Thames dismissed with a simple 'ibi aecclesia'[16] is disconcerting. More so is the fact that, of 12 east Kent minsters listed with their daughter churches in the Domesday Monachorum,[17] only six could have been recognized from Exchequer Domesday alone. The commissioners were concerned with the taxable assets of churches as property, not with their spiritual income or parochial rights. Hence Domesday Book is a poor guide to ancient minster status, if a relatively good one to the important and well-endowed churches of 1086.

The 'Circuit D' counties (Leicestershire, Northamptonshire, Oxfordshire and Warwickshire) are a problem to themselves. Here the selection seems more or less arbitrary: a few minsters appear, but many more which other circuits would have recorded do not.[18] Whatever the reason for this, any arguments based on the Domesday incidence of minsters must dismiss 'Circuit D' as a gap in the data.

With this reservation, Figure 7.1 suggests some *prima facie* conclusions. 'Superior' churches, in the broad sense defined above, are especially numerous in Hampshire, Wiltshire, Berkshire, north Somerset and west Sussex. On the other hand, most of these are relatively small within the range selected: royal churches with one or two hides but rarely more. The minsters of Devon and Cornwall[19] are fewer but more important, and in several cases size-

[14]This statement may need qualification in the light of local vagaries in data-collection. Dr Hase (pers. comm.) points out the under-recording of minsters on royal (in contrast to episcopal) demesne in Hampshire, and the omission of *all* churches on the main demesne manors of New Minster.

[15]Cf. Morris, *Church in British Archaeology*, p. 70. Dr Thacker (pers. comm.) points out that in Cheshire, where the returns for churches were made hundredally, the principal two or three ancient churches in each hundred tend to be the ones which appear.

[16]DB I 30b.

[17]Douglas, *Domesday Monachorum*; mapped in Barlow, *English Church 1000–1066*, p. 181.

[18]Cf. Gifford, pp. 106–8. It seems possible that the royal demesne churches were recorded separately, but then omitted from the circuit return.

[19]For a useful survey of the Cornish minsters in Domeday Book see B.L. Olson, 'Early Monasteries in Cornwall' (unpublished Toronto PhD, 1980), pp. 230–49.

able staffs are mentioned. Another notable area is western Mercia (Shropshire, Herefordshire, Worcestershire, north Gloucestershire and Staffordshire), where there are many 'two-priest' churches and some bigger communities. Mercian towns usually had at least one large collegiate minster, and some (Shrewsbury, Chester, Derby) had several. Elsewhere the incidence is lighter, decreasing progressively northwards, and eastwards into the Danelaw counties.

These contrasts seem to be genuine ones. For instance, the 'superior' category includes nearly all of the 32 churches listed in Wiltshire but hardly any of the 301 churches listed in Norfolk, even though glebe acreages are usually given in both counties. We can be confident that ordinary churches were more common in Norfolk, and almost equally confident that important ones were more common in Wiltshire. Similarly, the concentration of large minsters in west Mercia agrees with sources both earlier and later than Domesday Book; if the 'Circuit D' returns were better we would see it spreading over into west and central Oxfordshire, but not much further.[20] Figure 7.1 shows an incomplete picture, but basically it shows the true one.

How many of these churches were collegiate? Here Domesday Book is certainly inadequate. Several counties do not provide data for priests. Elsewhere, the entries (31 per cent of the total considered) which mention staffs of between two and 13 priests should probably be taken at face value. But are the statements '*X* presbyter tenet' or 'est ibi i presbyter' evidence that there was *only* one priest? Certainly not the first. The commissioners had little concern with priests holding under a named tenant; sometimes these are mentioned so casually as to suggest that they might easily not be mentioned at all, as at Lydbury North where a Frenchman and William the clerk held 'aecclesiam eiusdem manerii cum presbyteris et terra ibi pertinenti'.[21] Even 'est ibi presbyter' is inconclusive, since one possible application of it is to the head-priest or president of a college. This was evidently the case at Great Paxton (Hunts.), where Domesday records 'Ibi aecclesia et presbyter. . .; de hac terra pertinet ad aecclesiam una hida'. In the 1120s it was declared that 'prior et clerici . . . in religione canonice eidem ecclesie serviant', and the highly sophisticated building of *c.* 1050 supports the view that this collegiate arrangement was pre-Conquest.[22]

There are other stray references to communities, ignored by Domesday Book, which must have existed in 1086. The Cullompton (Devon) entry says that Battle Abbey 'habet i hidam terrae et i aecclesiam in Colitona quam tenuit Torbertus'; from another source we know that the land was held as five prebends.[23] Again, in 1086 the abbey of S. Wandrille had 'i aecclesiam aput

---

[20]External evidence suggests that the omitted 'Circuit D' minsters would have included Charlbury, Shipton-under-Wychwood, Bampton (where Domesday lists the endowment but not the church), Bicester, Dorchester, Thame, and perhaps Langford.

[21]DB I 252a.

[22]DB I 207a; C.A.R. Radford, 'Pre-Conquest Minster Churches', *Archaeological Journal* CXXX (1973), p. 133 (citing a charter of David I of Scotland printed *Scottish Historical Review* XIV (1917), pp. 370–2); H.M. and J. Taylor, *Anglo-Saxon Architecture* Vol. II (Cambridge, CUP, 1965), pp. 484–8.

[23]Exeter Domesday fo. 195; Lennard, *Rural England*, p. 397.

Warham quam tenet de rege Willelmo ad quam pertinet i hidam terrae'; a few decades later it was said that 'ecclesia beate Marie de Wareham erat ecclesia canonicorum prebendas habencium'.[24] The entry for South Stoneham (St Mary's, Southampton) suggests minster status but says nothing of the staff; the *custos* and his *clerici* do not appear in any known text until the 1190s, when they had already become a rare anachronism.[25] There is no reason to think these cases exceptional, except that they have external evidence. The Domesday record of clerical communities is a bare minimum, and far inferior to the record of the churches which housed them.

Recording of parochial rights is worse still. The occasional references to church-scot and tithe seem little more than arbitrary, or determined by non-relevant factors.[26] Links between mother and daughter churches are mentioned in a few exceptional entries, as at Southampton: 'Huius manerii aecclesiam tenet Richerius clericus cum duabus aliis aecclesiis iuxta Hantone quae ad hanc aecclesiam matrem pertinent, et ibi adiacet i hida terrae et omnis decima eiusdem ville et etiam de terra regis.'[27] But Domesday is silent in scores of other cases where, on external evidence of the kinds discussed below, similar payments and rights cannot possibly have failed to exist in 1086. The absence of any hint in Domesday Book of a church's local authority is not negative evidence, but simply *no* evidence.

So England in 1086 contained hundreds of 'superior' churches, many of which were staffed by more than one priest. The Domesday entries suggest much variety in status and, less explicitly, in age. A few churches were wealthy and had 'full convents' of 13 canons; more held three or four hides and were staffed by three or four priests; and it remains likely that many housed no communities at all, or had lost whatever communities they once had. Some seem to be young, others in decay, while the later layers on the palimpsest reflect the political geography and royal power of post-Viking England: well-endowed churches were thickest on the ground where late Saxon kings had their main estates and conducted their main activities.[28] These patterns can only be understood by reviewing the previous and subsequent fortunes of the greater Domesday churches.

II

The churches which can be defined as secular minsters by the eleventh century are very diverse in origin. Some had been, in the strict sense, monastic. Many

[24]Exeter Domesday fo. 28ᵛ; M. Brett, *The English Church under Henry I* (Oxford, OUP, 1975), p. 139n.

[25]DB I 41b; Hase, pp. 177–9.

[26]On church dues see Barlow, *English Church 1000–1066*, p. 195; Gifford, pp. 189–218.

[27]DB I 41b (South Stoneham). The Taunton entry (Exeter Domesday fo. 174) includes burial and other mother-church rights among the manorial assets.

[28]Compare Fig. 7.1 with P. Stafford in D. Hill (ed.), *Ethelred the Unready* (BAR, Oxford, 1978), Figs. 2.1, 2.2, 2.4 and 2.5. The fact that there are so many more 'superior' churches in Wessex than in Western Mercia does suggest that we are not looking at a wholly pre-Alfredian pattern.

south-western minsters perpetuate Celtic monasteries, and the arguments for a more general Celtic influence behind other Anglo-Saxon religious centres have recently been re-stated.[29] It is also apparent that seventh- and eighth-century monasteries in the Roman tradition, often double houses ruled by royal abbesses, could be linked to the local geography of royal *villae* and their districts in the way characteristic of later secular minsters.[30]

The frequent assumption that all clerical minsters were 'devolved' or 'degraded' monasteries is nonetheless wrong, for another tradition had existed from the beginning. The normal priestly organization of the early church was based on communities: priests no less than monks were expected to lead a common life, as members of the 'canonical order' which stood alongside the monastic order. Augustine of Hippo's clerks lived in an episcopal *monasterium clericorum*, serving the needs of the outside world while renouncing private property and living in monastic strictness. In fifth-century Europe, such a community was the normal staff of a cathedral or mother church.[31]

The years of disruption and decay which saw 'the obliteration of the erstwhile well-defined boundary between the *ordo canonicus* and the *ordo monasticus*'[32] also saw the conversion of England. So it is entirely natural that seventh- and eighth-century English communities are hard to define: they were as diverse as the models available to their founders. To draw a hard line between 'minsters' which had parochial duties and 'monasteries' which did not is impossible in practice, and probably anachronistic. Monastic *parochiae* seem more acceptable in the light of Professor Constable's recent survey, which argues that monks always took part in normal pastoral work, and that the early ninth-century reforms 'did little to stem the rising tide of ordination of monks and of monastic performance of the *cura animarum*'.[33] In all likelihood, communities with oversight over parochial territories ranged from the strictest monasteries to the most loosely ordered groups of priests.[34]

It is a recurring problem that nearly all our evidence for the non-regular minsters comes from the acid pens of monastic purists. Bede's famous attack on 'fraudulent' monasteries judges the motley communities of his day by one

[29]H.R. Loyn, 'The Conversion of the English to Christianity: some Comments on the Celtic Contribution', in R.R. Davies *et al.* (eds.), *Welsh Society and Nationhood: Historical Essays Presented to Glanmor Williams* (Cardiff, University of Wales Press, 1984), pp. 5–18. See also Olson, 'Early Monasteries in Cornwall', which stresses their Celtic origins. Dr Olson (pers. comm.) informs me that current research is detecting a bigger clerical (as against monastic) element in the Church in Celtic regions.

[30]Cf., for instance, the group of Kentish monasteries discussed by D.W. Rollason, *The Mildrith Legend* (Leicester UP, 1982), especially pp. 48–9, 53.

[31]See J.C. Dickinson, *The Origins of the Austin Canons and their Introduction into England* (London, SPCK, 1950), pp. 7–16.

[32]Ibid., pp. 14–15.

[33]G. Constable, 'Monasteries, Rural Churches and the *Cura Animarum* in the Early Middle Ages', *Settimane di Studio del Centro Italiano di Studi sull'Alto Medioevo*, XXXVIII, 1 (Spoleto, 1982), pp. 349–89.

[34]For the similarities between monasteries and clerical minsters, see M. Deanesly, 'Early English and Gallic Minsters', *TRHS.* 4th series XXIII (1941), pp. 25ff.; H. Mayr-Harting, *The Coming of Christianity to Anglo-Saxon England* (London, Batsford, 1972), pp. 244–6; Franklin, pp. 124–37. On the early clerical tradition at Canterbury see N. Brooks, *The Early History of the Church of Canterbury* (Leicester UP, 1984), pp. 87–91.

standard, and begins the chorus of abuse which the members, however conscientious in other ways, were to suffer for their wives: '[it is] a most disgraceful and unheard-of spectacle, [that] the very same men now occupy themselves with their wives and begetting children, now rise from their beds and perform with assiduous care whatever needs to be done within the monastery'.[35] This is, of course, an extreme statement; it may well be that most monks and clerics with pastoral duties were neither austere nor corrupt, but simply respectable enough in the eyes of their patrons and parishioners.

Some and possibly all of the English kingdoms seem to have acquired a framework of minster *parochiae* by the early eighth century. The minsters' functions and financial rights were moulded around those of the royal administrative centres where they so often stood, and often their parishes were coterminous with the districts which the centres controlled.[36] Church-scot and soul-scot, the primary, basic mother-church dues, were established early under royal authority and sometimes survived the Conquest as the clearest 'hard' test of ancient minster status.[37]

Yet if 'primary' foci, both secular and religious, often lasted for centuries, there was also expansion and change. Eighth-century kings and nobles founded numerous small minsters; if these had *parochiae* (as some certainly did), their advent must have modified the existing pattern. The exceptional size and number of colleges in western Mercia can be traced partly to minster foundations by Hwiccian aristocrats during the seventh and eighth centuries,[38] partly to the promotion of Mercian royal cults during the eighth and ninth,[39] and partly to continued patronage after 900. The expansion of Wessex during the ninth and tenth centuries must have created a need for more royal residences, and a new *villa regia* might in its turn have merited a new collegiate church.

The Carolingian reforms in the western church re-defined standards of monasticism, and it was perhaps the influence of these definitions which first set the majority of English minsters firmly outside the monastic fold.[40] On the

[35]*Venerabilis Baedae Opera Historica*, ed. C. Plummer, vol. I, (Oxford, OUP, 1896), p. 416 (translation in *English Historical Documents*. Vol. I (ed. D. Whitelock, 2nd edn, London, Eyre Methuen, 1979), pp. 805–6). P. Wormald, 'Bede, "*Beowulf*" and the Conversion of the Anglo-Saxon Aristocracy', in R.T. Farrell (ed.), *Bede and Anglo-Saxon England*, BAR XLVI (1978), pp. 49–58, graphically evokes the world of Bede's 'fraudulent' minsters. For eighth-century opposition to secularized monasteries and lay Lordship, see Brooks, *Early History of the Church of Canterbury*, pp. 175–80.

[36]See for instance J. Campbell (ed.), *The Anglo-Saxons* (Oxford, Phaidon, 1982), p. 61. A survey of systems of obligation based on *villae regales* is provided by G.W.S. Barrow, *The Kingdom of the Scots* (London, Edward Arnold, 1973), pp. 7–68. On royal vills see also P. Sawyer, 'The Royal *Tun* in pre-Conquest England', in P. Wormald (ed.), *Ideal and Reality in Frankish and Anglo-Saxon Society* (Oxford, Blackwell, 1983), pp. 273–99.

[37]Occasionally in Domesday Book, and often thereafter, church-scot appears as a secular due. Its continued payment to a church, on the other hand, seems to be good evidence for minster status. See F.M. Stenton, *Anglo-Saxon England* (3rd edn, Oxford, OUP, 1971), pp. 152–4; Gifford, pp. 189f.; N. Neilson in P. Vinogradoff (ed.), *Oxford Studies in Social and Legal History*, vol. II (Oxford, OUP, 1910), pp. 192–6.

[38]C. Dyer, *Lords and Peasants in a Changing Society* (Cambridge, CUP, 1980), pp. 13–16; cf. Campbell, *The Anglo-Saxons*, map p. 71.

[39]See A.T. Thacker, 'Kings, Saints and Monasteries in pre-Viking Mercia', forthcoming.

[40]I owe this idea to Mr C. Hohler.

other hand, the same reforms produced new rules for the common life of canons. The most important were the Rule of St Chrodegang (*c.* 755), and the *Institutio Canonicorum* ascribed to Amalarius of Metz and promulgated at the Council of Aachen in 816–17. As an ideal, they advocate a quasi-monastic regime with refectory, dormitory and assets held in common. Yet they are flexible and (especially Amalarius) eclectic, offering a wide range of precepts on which a life of greater or lesser austerity could be founded.[41] The influence of Chrodegang can be traced in England as early as the 786 Legatine Statutes, which include a decree on the conduct of *canonici*. In 808 x 13 Archbishop Wulfred gave the secular canons of Christ Church, Canterbury, a Chrodegang - based rule with a refectory and dormitory, though members could still hold separate houses and bequeath them to their successors.[42]

The orthodox view that the old minsters never recovered from the Vikings is misconceived. Certainly the Danelaw has few 'superior' churches in Domesday and little sign of minster rights influencing later parochial arrangements,[43] though even here there are some minsters (notably Grantham) whose status must be of pre-Viking origin.[44] In Wessex and its near dependences, there is no evidence for the long-term decline of the system until well after Alfred's day. Asser's well-known comment, though written with a strong monastic bias, shows that there were many non-regular communities in the late ninth century: 'for many years past the desire for the monastic life had been totally lacking in that entire race . . ., even though quite a number of monasteries which had been built in that area still remain but do not maintain the rule of monastic life in any consistent way.'[45] Asser himself received from Alfred the minsters of Banwell, Congresbury and Exeter,[46] foreshadowing a type of patronage that was to be normal in the eleventh century (below p. 124).

Unless corporate clerical life often survived through these years, it is hard to see how so many small minsters founded in the seventh and eighth centuries could still have been functioning in the eleventh. Such priests as figure in Alfred's laws live in communities. A priest who kills another man 'is to be handed over, and all of the minster property which he bought for himself, and . . . is to be delivered up out of the minster'. If a criminal takes refuge in 'any church which a bishop has consecrated', he is to be moved elsewhere 'if the

[41]On the Carolingian canonical tradition see J. Chatillon, 'La Spiritualité Canoniale', in *Saint Chrodegang* (Metz, 1967), pp. 111–22, and other papers in the same volume; Dickinson, *Origins of Austin Canons*, pp. 16–23; C.N.L. Brooke in W.R. Matthews and W.M. Atkins (eds.), *A History of St Paul's Cathedral* (London, Phoenix House, 1957), pp. 10–12.

[42]W. Levison, *England and the Continent in the Eighth Century* (Oxford, OUP, 1946), pp. 104–6; E. John, 'The King and the Monks in the Tenth-Century Reformation', *Bulletin John Rylands Library* XLII (1959–60), pp. 71–5; Brooks, *Early History of the Church of Canterbury*, pp. 155–60.

[43]See D.M. Owen, *Church and Society in Medieval Lincolnshire* (Lincoln, 1981), pp. 1–5.

[44]DB I 337b, 377a–b. On the effects of the Vikings see P.H. Sawyer, *The Age of the Vikings* (2nd edn, London, Edward Arnold, 1971), pp. 143–4. Professor Sawyer (pers. comm.) suggests that Kirkby names often refer to old minsters (as *the* churches). In Suffolk, three secular minsters (Mendham, Hoxne and Bury) appear in a will of 942 x *c.* 951 (*C & S*, pp. 74f).

[45]Trans. from S. Keynes and M. Lapidge (eds.), *Alfred the Great* (Harmondsworth, Penguin, 1983), p. 103.

[46]Ibid., pp. 97, 264–5.

[47]Alfred 21, 5–5.2; *C & S*, pp. 29–30, 24–5.

community have more need of their church', and the 'elder' of the church (*thaere cirican ealdor*) is to supervise him.[47] The Chrodegang rule for canonical life was being copied in England during Aethelstan's reign.[48] In 942 x 6 Archbishop Oda classified religious men in ascending order of strictness as *presbyteri*, *clerici* and *monachi*; the *clerici*, who must be the minster-priests, are to 'live canonically with all honesty and reverence according to the decrees of the holy fathers'.[49]

Alfred's heirs augmented old secular minsters and founded new ones.[50] In Wessex, Edward the Elder's New Minster at Winchester is an obvious case. In western Mercia, the old tradition of minster patronage continued under the semi-autonomous government of Alderman Aethelred and Aethelflaed. In 887, for instance, Aethelred gave fourteen hides and six men to Worcester Cathedral's minster of Pyrton (Oxon.).[51] The great Mercian minsters owed much to Aethelflaed, who re-founded St Werburh's at Chester, St Oswald's at Gloucester, and perhaps St Alkmund's at Shrewsbury.[52] The royal college at Stafford was established in *c.* 913; other West Midland colleges, which later claimed foundation by the prestigious Edgar, may in fact be the work of his forbears.[53] It has been suggested that the house of Wessex had political motives for supporting Mercian cults and minsters;[54] at all events, it was a notable benefactor to the big collegiate churches which were still so prominent here in 1086.

Changes in local government could affect minster *parochiae*. W. Page's pioneer study emphasized the 'hundredal' churches of Domesday Book: the cases in which there is only one 'superior' church in each hundred, and that at the hundred centre.[55] It is clear enough that tenth-century hundreds were re-fashioned from older territories. But re-fashioned they were: alongside ancient features, they show the marks of rationalization and division. It may not have been especially unusual in Edgar's reign to find a hundred centre and its hundred church which were both fairly new. There are regional contrasts here: the correlation between hundred and minster is strong in the south-east, for example, but not in Devon.[56] For the western Danelaw, it has recently been

[48]M. Wood in Wormald (ed.), *Ideal and Reality*, p. 270, who sees this as one instance of scribes under Aethelstan 'assimilating some of the intellectual legacy of the Carolingian Renaissance'. For minsters in Aethelstan's reign cf. V Aethst. 3; *C & S*, p. 54.
[49]*C & S*, pp. 71-2.
[50]For this paragraph cf. J. Campbell, 'The Church in Anglo-Saxon Towns', in D. Baker (ed.), *The Church in Town and Countryside: Studies in Church History*, XVI (1979), pp. 125-6.
[51]S. 217.
[52]A.T. Thacker, 'Chester and Gloucester: Early Ecclesiastical Organization in Two Mercian Burhs', *Northern History*, XVIII (1982), pp. 199-211. For the excavation of Aethelflaed's church at Gloucester, see C. Heighway in *Medieval Archaeology* xxviii (1984), pp. 219-20.
[53]D. Knowles and R.N. Hadcock, *Medieval Religious Houses: England and Wales* (London, Longman, 1971) [hereafter cited as 'K & H'], p. 439; A. Hamilton Thompson, 'Notes on Colleges of Secular Canons in England', *Archaeological Journal* LXXIV (1917), pp. 141-2.
[54]Thacker, 'Chester and Gloucester', p. 211.
[55]'Some Remarks on the Churches of the Domesday Survey', *Archaeologia* 2nd series XVI (1915), pp. 66ff.
[56]See Page, 'Some Remarks on the Churches', pp. 79-83 (Kent and Sussex); Hase, p. 39 (Hampshire); Blair, pp. 233-4 (Surrey); O.J. Reichel, 'The Church and the Hundreds in Devon', *Transactions Devonshire Association* LXXI (1939), pp. 331-42 (Devon). Dr Hase (pers.

argued that 'the re-conquest was marked by the planting of new hundred churches by the kings', financed from land and tithe but not from the ancient church-scot payments.[57]

But by the 940s, private churches were tipping the balance of pastoral organization in the countryside. If many of the tenth-century royal foundations were collegiate, they shade imperceptibly into the ranks of larger manorial churches. Some counties contained 'hundredal' churches (in private franchisal hundreds as well as in royal ones) which, while distinctly superior to their neighbours, have no sign of the normal minster attributes.[58] 'One-priest' churches were becoming the norm: the minsters remained, but their corporate ministry declined.

This brought financial problems. The tenth-century law-codes display a new emphasis on tithe, which first appears as an obligatory payment in 926 x *c.* 930.[59] It can be argued that tithe became important as a basis of finance for new minsters;[60] the urgent need to protect the incomes of old ones against thegnly encroachments may explain the legislation better. Edgar's second code (960 x 62) defends the principle of *parochiae* while conceding limited rights to private churches. All tithe is to be paid 'to the old minster to which the obedience pertains' (*to tham ealdan mynstre the seo hernes to hyrth*), except that a thegn whose church has a graveyard may endow it with one-third of his demesne tithes.[61] Whatever the gap between theory and practice,[62] this seems a clear attempt to find a *modus vivendi* in a world where social change ran counter to the minsters' vested rights.

If Edgar protected the incomes of clerical communities, he also sponsored a celebrated attack on their way of life: the expulsion of canons from some of the greater minsters to make way for reformed monasticism. Compared with the reformers' well-documented campaign, the 'anti-monastic' movement after 975 may seem of little consequence to the mainstream of religious history.[63] It should not be so lightly dismissed: St Aethelwold and his colleagues may have been more isolated than their own prolific writings tell us. Obviously enough,

---

comm.) believes that the royal minsters of Hampshire are generally ancient, and to be distinguished clearly from late-Saxon churches, founded on large episcopal (and often hundredal) manors, which lack minster attributes. Regional contrasts require further study.

[57]Franklin, pp. 11–13, 179–96, 313–33 (especially the cases of Towcester and Daventry).

[58]E.g., in Surrey: Shere, Dorking, Wotton, Reigate, Shalford, Walton-on-Thames (Blair, pp. 257–9). Cf. Hase, pp. 293–309.

[59]I Aethst.; *C & S*, pp. 43–7.

[60]As argued by Franklin, pp. 11–13.

[61]II Edgar 1–3.1; *C & S*, pp. 97–9; reissued by Cnut (I Cnut 11, 11.2; *C & S*, pp. 476–7).

[62]Stenton, *Anglo-Saxon England*, p. 156, claims that 'the right of a lord to build a church and endow it with tithe was fully recognized in the last years of the Old English state'. But he only gives one example; such freedom must have depended very largely on the vitality or otherwise of the minster within whose *parochia* the new church was built.

[63]On the reaction see *C & S*, pp. 155–65; D.J.V. Fisher, 'The Anti-Monastic Reaction in the Reign of Edward the Martyr', *Cambridge Historical Journal* X (1952), pp. 254–70; John, 'The King and the Monks', pp. 80–4. On its most notorious supporter see A. Williams, '*Princeps Merciorum Gentis*: the Family, Career and Connections of Aelfhere, Ealdorman of Mercia, 956–83', *Anglo-Saxon England* X (1982), pp. 143–72 (who argues, with Fisher, that Aelfhere's opposition to the reformers was more political than religious).

their vilification of minster-priests gives a one-sided view: the 'degraded and lascivious' clerics probably considered themselves lawfully married, and were respectable enough by ordinary standards.[64] But the abuse may also betray insecurity in a world where clerical communities remained familiar, accepted objects of patronage for many lay nobles. Even supporters of the monks did not necessarily abandon traditional loyalties: Aethelgifu's will of the 980s has bequests for St Alban's, but also for eight secular minsters (four of them traceable in Domesday Book) in Hertfordshire and Bedfordshire.[65] On Edgar's death, wrote Byrhtferth of Ramsey, 'monks were smitten with fear, the people trembled; and clerics were filled with joy, for their time had come. Abbots were expelled with their monks, clerics were installed with their wives, and the last state was worse than the first'.[66]

Vested interests, tradition, and the legitimate pastoral needs of *parochiae* whose minster-priests were threatened,[67] stood alike in the path of reform. St Oswald's Worcester continued to support clerks, and in 987 a priest of the community took up a lease for three lives.[68] A law of 1008 considers the plight of monks whose monasteries have been taken over by canons or nuns.[69] This glimpse of expropriated, wandering monks recalls the fate of Evesham[70] and other reformed houses, which passed through another clerical phase before being reformed again. Bedford and Cholsey were both Benedictine houses with abbots at the end of the tenth century, and both appear as secular minsters in Domesday.[71] It may be that, in the absence of strong and vigilant control, monasteries often showed a natural tendency to revert to the clerics.

Beside these cases may be set the many others of old minsters enlarged or rebuilt and new ones founded. Royal patronage is illustrated by Eadwig's grant to Bampton minster (955 x 7), Aethelred's charter for St Frideswide's Oxford (1004),[72] and Edward the Confessor's writ protecting the lands and rights of Bromfield minster (1060-1).[73] Tenth-century kings were active

---

[64] John, 'The King and the Monks', pp. 70-2. To quote W.J. Corbett (*Cambridge Medieval History*, vol. III (CUP, 1922), pp. 378-9): 'In judging this movement no reliance can be placed on the accounts of it which have survived, for they originate without exception from the side of the monks and depict all sympathizers with the clerks as the blackest scoundrels.'

[65] *The Will of Aethelgifu*, eds. D. Whitelock, N. Ker and Lord Rennell (Roxburghe Club, Oxford, 1968), pp. 29-32, 69-72. The minsters were at Ashwell, Bedford, Braughing, Flitton, Henlow, Hertingfordbury, Hitchin and Welwyn.

[66] *C & S*, p. 161.

[67] It seems likely that the royal nunneries of Nunnaminster, Wherwell, Romsey and Shaftesbury were founded in old secular communities, which thereafter coexisted with the nuns. The strange arrangement at Wherwell, where the canons controlled the subordinate parishes and had separate incomes, seats in chapter and voices in elections (Hase, pp. 84-5) is hard to explain except on the view that the canons preceded the nuns and retained their old pastoral functions. I owe this information to Dr Hase.

[68] P.H. Sawyer, 'Charters of the Reform Movement: the Worcester Archive', in D. Parsons (ed.), *Tenth-Century Studies* (Chichester, Phillimore, 1975), pp. 84-93.

[69] V Aethr. 6, VI Aethr. 3.1; *C & S*, pp. 348, 364-5.

[70] K & H, p. 65.

[71] K & H, pp. 420, 62; DB I 210b-211a, 56b-57a.

[72] The Oxford charter is S. 909; for Bampton see below, note 115.

[73] S. 1162; F. Harmer, 'A Bromfield and a Coventry Writ of King Edward the Confessor', in P. Clemoes (ed.), *The Anglo-Saxons: Studies presented to Bruce Dickins* (London, 1959), pp. 89-103. Cf. Edward's writ granting Axminster minster (S. 1161; *C & S*, pp. 557-9).

patrons of the ancient Cornish houses, most of which had by now assumed the character of collegiate minsters.[74] St Martin-le-Grand, London, may have been founded (or re-founded) under Edward the Confessor by the priest Ingelric as a royal college.[75]

Earl Leofric and Godiva, if we can trust 'Florence' of Worcester, were princely patrons of Mercian minsters, enriching Leominster, Wenlock, Stow, and St John's and St Werburh's in Chester.[76] Earl Godwin may have had a hand in the great minster of Bosham,[77] and his wife Gytha is said to have established secular priests at Hartland (Devon) where twelve *canonici* appear in 1086.[78] Another of Gytha's churches was Nether Wallop (Hants.), revealed as an old minster by its church-scot payments; in the early eleventh century it was rebuilt on an innovative plan and adorned with fine 'Winchester School' wallpaintings.[79]

Odd references show lesser aristocrats founding or re-founding minsters, such as Wulfrun at Wolverhampton in 994 and perhaps Urki at Abbotsbury during Cnut's reign.[80] Domesday Book says that in King Edward's time Aelfric son of Wisgar had given Stoke-by-Clare (Suffolk) to St John's church there, 'et quendam sacerdotem Ledmarum et alios cum illo imposuit'.[81] Of the many others which must have vanished without written record, some can be inferred on architectural grounds.[82] To judge from the known fragments, a typical late Anglo-Saxon minster church had a tall aisleless nave, a pair of north and south *porticus* towards the east end, and a rectangular chancel (Figure 7.2, Nos. 1–2). It is a fact worth noting that of the three best remaining examples (St Mary's Dover, Breamore and Worth)[83], only the first has documentary evidence for collegiate status. At Kirkdale (Yorks.), the remains of a high-quality late Saxon church are dated by the inscription 'Orm son of Gamal bought St Gregory's minster when it was broken and fallen, and has rebuilt it from the ground in honour of Christ and St Gregory, in the days of Edward the king and Tosti the earl'.[84] This unique witness may tell a common story.

[74]See Olson, 'Early Monasteries in Cornwall', Ch. III. W.M.M. Picken, 'The Manor of Tremaruustel and the Honour of St Keus', *Journal of the Royal Institution of Cornwall* n.s. VII (1973-7), pp. 220–30, argues that in Edgar's reign St Kew had two canons supervised by the larger collegiate minster at Plymouth.

[75]R.H.C. Davis, 'The College of St Martin-le-Grand and the Anarchy', *London Topographical Record* XXIII (1972), pp. 24–5.

[76]Stow: *C & S*, pp. 538–43 (Cf. Lennard, *Rural England*, pp. 397–8). For the others see Florence of Worcester, *Chronicon ex Chronicis*, ed. B. Thorpe (London, English Historical Society, 1848), vol. I, p. 216.

[77]Barlow, *Church 1000–1066*, pp. 190–1. Harold's visit to Bosham minster, depicted on the Bayeux Tapestry, underlines its importance for his family.

[78]K & H, p. 426; Exeter Domesday fo. 456ᵛ.

[79]DB I 38b; R. Gem and P. Tudor-Craig, 'A "Winchester School" Wall-Painting at Nether Wallop, Hampshire', *Anglo-Saxon England* IX (Cambridge, 1981), pp. 115–36.

[80]J.H. Denton, *English Royal Free Chapels 1100–1300* (Manchester, University Press, 1970), pp. 41f.; *C & S*, p. 516.

[81]DB II 389b; cf. K & H, p. 423, and *VCH Suffolk*, vol. I, p. 527n.

[82]E.g. the churches listed by Radford, 'Pre-Conquest Minster Churches', pp. 127–37.

[83]Taylor and Taylor, *Anglo-Saxon Architecture*, vol. I, pp. 214–17, 94–6, vol. II, 688–93. I am grateful to Mr T. Tatton-Brown for the view that St Mary's Dover was the collegiate predecessor of St Martin's.

[84]Ibid., vol. I, pp. 357–61.

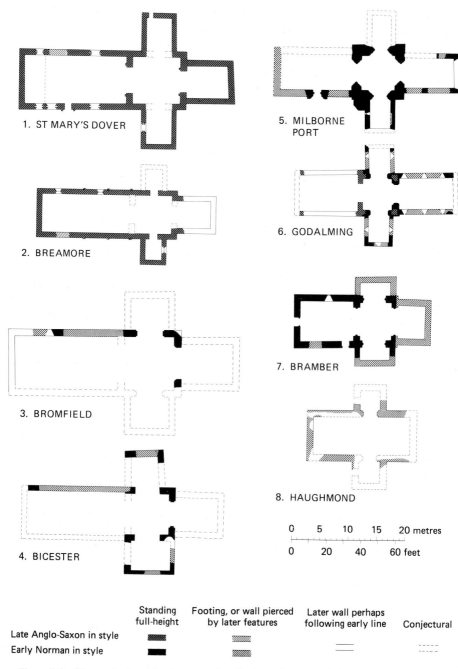

1. ST MARY'S DOVER

2. BREAMORE

3. BROMFIELD

4. BICESTER

5. MILBORNE PORT

6. GODALMING

7. BRAMBER

8. HAUGHMOND

	Standing full-height	Footing, or wall pierced by later features	Later wall perhaps following early line	Conjectural
Late Anglo-Saxon in style				
Early Norman in style				

Figure 7.2 Plans of selected minster and collegiate churches of the tenth, eleventh and twelfth centuries. (Dover, Breamore and Milborne Port after Taylor and Taylor, *Anglo-Saxon Architecture*; Bromfield and Godalming from surveys by the author; Bicester after *VCH Oxfordshire* vol. VI, p. 45; Bramber after E.F. Salmon in *Sussex Arch. Collns.* LXXIII, p. 190; Haughmond after J.J. West in *Medieval Archaeology* XXIV, pp. 240–1.)

The clearest testimony to the vitality of the old secular tradition is Waltham Holy Cross, founded by Earl Harold and dedicated in 1060. A twelfth-century narrative describes how Harold established a dean and 12 canons, built them a sumptuous church and filled it with splendid ornaments.[85] Harold's Waltham, not Edward's Westminster, is the house most intimately associated with the last days of Anglo-Saxon kingship. Here, in the canons' own tradition, Harold prayed before Hastings; a few days later it was two canons of Waltham who searched for his corpse on the battlefield.[86]

The data admit the possibility that during the last Anglo-Saxon century, more old minsters acquired a renewed collegiate life than were reformed as Benedictine abbeys. Others, like Waltham, were new. This patronage cannot have been wholly, or even mainly, for the old reasons. Where *parochiae* were still relatively intact, the minsters could still serve them: their *raison d'être* was what it had always been.[87] But in most of England, the manorial churches now bore the main burden of pastoral care. Even if a well-protected old minster could restrict the building of private churches in its *parochia*, a new college such as Waltham can never have had any *parochia* in the old sense. It seems clear, in fact, that the role of the minsters had shifted. Parochial rights and duties, where they existed from of old, often survived and sometimes remained important; but these were no longer the main reasons for lay support. It is more important that clerical colleges were still regarded, at least among the laity, as worthy objects of patronage; and that their advantages for their patrons could be practical as well as spiritual.

The *mynster-preost* or *riht-canonicus* had a distinct status in early eleventh-century society, higher than that of the ordinary mass-priest,[88] and a stricter life was required of him. Aethelred's 1008 code ordains that 'canons, where there is property, such that they can have a refectory and dormitory, are to hold their minster with right observance and with chastity, as their rule directs'.[89] This sounds like a rule based on Chrodegang or Amalarius, and reflects Archbishop Wulfstan's exacting standards.[90] St Paul's had a version of Amalarius, which Leofric and Godiva may have had in mind when they established 'service' (*theowdom*) at Stow 'exactly as one has at St Paul's in London'.[91] During Edward's reign the reforms of cathedral chapters by bishops Giso at Wells, Leofric at Exeter, Walter at Hereford and Ealdred in the Yorkshire minsters were along the same strict lines; Leofric especially is notable for giving his canons an English version of the enlarged Chrodegang rule.[92]

[85] *The Foundation of Waltham Abbey*, ed. W. Stubbs (Oxford and London, 1861). I am grateful to Miss Rosalind Ransford for advice on Waltham.

[86] Ibid., pp. 26–31.

[87] For the survival of minster organization in Cornwall, Devon and Somerset into the eleventh century, see S.M. Pearce, *The Kingdom of Dumnonia* (Padstow, Lodenek, 1978), pp. 116–21.

[88] VIII Aethr. 19–21, and other texts; *C & S*, pp. 278, 198, 394–5.

[89] V Aethr. 7; *C & S*, p. 348.

[90] Cf. Aelfric's pastoral letter for Wulfsige (993 x c. 995), in which the bishop is made to say to his unruly clerics: 'you also have a rule, if you were willing to read it' (*C & S*, p. 216).

[91] D. Whitelock, *Some Anglo-Saxon Bishops of London*: the Chambers Memorial Lecture 1974 (London, H.K. Lewis, 1975), pp. 27–9; *C & S*, p. 540.

[92] R.R. Darlington, 'Ecclesiastical Reform in the Late Old English Period', *EHR* LI (1936), pp. 385–428; K. Edwards, *The English Secular Cathedrals in the Middle Ages* (2nd edn, Manchester,

So the ideal remained the strict regime prescribed by the Carolingian reformers. But how many communities followed it? Domesday Book shows the canons of the two Chester colleges (one headed by a *custos*, the other by a *matricularius*) living in the town in separate houses.[93] Even at St Paul's a rudimentary prebendal system existed by the Conquest.[94] Waltham is revealing here, for Harold's college was thoroughly respectable, and his adviser was a Lorrainer like some of the reforming bishops. The canons, if we may trust their twelfth-century chronicler, had their own houses and prebends, and could evidently marry. Their allowances of food and drink (more ample than in Chrodegang's scheme) were financed from charges on the prebendal manors, and other revenues were set aside for their clothing.[95] A 'mixed' system such as this, in which a measure of common life and control did not preclude a fair degree of freedom, may have been normal in eleventh-century minsters.

So flexible an establishment was potentially more useful to its patron than a monastery could ever be. The canons could be active in the world outside (Waltham seems to have run a school);[96] conversely, canonries could be given to the patrons' servants without greatly hindering their normal duties. Hence the distinctive character so often revealed by the TRE data for minsters: less communities in their own right than groups of royal, episcopal and perhaps noble clerks. At the top level, the great minsters which became known as the 'king's demesne chapels' were exactly that: chapels of high-ranking clerks whose main duty was to serve the king.[97]

The Domesday data for 1066 show a high proportion of the king's 'superior' churches applied to such ends. The important men, such as Spirites in Shropshire and Herefordshire, Ernuin in Lincolnshire, and above all the great clerk Regenbald, tended to have whole minsters of ordinary size or shares in the very big ones; Regenbald alone held five minsters.[98] The great collegiate churches of Dover and Bosham were especially useful patronage resources. At least five of King Edward's clerks had canonries at Dover, and grants of this kind may have been normal practice.[99] Minster assets could be negotiable: at Huntingdon Edward gave St Mary's church to two of his clerks, who sold it to a royal chamberlain, who sold it in turn to two local priests.[100]

So it seems clear that by 1066 many old minsters, together with a certain number of new colleges, maintained groups of 'canons' which were only communities in the loosest sense. Probably a high proportion were not pastorally active, and certainly some were non-resident. Active or not, they

---

1967), pp. 3–12; *The Old English Version of the Enlarged Rule of Chrodegang*, ed. A.S. Napier (Early English Text Society, CL, 1916).

[93]DB I 263a.

[94]*Early Charters of St Paul's Cathedral*, ed. M. Gibbs, Camden 3rd series LVIII (1939), pp. xvii–xxiii; Franklin, pp. 203–6.

[95]*Foundation of Waltham Abbey*, pp. 15–17.

[96]Ibid., p. xii.

[97]Cf. Denton, *English Royal Free Chapels*, pp. 133–40.

[98]On Edward's pluralists see Barlow, *English Church 1000–1066*, pp. 129–36; Campbell, 'Church in Anglo-Saxon Towns', pp. 130–2.

[99]Cf. Barlow, *English Church 1000–1066*, pp. 130–1, 156–8, 190–1.

[100]DB I 208a.

took the church-scot, tithe, and other revenues which had once supported the public role of their churches. A central problem is how this diversion of resources affected service of the *parochiae*. There can be no doubt that some minsters which we find in pluralists' hands in 1066 were still the mother churches of big *parochiae*. How were these served? By groups of deputy priests resembling later vicars? At present this problem cannot be satisfactorily resolved. Clearly the state of the old minsters had become very diverse, and the spectrum of their functions wide. Some evidently retained something of their former character, while others had been assimilated to a newer category of colleges which were to all appearance non-parochial. But even where the canonries had gone to pluralists, the old pattern may often have persisted better in local arrangements than at the level of formal tenure.

III

With the Norman settlement, minster churches were often faced with loss of lands and decay of parochial rights. The former leaves its trace in scores of Domesday entries;[101] of the latter Domesday says almost nothing, but we can make some guesses. The settlement produced its own crop of manorial churches,[102] whose founders may have cared little for a declining system of rights outside their own experience.[103] Norman attitudes to minster tithes must have been especially harmful. Edgar had allowed a thegn to give one-third of his demesne tithes to his own church, while reserving the other two-thirds, and all peasant tithes, to the old minster. Post-Conquest practice effectively reversed this: lords endowed Norman abbeys with two-thirds of the tithes (the presumed 'minster portions') from innumerable English demesnes, while by *c.* 1130 it was apparently usual for the local churches to take the tithes of peasants.[104] Although we cannot know how far the letter of Edgar's code was still observed in 1066, this large-scale diversion of demesne tithes, combined with a change of accepted practice in relation to peasant tithes, must have gone hard with minsters which still had parochial revenues to lose.

Some were not merely impoverished, but absorbed wholesale into larger establishments. Minsters controlled by cathedrals and monasteries were nothing new; but the movement of sees, the reformation of abbeys, and (after

[101]E.g. the Count of Mortain's seizures from the Cornish minsters of Bodmin, Constantine, Crantock, Launceston, Perranzabuloe, St Buryan, St Keverne, St Michael's Mount and St Neot's. J.H. Denton, 'Royal Supremacy in Ancient Demesne Churches', *Journal of Ecclesiastical History* XXII (1971), pp. 293-4, makes the same point in relation to St Oswald's, Gloucester.

[102]E.g., for the chronology of manorial church foundation in Surrey, see Blair, pp. 281-7.

[103]However, cf. a writ of Henry I (1114?) ordering that the churches of five royal manors in Yorkshire 'non perdant parochias suas quas habuerunt tempore Regis Edwardi propter socas quas inde dedi quibusdam baronibus meis' (*Regesta Regum Anglo-Normannorum*, vol. II, eds. C. Johnson and H.A. Cronne (Oxford, OUP, 1956) No. 1046; quoted Brett, *Church under Henry I*, p. 223n).

[104]Cf. Stenton, *Anglo-Saxon England*, pp. 155-6; Brett, *Church under Henry I*, pp. 225-7 (esp. p. 226 note 3); Franklin, pp. 13-14. I am grateful to Dr Franklin for ideas embodied in this passage.

1100) the foundation of Augustinian priories created within a couple of generations a wholly exceptional demand for endowment. It was the fate of many
collegiate churches to be annexed to Lincoln, Salisbury and other chapters as
prebends for their canons.[105]

The individual minster tenants in 1086 seem much like King Edward's men,
except that there were probably rather more of them. A few English survivors,
notably Regenbald, still retained their minsters. Nigel, William I's physician,
had acquired Spirites's churches more or less *en bloc*; other new figures are
Bollo in Dorset, Ulviet in Lincolnshire, and Osbern de Eu who held the Surrey
minsters of Farnham, Leatherhead and Woking. Sometimes Norman
ecclesiastics had been interposed between the king and his clerical communities: at Hartland (Devon), Gerald the chaplain held two hides 'quam
tenuerunt canonici eiusdem mansionis . . .; has tenent ipsi xii canonici de
G[iroldo], qui eas antea tenuerunt, et reddunt per annum xl sol. ipsi
G[iroldo]'.[106] Royal churches held in shares by several priests are more evident
in the 1086 data, which also reveal clerics holding from the minsters of bishops
and lay lords. Well-endowed churches on seven of the bishop of Winchester's
Hampshire manors supported the priests Aelfric, Ralph and Vitalis and the
clerks Richer, Robert and Wibert.[107] In Berkshire, Geoffrey de Mandeville's
priest Wibert held Streatley church with one hide, and probably another hide
at Warfield.[108]

Few laymen in 1086 can have had more clerks than Roger earl of
Shrewsbury,[109] and none had so many minsters. His Domesday holdings
include 12 'superior' churches in Shropshire and six in Sussex. He exploited
the Shropshire churches systematically, annexing six to his abbey in Shrewsbury and giving Wenlock minster's manor of Stoke St Milburgh to his
chaplains;[110] at Morville he depleted the once-prosperous minster for both
purposes:

> Aecclesia huius manerii est in honore S. Gregorii, quae TRE habebat de hac
> terra viii hidas, et ibi serviebant viii canonici. Hanc aecclesiam cum v hidis
> terrae tenet aecclesia S. Petri [Shrewsbury Abbey] de comite. . . . Ibi . . . iii
> presbyteri. . . . Reliquas iii hidas tenent capellani comitis, et v homines de
> eis . . .[111]

Another Domesday tenant with many clerical mouths to feed was Robert of
Lorraine, bishop of Hereford: in 1086 his *clerici* and *capellani* held land on 13 of

[105]There are examples of this in, for instance, *The Register of St Osmund*, ed. W.H.R. Jones,
vols. I–II (Rolls Series, 1883–4), and *The Registrum Antiquissimum of Lincoln Cathedral* (Lincoln
Records Society, passim).
[106]Exeter Domesday, fo. 456a–b.
[107]Highclere, Houghton, Hurstbourne Tarrant, South Stonham, Overton, Bishop's
Waltham, Whitchurch.
[108]DB I 62a, 57a.
[109]See J.F.A. Mason, 'The Officers and Clerks of the Norman Earls of Shrewsbury', *Transactions Shropshire Archaeological Society*, LVI (1957–60), pp. 244–57.
[110]DB I 252b.
[111]DB I 253a.

his cathedral canons' estates.[112] So it is interesting to find him also acquiring minsters. At Writtle (Essex) he had three hides in 1086, of which one had belonged to the church in King Edward's day, another had been given by Harold to one of his priests, and the third had been royal demesne.[113] This trail leads to a well-endowed minster lurking in the unpromising folios of 'Circuit D'. At Bampton (Oxon.) we read that the bishop of Exeter holds six hides of the king, that 'Bishop Robert' holds them of him, and that Bishop Leofric had held them previously.[114] This was minster land, as is proved by a royal grant of the 950s 'to the saint at Bampton and the community'; Edward the Confessor had given the minster to Leofric while he was still a royal clerk, and Leofric had given it to Exeter.[115] Here and at Writtle, Robert's involvement is best explained by the hypothesis that each church was providing prebends for his household clerks.

A certain type of Domesday entry, where two or more priests appear as co-tenants on a royal or episcopal manor, sometimes disguises a minster which has fragmented into separate tenancies. Two Sussex manors of the bishop of Chichester illustrate the point.[116] The Aldingbourne entry reads: 'Ibi aecclesia . . . De hoc manerio tenet presbyter i hidam, Robertus v hidas, Hugo iii hidas, Aluuardus i hidam; hi iii clerici sunt'. The knowledge that land at Aldingbourne was granted for a minster in *c.* 692[117] gives confidence that the Amberley entry, 'de isto manerio tenent Willelmus clericus ii hidas et Aeldred presbyter iii hidas', can be read in a similar sense, even though in this case there is no external evidence. At Alderbury (Wilts.), we read that 'Alwardus presbyter habet v hidas quae pertinent ad aecclesiam Alwarberie de elemosina regis. . . .Huic eidem aecclesiae adiacet i hida quae nunquam geldavit. . . . Osbernus presbyter habet ii hidas de rege in aecclesia Alwaresberie'.[118] This 'Osbern the priest', who also appears as tenant of Britford minster and land at Homington,[119] may be the same Osbern de Eu who held three minsters in Surrey and land from the count of Eu in Sussex.[120] There must have been a tendency for these clerical specialists, whose names constantly recur, to establish hereditary tenure, thus impoverishing the ex-minsters for good.

Alongside such cases of division imposed from without are others in which minsters dissolved spontaneously into federations of separate village priests. A canon who regularly served an outlying chapel might eventually come to make it his permanent base. The charters of Christchurch minster (Hants.), analysed by Dr Hase, show this happening shortly after 1086. In *c.*1110 a priest there recalled how, in 1070 x 98, one Aelfric the Small had obtained leave from Godric dean of Christchurch to found a church within the *parochia*, and

[112]DB I 181–2.
[113]DB II 5a–b.
[114]DB I 155a.
[115]J. Blair, 'Saint Beornwald of Bampton', *Oxoniensia* XLIX (1984), pp. 47–55.
[116]DB I 16b–17a.
[117]S. 45, 1172.
[118]DB I 68b.
[119]See *VCH Wiltshire*, vol. II, p. 33.
[120]*VCH Sussex*, vol. I, p. 406 n .5; *Regesta Regum Anglo-Normannorum*, vol. II, addenda p. 391, No. 59a.

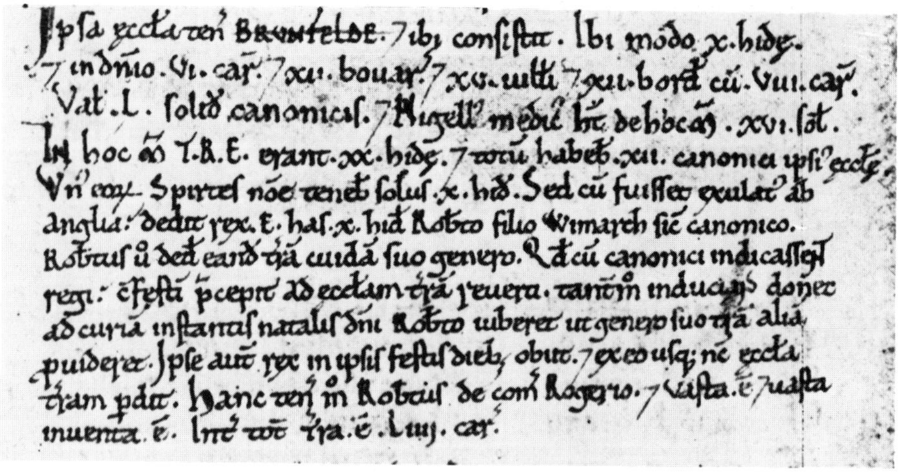

Plate 7.1 The Domesday entry for Bromfield minster. (DB I 252b. Reproduced by permission of the Controller of Her Majesty's Stationery Office.)

how Godric appointed 'a certain priest of Christchurch called Eilwi' to serve it periodically. But by the mid-twelfth century, when Bishop Henry of Blois established formal vicarages, the successors of Eilwi and his colleagues in the other chapels seem more like parish priests, 'personae ecclesiarum vel capellarum ad Christi Ecclesiam pertinent[ium]'.[121]

Something of the same kind happened at Bromfield (Salop.), a minster of 12 canons patronized by Edward the Confessor (see Figure 7.3).[122] The long Domesday entry (Plate 7.1) recounts how the pluralist Spirites had held 10 of the 20 hides in the early 1060s; how King Edward had banished him and given the land to Robert fitz Wimarch *sicut canonico*; how Robert passed it on to his son-in-law; and how death prevented Edward from answering the complaints of the canons, who never recovered the prebend.[123] But they kept their other 10 hides, and survived, thanks to their status as a royal demesne chapel, until 1155. In that year, Henry II's charter annexing the church to Gloucester Abbey (Plate 7.2) reveals a minster community in transition. Henry grants the church with

> all the prebends which Frederick clerk of Burford, and Robert Colemon of Pontesbury, and Eadric priest of Bromfield, and Robert priest of Felton and the other canons held in the obedience (*hernesse*) of Bromfield in the time of King Henry my grandfather or in my time: that is, all the lands and vills of Halford, and of Dinchope, and of Ashford [Bowdler], and of Felton, and of

[121]Hase, pp. 211–16; Lennard, *Rural England*, p. 399. The 'chapels of the prebendaries' at Dorchester (Oxon.) are a similar case; see *VCH Oxfordshire*, vol. VII, pp. 52–3.
[122]See *VCH Shropshire*, vol. II, pp. 27–9, and note 73 above.
[123]DB I 252b.

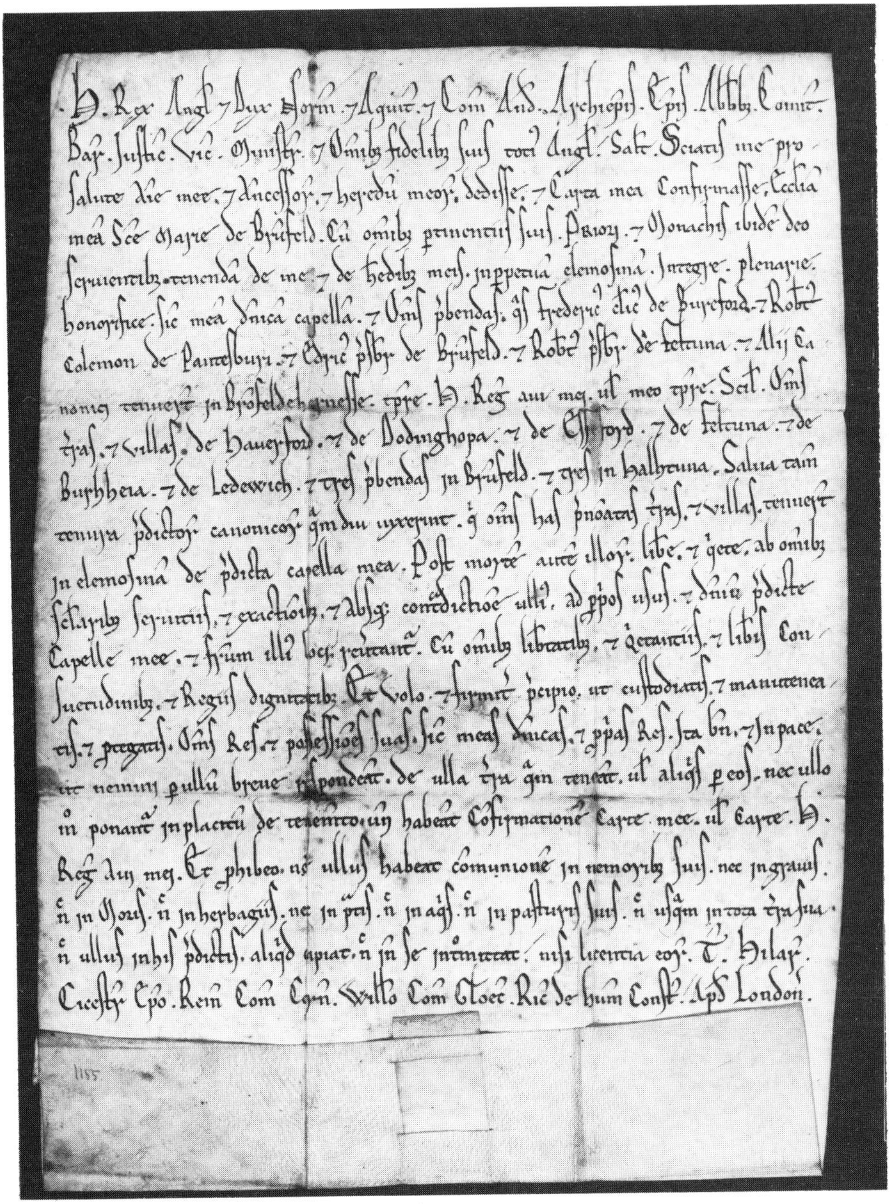

Plate 7.2 Charter of Henry II granting Bromfield minster to Gloucester Abbey in 1155. (British Library Cotton Charter xvii.4. Reproduced by permission of the British Library.)

Figure 7.3   Bromfield minster parish and the prebends of its canons. (Interpretation of the 1155 charter, based on post-medieval topography and parish boundaries.)

Burway, and of [Lower] Ledwyche, and three prebends in Bromfield, and three in Halton; saving nonetheless the tenure of the said canons while they live.[124]

If the 12 prebends were originally for 12 canons in the minster, 'Robert priest of Felton' and others sound more like local priests with their local churches. Norman work in fact remains at Halford and Ashford Bowdler, while at Felton

[124]British Library, Cotton Ch. xvii. 4; printed *Historia et Cartularium Monasterii Sancti Petri Gloucestriae*, ed. W.H. Hart, vol. II (Rolls Series XXXIIIb, 1865), pp. 213–14).

a tiny apsidal chapel, doubtless Robert's, was excavated in 1885.[125] Presumably the six prebendaries of Bromfield and Halton still frequented the minster in 1155, but it may be suspected that the lives of the other six were more firmly based in their own villages.

In Domesday Book such cases are hard to distinguish from minsters held in shares by pluralists, but occasional entries are suggestive. On the royal manor of Odiham (Hants.) 'pertinent ii hidae duabus aecclesiis eiusdem manerii, et ibi habet presbyter i villanum . . .; de eodem manerio tenent alii ii presbyteri ii aecclesias cum ii virgatis terrae . . .'.[126] There is a suggestion here of a $2\frac{1}{2}$-hide minster which has broken down into four separate churches. The Dorset folios record the royal demesne minster of Wimborne and, separately, three priests at Hinton Martell five miles away. The first held 1 hide, the second $2\frac{1}{2}$, and the third, called 'presbyter hujus manerii', $1\frac{1}{2}$; a fourth priest, living at Tarrant Keynston, had $1\frac{1}{3}$ hides of the same land.[127] Again, it looks as though some of the Wimborne priests have been distributed within the big royal manor which they once served as a team. Such cases may be commoner than they seem. A priest who had come to identify more strongly with the local than with the mother church might seek the patronage of a landowner eager to support such separatist claims. The origins of most local churches are obscure: some which seem wholly proprietary may have begun as legitimate daughters of their mothers, founded from the centre.

IV

Despite pluralism and fragmentation, the Norman impact on secular minsters had its positive side. The new order of things was at a reduced level: there was no return to the wealth and status of the great pre-Conquest minsters. Nor could the long-term decline of their parochial influence ever be halted. Yet secular colleges were not mere relics in the Anglo-Norman world: they belonged to it more naturally than hindsight suggests.[128] Many – perhaps more than we shall ever know – were rebuilt, reorganized or newly founded during the half-century after the Conquest, only to be extinguished within a few decades.

It is useful here to remember the reforms of cathedral canons carried out by Archbishop Thomas at York, St Osmund at Salisbury, Remigius at Lincoln

---

[125]D.H.S. Cranage, *An Architectural Account of the Churches of Shropshire*, vol. I (Wellington, Hobson, 1901), pp. 95, 64; C. Fortey, 'Discovery of a Chapel at Felton near Ludlow', *Transactions, Shropshire Archaeological and Natural History Society* VIII (1885), pp. 450–3. Stanton Lacy and Burford were independent mother churches, each with a pair of priests in 1086 (DB I 260a–b), and the former with remains of a large pre-Conquest church (Taylor and Taylor, *Anglo-Saxon Architecture*, vol. II, pp. 569–71).

[126]DB I 38a.

[127]DB I 76a.

[128]It is worth remembering that Ailred of Rievaulx was born in *c.* 1110 to a line of married canons of Hexham, 'learned, respectable, conscientious': *The Life of Ailred of Rievaulx*, ed. F.M. Powicke (London, Nelson, 1950), pp. xxxiv–xxxv.

and their contemporaries elsewhere.[129] The steps of late Anglo-Saxon bishops towards a common life and common funds were reversed, and secular chapters established on the north French model, though often retaining pre-Conquest elements.[130] Reorganization generally produced separate and stable territorial prebends. At St Paul's, the 'embryo' prebendal system shown by Domesday Book was remodelled by Bishop Maurice into a structure of named prebends, whose incumbents from *c.* 1090 are recorded in a series of lists.[131] These include some familiar names from the minster-owning fraternity: Osbern de Eu; Robert bishop of Hereford; Ingelric, the re-founder of St Martin-le-Grand; and Ranulf Flambard, who held the great minster of St Martin's Dover[132] and whom we will meet again at Christchurch and Godalming. Prebends at St Paul's could, in fact, be of much the same kind as absentee tenancies in ordinary minsters, and the same kinds of people sought them.

Some great royal minsters, and others linked especially closely to sees, were reorganized for chapters of prebendal canons along lines similar to the cathedrals. The most obvious cases are the archbishop's chapters in the great northern minsters at Beverley, Ripon and Southwell.[133] The ex-cathedrals of Crediton, Ramsbury, Lichfield and Dorchester were left with secular canons; at Crediton in 1107 x 37 the bishop reorganized the 18 prebends, 'quia admodum pauperes sunt', into 12 adequate ones.[134] There is a tradition (though not necessarily a reliable one) that the portionary churches of Easington, Norton, Darlington and Auckland St Andrew were founded by Bishop William de St Calais in 1083 to house seculars displaced by the new monastic chapter at Durham.[135]

The Anglo-Norman kings had a strong interest in maintaining the greater minsters in a way which enabled royal clerks to live off the prebends.[136] St Martin-le-Grand in London 'developed into a college of civil servants, its Dean was the King's chief minister, many of its canons were clerks of his Chancery or Chamber, and its school . . . could easily have served as the natural training ground for the royal service'.[137] Of St Martin's at Dover,

[129]See especially Edwards, *English Secular Cathedrals*, pp. 11–22; R.M.T. Hill and C.N.L. Brooke in G.E. Aylmer and R. Cant (eds.), *A History of York Minster* (OUP, 1977), pp. 20–8.

[130]See F. Barlow, *The English Church 1066–1154* (London, Longman, 1979), p. 211. At Exeter the change happened slowly, and Leofric's Chrodegang Rule remained influential well into the twelfth century: see D. Blake, 'The Development of the Chapter of the Diocese of Exeter, 1050–1161', *Journal of Medieval History* VIII. 1 (March, 1982), pp. 1–11.

[131]See *Early Charters of St Paul's*, pp. xxi–xxvii; C.N.L. Brooke, 'The Composition of the Chapter of St Paul's, 1086–1163', *Cambridge Historical Journal* X (1951), pp. 111–32; *Fasti Ecclesiae Anglicanae 1066–1300: I: St Paul's*, ed. D.E. Greenway (London, Athlone Press 1968), pp. 27ff.

[132]*Regesta Regum Anglo-Normannorum*, vol. II, No. 562.

[133]See Hamilton Thompson, 'Notes on Colleges', pp. 174–83; Brett, *Church under Henry I*, pp. 198–9.

[134]*The Crawford Collection of Charters*, eds. A.S. Napier and W.H. Stevenson (Oxford, 1895), No. XIII. For Lichfield see Brett, *Church under Henry I*, p. 199; for Dorchester see *VCH Oxfordshire*, vol. VII, pp. 52–3; for Ramsbury see K & H, p. 480.

[135]I am grateful to Mr M.G. Snape for advice on this tradition, which seems to derive from a thirteenth-century interpolation in Simeon of Durham's *Historia Dunelmensis Ecclesie* (York Minster Library, MS XVI.1.12, f. 149). See also A. Hamilton Thompson, 'The Collegiate Churches of the Bishoprick of Durham', *Durham University Journal* XXXVI (1944), pp. 33–42.

[136]Cf. Denton, *English Royal Free Chapels*, pp. 23ff.

[137]Davis, 'College of St Martin-le-Grand', p. 25.

Domesday says that 'TRE erant prebendae communes, et reddebant lxi libras inter totum; modo sunt divisae per singulos per episcopum Baiocensem'.[138] The 12 prebends at Bromfield in 1155 had presumably been apportioned since the loss of Spirites's 10 hides in the 1060s. At Stafford, where the king had 13 *canonici prebendarii* in 1086, there remained a dean and 12 prebendal canons until the Dissolution.[139]

When we turn to the private colleges, which were so much at the mercy of their new lords, it is relevant to look across the Channel.[140] In Normandy there is evidence, during the period 960–1110, for the existence of some 24 secular *collégiales*, at least 14 of which were founded between 990 and 1066. Most were new: the entrenched rights of the English minsters had practically no counterpart in tenth-century Normandy. The colleges were small and (apart from Cherbourg, *c*. 1063, and Mortain, *c*. 1082) modestly endowed, and were tied firmly to their noble founders and patrons. The canons lived in their own houses and had individual prebends, though most colleges maintained a common table from tithes and oblations. Canonries were usually filled by seigneurial nomination; many colleges adjoined their lords' residences, and some canons served castle chapels and dined at castle tables.

The movement was short-lived. Only four *collégiales* were definitely founded after 1066, and the whole group was either regularized or suppressed during the twelfth century. The main threat was, of course, the rapid growth of monasticism, hostile as ever to the 'carnal canons', as the Fécamp foundation narrative calls them. From the end of the eleventh century the Gregorian ideal, the growing pretensions of bishops and the advent of regular Augustinian canons combined to achieve the rapid eclipse of the seculars.

With these parallels it comes as no surprise to find in Norman England a widespread support for secular canons, non-pastoral in its motivation but grafted onto the old parochial base. The new aristocracy, like their English predecessors, found collegiate churches acceptable in their own right, and useful sources of maintenance for clerical servants. We might equally expect the English colleges to suffer the fate of their Norman counterparts, as patronage came to be diverted to more fashionable ends. The proprietary character of several Anglo-Norman alien priories, established in their founders' *capita baroniae* and main churches, enabled some lords to satisfy the urge for 'personal monasteries' within a Benedictine context; it is interesting to see a few minsters (for example Wing, Wootton Wawen and Minster Lovell) re-born as alien priories.[141] On the other hand, the secular college must have been an

---

[138]DB I 1b.

[139]DB I 247b, K & H, p. 439.

[140]For this paragraph see L. Musset, 'Recherches sur les Communautés de Clercs Séculiers en Normandie au XIᵉ Siècle', *Bulletin de la Société des Antiquaires de Normandie*, LV (1961, for 1959–60), pp. 5–38.

[141]I am grateful to Dr Richard Gem for advice on Wing (Bucks.), where the minster land seems to appear in Domesday Book as $2\frac{1}{2}$ hides in Craston (DB I 146a); these were granted with the church to the monks of Angers during *c*. 1070 x 86. On the proprietary overtones of the alien priories see D.J.A. Matthew, *The Norman Monasteries and their English Possessions* (Oxford, OUP, 1962), pp. 58–65; cf. comments by Brett, *Church under Henry I*, p. 230 n. 5, and by B.R. Kemp in *Journal of Ecclesiastical History* XXXI (1980), pp. 144–5n.

attractively cheap alternative in a land where old minsters were so numerous and so easy to come by.

It is a question how far the great Domesday *curiales* were concerned to reform or re-endow minster communities in their hands: what level of personal involvement is implicit in the phrase '*X* presbyter tenet aecclesiam'? Regenbald, the great survivor from King Edward's day, seems to have taken more than a financial interest in his churches. He is said to have been dean of his minster at Cirencester, and apparently he was buried there.[142] It may be worth mentioning here the odd discrepancies between the Exon and Exchequer entries for his Somerset minsters. At Milborne Port, Exon Domesday reads 'Rainbaldus presbiter tenet hanc qui servit ecclesie', which Exchequer Domesday amends to 'Reinbaldus tenet aecclesiam'; at Frome, Exon reads 'modo tenet hanc Rainbaldus et tenuit tempore E.', which Exchequer amends to 'Reinbaldus ibi est presbyter'.[143] While the scribe of Exchequer Domesday might well baulk at the absurdity of Regenbald as a village priest, the re-casting of the Frome entry is in the direction of *greater* personal involvement. If anything at all is to be read into this (though it may be that nothing should), it strengthens the suspicion that *est ibi presbyter* can mean more than it seems.

This is supposition; the events at Christchurch (Hants.) are clear fact. In 1086 the 'canons of the Holy Trinity of Twynham' were tenants-in-chief in their own right.[144] Rufus gave the minster to Ranulf Flambard (over the head of one Godric whose canons respected him 'non pro decano, quasi nominis ignorantes, sed pro seniore et patrono'), and Flambard held it as dean until his fall. Soon afterwards the canons compiled a narrative of their fortunes since William I's reign, and this, with related documents, has been studied by Dr Hase.[145] The canons seem to have followed a laxer code than the Chrodegang Rule, not unlike the regime in contemporary Norman *collégiales*: they had prebends and separate houses, but said the hours together and maintained a common table from a common fund. Much is said of Flambard's rapacity, but one passage shows that his influence was not wholly destructive:

> The bishop [i.e. Flambard] demolished the primitive church of that place and nine others which stood around in the cemetery, with the houses of certain canons near the cemetery, and adapted the place as lord. . . . Bishop Ranulf also founded this church which is now at Twynham [i.e. Christ-church], and houses and offices for each religious. When any canon died he held his benefice in his power. . . . So Godric the elder died, and likewise 10 canons of the convent not long afterwards, whose prebends the bishop granted to the remaining 14 to supplement their food during their lives.

[142]The evidence is reviewed by B. Evans, 'The Collegiate Church at Cirencester: a Critical Examination of the Historical Evidence', in A. McWhirr (ed.), *Archaeology and History of Cirencester*, (BAR 30, 1976), pp. 46–60 (who takes, however, a perversely destructive view).

[143]DB I 86b; Exeter Domesday, fos. 91ᵛ, 90ᵛ.

[144]DB I 44a.

[145]Hase, pp. 181–222; the narrative is printed W. Dugdale, *Monasticon Anglicanum*, vol. II (London, 1661), pp. 177–8.

In England as in Normandy, a common type of clerical community under lay patronage was the college at the castle gates. Some were entirely new, the adjuncts of new baronial *capita*, and hence non-parochial; others (especially when attached to urban castles) could be re-foundations.[146] Doubtless they were linked more or less closely to the patron's household, the service of his chapel, and perhaps the staffing of his secretariat. Some magnates may have chosen between endowing such a community and endowing an alien cell, but patronage of monks and canons were not mutually exclusive. As well as exploiting minsters for Shrewsbury Abbey and for his own clerks, Earl Roger seems to have maintained small groups of priests at Arundel, Boxgrove, Singleton and Wroxeter.[147] He may have founded St Michael's college in Shrewsbury castle;[148] he certainly founded the college by Quatford castle (later at Bridgnorth), where formal prebends can be traced from the early twelfth century onwards.[149]

The smaller colleges, new and old, are indeed shadowy during these years. It is worth remembering how few of those in Normandy survived more than two generations beyond 1066;[150] perhaps we should expect the same in England. This may apply above all to new communities, which had no basis of ancient parochial rights. In 1073 William de Braoze founded a college at Bramber castle (Sussex); in 1080 it was handed over to Sele Priory with reservation of the canons' life-interests, though the small cruciform church remains (Figure 7.2 No. 7).[151] This eight-year college may stand for many which vanished without record. Monks and regular canons seldom concerned themselves with their predecessors' affairs: in England as in Normandy, 'c'est que, pour nous, les séculiers vaincus sont une ombre à peine consistante; ils n'ont pratiquement laissé ni archives, ni écrits, alors que nous croulons sous les poids des parchemins légués par les réguliers victorieux'.[152]

Patronage of secular colleges, both new and old, in the post-Conquest period is sometimes implied by physical evidence. Christchurch and St Martin's Dover, the two large minsters controlled by Flambard, had grand Norman churches. Milborne Port church (Figure 7.2 No. 5) is in a sumptuous if rather unorthodox Romanesque style now dated to the later eleventh century;[153] was it commissioned by Regenbald himself? At Bromfield, the community recorded in 1155 could almost be inferred from the building alone (Figure 7.2

---

[146]See for instance J. Cooper, 'The Church of St George in the Castle', *Oxoniensia* XLI (1976), pp. 306–8.

[147]DB I 23a, 25b, 23a, 254b.

[148]DB I 252b.

[149]Founded at Quatford 1086, transferred to Bridgnorth 1098. Originally there were six canons; W.G. Clark-Maxwell and A. Hamilton Thompson, 'The College of St Mary Magdalene, Bridgnorth', *Archaeological Journal* LXXXIV (1927), p. 6, suggests that Henry I reconstituted the college with a dean and five canons, and assigned the prebends, after it was forfeited to the crown in 1102. See also *VCH Shropshire*, vol. II, pp. 123f.

[150]Musset, 'Recherches sur les Communautés', p. 14.

[151]*Calender of Documents: France*, pp. 405, 396–7, 37–8; E.F. Salmon, 'St Nicholas, Bramber', *Sussex Arch. Colls.* LXXIII (1932), pp. 187–91.

[152]Musset, 'Recherches sur les Communautés', p. 5.

[153]Taylor and Taylor, *Anglo-Saxon Architecture*, vol. I, pp. 424–8; G. Zarnecki, '1066 and Architectural Sculpture', *Proceedings of the British Academy*, LII (1966), pp. 98–9.

No. 3). Its masonry is Norman in character and the carved details are of *c.* 1120–30, though very clumsy; but the form is that of a pre-Conquest minster such as Dover or Breamore, a nave with porticus rather than a Romanesque church with integrated crossing and transepts.[154] Nothing could better evoke the character of an old minster surviving into Henry I's England than this big, old-fashioned building.

Behind the church of Godalming (Surrey) must lie a forgotten but somewhat complex story.[155] The Domesday entry suggests an old minster with its chapel: 'Rannulfus Flanbard tenet de hoc manerio aecclesiam, cui pertinent iii hidae. Ulmaerus tenuit de rege E. Nunquam geldum reddidit. . . . Ibidem tenet isdem Rannulfus alteram aecclesiam quae reddit xii sol. per annum.'[156] A survey of 1220 describes the present parish church, and then mentions a chapel about a mile away 'where was first sited the church of Godalming; [mass] is only celebrated there three times yearly, . . . and that on account of the reverence in which this place is held'.[157] The parish church (Figure 7.2 No. 6) began as a typical late-Saxon estate church, greatly enlarged in *c.* 1100 by raising a tower over the old chancel and adding transepts and a two-bay choir.[158] Clearly the hierarchy of mother and daughter churches was reversed,[159] and the latter enlarged to suit some purpose which was surely beyond the ordinary parochial ones: Flambard's activities at Christchurch spring to mind. There is no clear evidence for collegiate life; but according to John Aubrey in 1673, 'the tradition here is that it was heretofore a cathedral, and that here was a bishop, dean and canons, . . . and that it was before the Conquest; . . . the street here is called Church Street, [and] was the street of the canons' houses.'[160]

Sometimes architectural evidence strengthens what would otherwise be the feeblest of hints or suspicions. Bicester (Oxon.) was within 'Circuit D', so Domesday is unhelpful. We know that the church housed the relics of a Mercian royal saint; that it exercised burial rights over two chapelries; that there were at least three clerics at Bicester in the 1150s; and that an Augustinian priory had been established there by 1182.[161] The parish church (Figure 7.2 No. 4) is of the late eleventh or early twelfth century, and comparable in scale and conception to Bromfield; it corroborates the other signs of minster status, and testifies to a major rebuilding before the Augustinians came.

[154]Cranage, *Account of the Churches of Shropshire*, pp. 70–2; J. Blair in *Archaeological Journal* CXXXVIII (1981), pp. 29–31 (where the alleged evidence of a string-course on the external NE angle of the nave should be discounted).

[155]See Blair, pp. 220–1.

[156]DB I 30b.

[157]*The Register of St Osmund*, ed. W.H.R. Jones, vol. I, (Rolls Series LXXVIII, 1883), pp. 296–8.

[158]Taylor and Taylor, *Anglo-Saxon Architecture*, vol. I, pp. 258–61; *VCH Surrey*, vol. III, pp. 37–42.

[159]This reversed hierarchy is paralleled by the case of Basing and Basingstoke (Hase, pp. 313f.)

[160]Bodleian Library, MS Aubrey 4, f. 153.

[161]*VCH Oxfordshire*, vol. VI, pp. 16, 40, 44–5; *The Boarstall Cartulary*, ed. H.E. Salter (Oxford Historical Society LXXXVIII, 1930), pp. 101, 103; White Kennett, *Parochial Antiquities* (Oxford, 1695), pp. 134–8.

It may be that transeptal and cruciform churches from before the 1130s, even very small ones, often imply communities of more than one priest. Braoze's collegiate church at Bramber may be compared with the recently excavated predecessor of the Augustinian abbey at Haughmond (Salop.) (Figure 7.2 Nos. 7 and 8). The latter was built in *c.* 1080–1100, and quickly acquired a cemetery; a cloister added in *c.* 1130 may mark the arrival of regular canons. What was this establishment? The only historical evidence is a vague tradition of a 'hermitage', and a grant in the 1130s to 'Prior Fulk and his brethren' who could have been either seculars or Augustinians.[162] And what was the eleventh-century church excavated at Bargham (Sussex): only 16 metres in overall length, yet cruciform, with a triple-apsed east end and elaborate carved capitals?[163]

Archaeology cannot answer such questions, but it shows how much has been forgotten. Evasive though the evidence is, there is enough to suggest that in Henry I's reign there were still many small collegiate bodies, some based on old minsters and others recent, which bore the stamp of Anglo-Norman patronage. It is worth speculating how many secular canons England may have contained in 1100.

V

Only a handful of the Domesday 'superior' churches survived the twelfth century as secular colleges. Collegiate churches did not become popular again until the fourteenth century, and then for very different reasons. Of some 170 foundations existing in 1535 (excluding cathedral chapters and academic colleges), only about a quarter had existed before 1120, and very few had been founded between 1120 and 1250.[164] As religious institutions, colleges of priests were not popular with the twelfth-century hierarchy: new enthusiasm for reform reinforced old charges of laxness, and bishops viewed them with increasing hostility.[165] Nor could a community of ancient origin continue to draw much strength from its old parochial status. The emerging diocesan structure of archdeacons and rural deans made mother churches interposed between parish and diocese seem the more anomalous, while strengthening bishops' hands against them.

Some important pre-Conquest minsters survived simply because, as royal demesne chapels, they were protected from their diocesan bishops.[166] That the

---

[162]See J.J. West in *Medieval Archaeology* XXIV (1980), pp. 240–1; *VCH Shropshire*, vol. II, pp. 62–3.

[163]A. Barr-Hamilton, 'The Excavation of Bargham Church Site', *Sussex Arch. Colls.* XCIX (1961), pp. 38–65.

[164]From list in K & H, pp. 413–19.

[165]Cf. the case of Damerham (Wilts.) in Lennard, *Rural England*, p. 402. As Lennard comments, 'the contemptuous reference to "so-called canons" is significant'.

[166]The 'ancient demesne chapels' include a high proportion of the most important Domesday minsters. See Denton, 'Royal Supremacy in Ancient Demesne Churches'.

latter would have interfered if they could is suggested by Archbishop Corbeil's plea to Henry I in 1124 to discipline the unruly canons of Dover.[167] In *c.* 1200, Peter of Blois wrote thus of Wolverhampton college to Pope Innocent III: 'The clergy there were completely undisciplined as though they were Welshmen or Scots, and so greatly had their life been overtaken by vice that their wickedness passed into contempt of God, peril to souls, infamy to the clergy . . . And while I was preaching the meaning of the Scriptures they would be singing their disgraceful songs. . . . Indeed, fornicating publicly and openly they proclaimed like Sodom their own sin, and they took as wives each other's daughters and nieces. . . . Convert this sty of pigs, this whore-house of Satan, into a temple of God. . . .'[168] Just or unjust, such a view of the unreformed minsters may have been held by many leading churchmen. Wolverhampton was a privileged royal chapel; the disappearance of more vulnerable colleges is hardly surprising.

After *c.* 1100 the regular (Augustinian) canons provided a new alternative to the seculars. It is clear enough that they appealed because they combined a relatively strict rule with the sort of involvement in the world around that minster-priests must once have had; and that this is why so many old minsters were given to them.[169] For some 18 out of 43 Augustinian houses founded by 1135 there is evidence of a 'pre-regular' stage, whether Anglo-Saxon or early Norman.[170] It is often noted that the Augustinians' dramatic growth owed a great deal to the patronage of Henry I's *curiales* and bishops.[171] Put another way, they appealed to the same circle of courtiers and clerics who had held the biggest stake in minster revenues during the previous half-century. Patronage of regular canons often seems to grow naturally out of involvement with the old minsters; once the choice existed, some founders of secular colleges were swift to reform them on Augustinian lines.[172] The honoured founders of twelfth-century priories are sometimes not far removed from the pluralists of Domesday minsters.[173]

So by Richard I's reign the eleventh-century colleges had, with a few exceptions, lost their collegiate character in any formal sense. But the local roots of ancient minsters still proved oddly resilient; the churches which continue to stand out are those which once had large *parochiae*. Reduced though they were, minster parishes remained not merely bigger but distinctly different

[167]Denton, *English Royal Free Chapels*, p. 59.

[168]From translation in ibid., pp. 148–9.

[169]The question of their pastoral work is a vexed one, but it is at least clear that they *sometimes* served *some* of their churches. See Dickinson, *Origins of Austin Canons*, pp. 214–41.

[170]Ibid., pp. 98–124.

[171]Ibid., pp. 125–31; Brett, *Church under Henry I*, pp. 138–40.

[172]See, for instance, the cases of Merton (M.L. Colker, 'Latin Texts Concerning Gilbert, Founder of Merton Priory', *Studia Monastica* XII (1970), pp. 241–70), and of St Osyth (Brett, *Church under Henry I*, p. 139).

[173]For instance, William Giffard, bishop of Winchester, Augustinianized the old minster at Southwark in 1106 and later patronized several other monasteries (cf. Brett, *Church under Henry I*, pp. 138–40). He had been a royal clerk, William II's chancellor and a canon of St Paul's; the king probably gave him Southwark minster, where he is said initially to have established *secular* canons (Bodleian Library, MS Corpus Christi D 256 f. 197). His career until *c.* 1100 might seem much on the lines of Flambard's.

from ordinary local parishes. The latter had been fashioned for their immediate purpose; the former were the residue of something older, and their sprawling, irregular boundaries with 'bites' out of the edges stand out from early editions of the Ordnance Survey.

Definitions of parochial rights by early twelfth-century bishops generally concern the parishes of ex-minsters,[174] as do most thirteenth- and fourteenth-century disputes about chapelries, tithes and burial duty. The right, where it survived, to receive corpses (and mortuary fees) from all townships of the old *parochia* was jealously guarded, with results that can be seen in, for example, the huge collection of grave-slabs at Bakewell (Derbs.). The numerous conflicts between mother and daughter churches are a sign of genuine uncertainty, as ex-minster proprietors clung to a rag-bag of pensions, portions and other vested rights which grew ever more tenuous with distance from the mother church.

This raises again the hard question of actual parochial arrangements: were minster rights still defended for reasons beyond the merely financial? We can do little except note certain cases in which early groups of clergy seem to be perpetuated in a late medieval guise. At Thatcham (Berks.) there were two *clerici* in 1086 and still two in 1201, when they were called 'perpetual vicars'.[175] Wroxeter (Salop.) had four *presbyteri* in 1086 and later three portionary rectors;[176] Bisley (Glos.) had two *presbyteri* and later two portioners.[177] Even in the absence of Domesday evidence, a staff of two or three rectors or vicars in the later Middle Ages is often a sign of former minster status. At Bampton (above, p. 127) the community recorded in the 950s was succeeded from the thirteenth century onwards by three vicars,[178] whose houses stood around the churchyard (Figure 7.4) and who feuded with neighbouring clergy over tithes and burial jurisdiction.[179] The vicars served the large, multi-vill parish as a team, remaining for all practical purposes a minster staff on the mid-Saxon model until 1845.[180]

An echo of minster organization was the service of out-chapels by priests from the mother church. The tendency for chapels to split away has already been noted, but in some areas, especially the big parishes of north-west England, they kept their original character into modern times. Even in the south, this may have been commoner than sources suggest: written agreements were necessary with other people's chaplains, not with one's own. As

[174]All the charters discussed by Brett, *Church under Henry I*, pp. 129–31, 224, were drafted to protect the rights of old mother churches.

[175]DB I 56b; Kemp, 'Mother Church of Thatcham', p. 16.

[176]DB I 254b; K & H, p. 445.

[177]DB I 166b; *VCH Gloucestershire*, vol. XI, p. 32.

[178]A. Hamilton Thompson in *Transactions, Bristol and Gloucestershire Archaeological Society* LIII (1931), pp. 41–3; J.A. Giles, *History of the Parish and Town of Bampton* (Bampton, 1848), pp. 23–5, 30–1.

[179]See J. Blair, 'Parish versus Village: the Bampton–Standlake Tithe Conflict of 1317–19', *Oxfordshire Local History* II. 2 (1985).

[180]Cf. letter from Bishop Fell to Archbishop Sancroft, 1684 (Bodleian Library, MS Tanner 32, f. 158), and draft scheme for separating the vicarages, 1845 (Bodleian Library, MS Oxf: Dioc. Pap. c. 746, ff. 114f.)

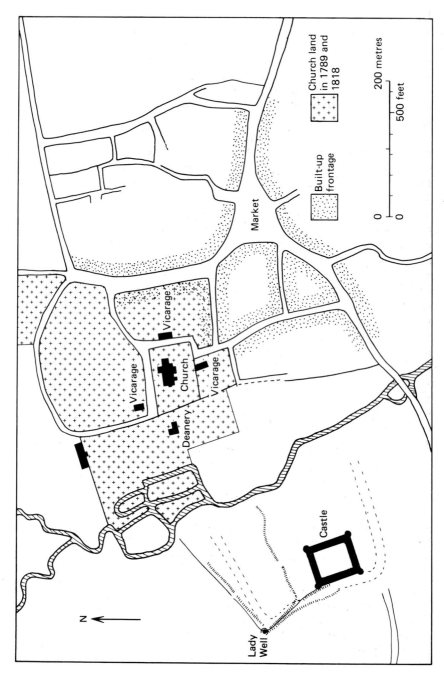

Market

Church land in 1789 and 1818

Built-up frontage

200 metres

500 feet

0

0

Vicarage

Vicarage

Vicarage

Church

Deanery

Castle

Lady Well

N

Figure 7.4 Bampton (Oxon.) in the late Middle Ages, showing the former minster church and the houses of its portionary vicars. (Based on the 1st edn OS 25 inch survey, with data from maps of 1789 (Exeter Dean and Chapter M/1) and 1818 (Exeter Dean and Chapter 13/74363a).)

late as the 1360s the vicars of Bampton sent a chaplain on certain feasts to Shifford chapel, where the landowner provided his wax and lodging.[181] And in Henry II's reign an outlier of Woking minster parish at Windlesham (Surrey) acquired 'a certain oratory, in which a chaplain of Woking sometimes celebrated [mass] and sometimes read the gospel'.[182] It is hard to penetrate the outward forms; could we do so more often, such survivals might prove commoner than they seem.

Finally, it may be noted that minsters often stimulated urban growth around them in the late Anglo-Saxon period,[183] and that sometimes the religious life of such towns shows continuing links with service of the old *parochiae*. Minsters attracted organized activity: it seems significant that the four extant sets of pre-Conquest gild statutes all come from minster towns (Cambridge, Exeter, Bedwyn and Abbotsbury), and that Urki, patron of the Abbotsbury gild, was also patron of its minster.[184] Since the main object of these gilds (and of later ones which could be of early origin) was to provide masses for deceased brethren, they would have coexisted easily and effectively with multi-priest minsters.[185] Such a relationship may be suspected, from later evidence, at Chesterfield (Derbs.). Though Domesday Book omits it, the location of this minster in a Roman fort suggests early origins. Following a familiar pattern, it was granted by William II to Lincoln Cathedral in 1093 and supported two portionary vicars in the late twelfth century.[186] By the thirteenth century Chesterfield had at least three gilds, the senior dedicated to the Holy Cross and another to the related cult of St Helen.[187] As well as praying for their own members, the Chesterfield gild-priests took a hand in serving the parish; in 1546 they were said to exist partly 'for the help and ministration of all manner of sacraments and sacramentals within the said parish, and other charitable deeds, forasmuch as the said parish is very large . . . and is divided into many hamlets and villages, being distant some two miles, some three miles or more from the said parish church, so that the vicar and his parish priest in the time of Lent and Easter and some other times cannot suffice to the ministration of behoveful matters'.[188] If only as a distant echo, such cases evoke some of the

[181] *The Eynsham Cartulary*, ed. H.E. Salter, vol. II (Oxford, Oxford Historical Society, 1908), p. 6.

[182] *Bracton's Note Book*, ed. F.W. Maitland, vol. II (Cambridge, 1887), pp. 586–8.

[183] See Campbell, 'Church in Anglo-Saxon Towns', pp. 120–3; A. Everitt, 'The Banburys of England', *Urban History Yearbook 1974* (Leicester University Press), pp. 28–38.

[184] *English Historical Documents* vol. I, pp. 603–7.

[185] I am indebted to the Revd. H.E.J. Cowdrey for this idea. For post-Conquest religious gilds see Toulmin Smith, *English Gilds* (EETS XL, 1870); G.E. Meersseman, *Ordo Fraternitatis* (Italia Sacra XXIV, Rome, 1977), pp. 169–78.

[186] *The Registrum Antiquissimum of Lincoln Cathedral*, ed. C.W. Foster, vol. I (Lincoln Records Society XXVII, 1930), No. 14; ibid., vol. III (Lincoln Records Society XXIX, 1932), Nos. 691, 703–5.

[187] *Records of the Borough of Chesterfield*, eds. P. Riden and J. Blair (Chesterfield, 1980), Chapter II. St Mary's Gild (the best-recorded) was founded in 1219, but the Holy Cross Gild seems to have been considered senior or superior to it. It is worth noting that other early minster towns (e.g. Worcester and Abingdon), had, like Chesterfield, subsidiary churches dedicated to St Helen.

[188] Ibid., p. 105.

factors in the mind of the late ninth-century translator who rendered Bede's *per urbana loca* as *thurh mynsterstowe*.[189]

If the later and lesser colleges have been underrated, the old parochial minsters still had the greatest lasting importance. With the royal *villae*, they were central points in what has been called 'the in some ways oddly orderly world of early England'.[190] Like the *villae*, they are buried deep under layers of better-recorded institutional development. It is worth remembering how much is implicit in the scores of minsters which are now so dimly visible: scores of forgotten shrines, the cult centres of their regions; scores of priestly communities, the immediate religious leaders of scattered settlements around them. At about the time of Domesday Book, the lord of a Hampshire manor wanted to found a chapel: his first approach was to Godric the 'elder' of Christchurch minster, who discussed it with Bishop Walchelin.[191] It may be that many minsters still commanded a local influence and respect, founded on long tradition. Habits so deep-rooted can scarcely have died in the first waves of Gregorian reform, however indisposed twelfth-century bishops may have been to countenance or record them.

The experience of recent decades has shown that the organization of early England must be reconstructed progressively, through local studies in which all the scattered traces are drawn together. In the coming years many lost *parochiae* will be reassembled, and latent references to minsters will doubtless emerge from Domesday entries which this paper has ignored. The more such work is done, the clearer may seem the enduring distinctness of both *parochiae* and minsters: reduced in size and status, yet still set apart from their younger neighbours through the twelfth century and beyond.

[189]Campbell, 'Church in Anglo-Saxon Towns', p. 121.
[190]J. Campbell, in P.H. Sawyer (ed.), *Names, Words and Graves: Early Medieval Settlement* (Leeds, 1979), p. 51.
[191]Hase, p. 212.

CHAPTER EIGHT

Domesday Book and the Boroughs

G.H. Martin

'Domesday Book is a mine of information which has not yet been sufficiently wrought.' (Sir Henry Ellis, 1836)

'Dark as the history of our villages may be, the history of the boroughs is darker yet.' (F.W. Maitland, 1897)

'The Domesday Book is far from being a straightforward document.' (Professor H.C. Darby, 1952)

The term borough (*burgus*) is used widely in Domesday Book, and with no more precision than it has been used at large in England over the centuries. In that respect, as in many others, and for all its Latinity, Domesday is a very English document. By their frequent appearances in its folios, boroughs and burgesses claim a substantial place in the picture of society that emerges from the Conqueror's survey of his kingdom. Their incidence is worth considering carefully, quite as much as an intrinsic feature of the text as for its contribution to the patchwork web of English urban history. From William Somner onwards, historians of the local community have mined Domesday enthusiastically, but with varying degrees of respect and discrimination. That the value of historical evidence depends on its context is a truism, but in studies of Domesday the context has still to be defined.[1]

The business of discerning and appraising the boroughs, let alone the Borough, in Domesday Book is beset both by particular and by general difficulties. Some of the places so designated are treated in a distinctive way in the text, implying though not defining a particular status. Yet it is also clear that the word *burgus* covers a variety of communities, and it appears to exclude

---

[1] W. Somner, *The antiquities of Canterbury* (London, 1640), pp. 4–5. The text of Domesday Book was made generally available by the version published between 1783 and 1816. On the genesis of that edition see M.M. Condon and E.M. Hallam, 'Government printing of the Public Records in the Eighteenth Century', *Journal of the Society of Archivists* 7, 1984, pp. 348–86. The volumes are succinctly described in V.H. Galbraith, *Domesday Book: its Place in Administrative History* (Oxford, Clarendon Press, 1974), pp. xx–xxii. References to the printed (Record Commission) edition here are distinguished as DB I (*etc.*), fo., and v (for *verso*), or p. in the paginated vols. Since 1900 scholarly introductions and translations of the entries for individual counties have appeared in *The Victoria History of the Counties of England*. In recent times the only major work of local history to ignore Domesday has been Sir Osbert Lancaster's *Drayneflete Revealed* (London, Murray, 1949).

others which we might wish to associate with them. Domesday counts properties and inhabitants without either distinguishing or equating them. It refers to burgesses and also to markets where no borough is mentioned, and offers descriptions of boroughs which seem to dwell on anything but their urban qualities. The consistency that contemporaries observed in their use of a word will often escape us.

Even more formidably, Domesday Book itself is unique; its purpose and its bulk set it above the other sources that survive from its time, and it has to be approached and can only be interpreted in its own terms. Its two constituent volumes, distinguished here as Great and Little Domesday, are the first of the Public Records of the kingdom, and mark the beginnings of the systematic registration of governmental business, which continues down to the present day. At the same time it has a commanding place in an even longer sequence of historical evidences which begins almost five centuries earlier, with the arrival in England of Christianity and written documents, and in which the deficiencies of one record have often been offset or made good by other testimony either earlier or later in time. Domesday Book is a national monument, and we expect it to make a monumental contribution to national history. The striking continuity of English institutions, which is largely to say the continuity of their records, is both a blessing and a bane to those who study English history. The evolutionary development of English society affords its commentators both a genuine familiarity and an illusory sense of unchanging values.

The continuity is real enough: the Norman Conquest was the last and perhaps the most potent intrusion of an alien force into English society, yet Domesday Book, which takes stock of the Norman settlement, is as much a record of the Normans' assimilation as of their triumph. It is therefore called upon to exemplify a process which is hardly recorded outside its own pages, and at the same time to answer all the other questions that we wish to ask of a society which we can perceive in outline, but which rarely explained itself. That society certainly included towns, in the sense of permanent settlements with multiple functions, too populous to live on their own agricultural resources, and therefore dependent on a trade which might, and usually did, serve other and wider purposes. A composite economic structure is unlikely and probably unable to stand by itself. By the eleventh century regular trade needed the protection of a sovereign power, and in a society open to change protection is apt to confer a civil status on the settlement which enjoys it.[2]

A community thus privileged is historically known in English as a borough. In eleventh-century England it was called variously a *burh* or a *port* by the English themselves, and sometimes a *tun*, meaning simply a place where people lived. Our own use of town, denoting a place where people live under stress, has moved further from *tun* than has current North American usage. To the

---

[2]For a valuable recent discussion, see S. Reynolds, *An Introduction to the History of Medieval English Towns* (Oxford, Clarendon Press, 1977). Archaeological and historical evidence are related in an interesting way in R. Hodges, *Dark-Age Economics: the Origins of Towns and Trade AD 600–1000* (London, Duckworth, 1982). A wide range of literature is listed and reviewed in G.H. Martin and S.C. McIntyre, *A Bibliography of British and Irish Municipal History*, 1, *General Works* (Leicester, Leicester University Press, 1972).

Normans a *tun* was a *ville*, and a *burh* or *port* was a *bourg*, which becomes *burgus* in the Latin of Domesday. Its inhabitants, who for the most part thought of themselves as *burhwaras*, or *portmen*, became *burgenses* in the text. There are, however, more communities of such *burgenses* in Domesday than there are places called *burgus*, and if we choose here to speak of boroughs and burgesses together as a shorthand for communities with some claim to a distinctive status, we usually have either to extend our view over other settlements with only the beginnings of an urban function, or limit it to those places which most closely accord, though with many qualifications, to our historical notions of a borough.

The reality behind the boroughs' assorted labels was even more various. *Burh* and its congeners originally signified a fortified place, large or small. The etymology of *port* is still open to argument, but by the eleventh century it had come to signify a place of trade, and more: a licensed place of trade, a cheaping or cheapstead, which under the Latinizing influence of the Normans came to be called a market. The two chief elements of defence and trade came together readily enough. Although a *burh* might be only a fortified house, the term was generally appropriated from the early tenth century to the communal fortresses raised against the Scandinavians by the West Saxons, and used to secure the areas brought back under English control. Many of the *burhs* were raised merely as campaigning quarters, but all had to be victualled, and some proved permanently valuable. Existing centres of trade and other places valuable in themselves required the protection of walls and garrisons. Both kinds of settlement developed into something new. The emergent borough attracted other functions to itself, partly by the efforts that brought it into being, partly as a result of the new strength which it brought to the kingdom.

By the early eleventh century therefore, the larger Old English borough was a distinct and complex institution.[3] It was fortified, and the maintenance of its defences fell to the shire in ways that emphasized its origins in successful wars and the communal efforts that had secured victory. Its revenues were apportioned between the king and the earl in a way that signalled its separation from the shire. It seems to have been a community distinguished by a particular form of tenure, with a locally uniform rent for its major units of property, which were usually called *haws* or *hagae*, and marked by a variety of seignorial interests in its lands and tenements. It had a market with an exclusive claim to trade in its hinterland, and in many instances a court which was differentiated from the courts of the shire and of the hundreds into which the rest of the shire was divided. It also housed a mint, and so was the seat of the most tightly controlled and consistent institution of the Old English polity.

Those are significant features, and their juxtaposition is significant. However diverse the origins of such boroughs, by the time of the Conquest everything inside their walls seems to have been directed towards, or powerfully influenced by, the interests of commerce. Even the defences themselves served not only to protect but also to control access to their market places, and facilitated the collection of tolls. The primary object of the borough courts was

[3] J. Tait, *The Medieval English Borough: Studies on its Origins and Constitutional History* (Manchester, Manchester University Press, 1936), pp. 130-8.

to maintain the peace between man and man, and in doing so to maintain the king's authority over all, but so far as we have indications of the customs that came to distinguish their practice from the shire and hundred courts that they may originally have matched, they related to the conventions of trade and to a freer exchange of property than obtained elsewhere. The coinage, which was subject to a closer control by the king's own officers than any operation of the local community, was nevertheless struck exclusively in the boroughs. Its quality and abundance were central to the maintenance of the king's household and to every manifestation of royal authority, but they depended in turn on a network of urban markets that could turn the agrarian surplus and the profits of foreign trade, however precarious, into silver tokens. In sustaining those operations, the towns grew in usefulness and complexity.

Domesday Book was an object of curiosity and respect from its earliest days, but the manner of its making began to concern historians only in the nineteenth century.[4] It perhaps required an age which regarded its own substantial achievements with a proper awe to appreciate the energy with which earlier societies had been constrained to sustain the mere business of living. The first and most enduring assessment of Domesday was made by Sir Henry Ellis, who concerned himself with a careful analysis of the texts which had passed under his hands as general editor for the Record Commissioners.[5] The busiest period of Domesday studies, however, came in the last quarter of the century, under the stimulus of the octocentennial celebrations of 1886. Two figures, those of John Horace Round and Frederic William Maitland, dominated the rest, and it was a misfortune for medieval scholarship in general that Maitland, whose mind was as far the more original as his nature was the more amiable, deferred to Round's judgements.

Round combined a talent for detailed argument and lucid exposition with an indomitable sense of rectitude, a quality which led him to pursue the real and supposed errors of others to the point of mania. It also led him into hypotheses about the making and import of Domesday Book that were inherently improbable, but that he sustained by convoluted and assertive argument, and successfully imposed not on his contemporaries alone but even upon subsequent generations. He was not greatly concerned with the boroughs, though he made valuable observations on several of them in his studies of Domesday Book for the Victoria County History. The gist of his general theory was that Domesday Book, which is marked on every folio by a tight and urgent sense of purpose, was the product of a lengthy process of trial and error, and that some whimsicality of the medieval mind induced the king and his ministers in making the survey to accept and perpetuate a system of tax assessment that bore no relation to the resources that were taxed.[6] The effect of his judgement was to make the anomalies in Domesday, which are abundant and challenging, pass

---

[4]For a general review of modern Domesday scholarship, see V.H. Galbraith, *The Making of Domesday Book* (Oxford, Clarendon Press, 1961), pp. 12–27.

[5]See n. 1, above.

[6]For a pungent recent *critique*, see J. McDonald and G. Snooks, *How Artificial were the Tax Assessments in Domesday England?*, Working Papers in Economic History, 7, Flinders University of South Australia, 1984.

for the substance of the book. Conceived without reason, it seemed a source from which little but bafflement could be expected.

The confusion bred by Round's theory about the manner in which the text evolved lasted until V.H. Galbraith's exposition of the making of Domesday Book in 1942. In the meantime Maitland accepted Round's dictum on assessments, though his own researches had led him towards other and better-founded conclusions. His own interests lay in the structure of Old English society, and the boroughs attracted his attention particularly. He remarked on their differentiation in the text, and seems to have been the first scholar to suggest that Domesday Book deserved codicological analysis, a suggestion unheeded for half a century.[7] In seeking reasons for the peculiar treatment accorded to the eponymous boroughs of the Midland shires and some other communities, he noted that besides paying seignorial dues to the king, they contained burgesses and properties appurtenant to rural manors in the hands of a variety of lords. He proceeded to argue that it was what he called the tenurial heterogeneity of their communities that set them apart, and elaborated a theory that it reflected their origins as communal garrisons maintained at the expense of the shire. The obligations set upon the localities, as indicated in the enigmatic pre-Conquest text known as the Burghal Hidage, had evolved into a distinctive though confused pattern of lordship in the boroughs, where the grandsons and great-grandsons of a county militia had become merchants and craftsmen.

That hypothesis was effectively refuted by James Tait, in a searching review,[8] but its constituents lingered to tease the mind. Whatever it may have been in 1086, or even in 1066, a *burh* was originally a fortified place. The boroughs 'above the line', as Maitland described them, have several distinctive characteristics, and undoubtedly had once discharged military functions. In Oxford there were certain tenements, members of rural manors, with an explicit liability to repair the town walls. Military services and their incidentals appear amongst the customs of such towns as Hereford and Leicester. Tait largely turned his mind from the history of towns for some 20 years, though he continued to ponder Domesday Book, and produced a model edition and study of a county section in *The Domesday Survey of Cheshire*, in 1916. In the meantime however Adolphus Ballard, a solicitor and town clerk, moved by the elegance of Maitland's work and a formidable antiquarian zeal of his own, launched into a study of municipal origins that led him through an analysis of the boroughs in Domesday to a comprehensive survey of borough charters.

Ballard began with an enthusiastic development of Maitland's theories in *The Domesday Borough* (1904). His reverence for Maitland's great gifts led him to seek out and display a developed system where Maitland had seen indications and possibilities. In doing so he strained what he saw as Maitland's central arguments and neglected the implications of their delicately allusive style. His own book is a competent survey of the complex and diffuse material in

[7]F.W. Maitland, *Domesday Book and Beyond: Three Essays in the Early History of England* (Cambridge, CUP, 1897), p. 178 n. The entire section on the boroughs, *ibid.*, pp. 172–219 is an acute and illuminating essay.
[8]*English Historical Review* 12, 1897, pp. 768–77.

Domesday, vitiated by an obsessive concern to illuminate the past by referring in detail to his own familiar world of local administration. Two examples may suffice to illustrate the weaknesses of a book that at large displays considerable shrewdness and learning. Ballard unquestioningly accepts, and several times repeats, Maitland's *dictum* that Domesday is a geld book. He goes on indeed to describe it as a valuation list, and 'probably the greatest valuation list in existence'. He then proceeds to quote a modern valuation list for his own borough, Woodstock, with a railway company and a Burial Board amongst its owners and occupiers, to show how closely the Conqueror's fiscal curiosity can be matched to the virtuous administrative procedures of Edwardian England.[9]

Turning to the association of burgesses and tenements with the lordship of rural manors, a feature of the Domesday borough with which Maitland made subtle and cautious play in his reconstruction of its origins, Ballard again finds a modern parallel of an enlightening kind:

> Nowadays, when any unit of local government joins with others for a specific purpose to be carried out in combination, we call each of these units a contributory place to that combination; for example, every parish in a poor law union is a contributory place to that union. I propose therefore to give the name of *contributory properties* to Faversham and other properties having houses or burgesses in Canterbury, and to style their houses or burgesses the *contributed houses* or *burgesses*, and to reckon all the contributions together, whether they be haws, masures, houses or burgesses.[10]

His subsequent mode of reckoning is a useful scheme of reference in itself, but the looming figures of the Poor Law Commissioners, the Board of Guardians, and the Rating Officer lend an air of surrealist farce to its invocation of medieval society.

In a later work, *The English Borough in the Twelfth Century* (1914), Ballard displayed a more tempered judgement, though he continued to argue his version of Maitland's views. His work on the constituents of borough charters from the eleventh century to 1215, which James Tait took up and extended to 1307, is a work of patient scholarship, and a valuable guide to the first substantial body of municipal records. Ballard also made another important contribution to the study of Domesday Book in *An Eleventh-Century Inquisition of St Augustine's, Canterbury*, edited in 1910 and published posthumously by the British Academy in 1920, but his artless concern with the business of local government had stamped his efforts with the stigmata of amateurism and provincial narrowness. His considerable talents have been correspondingly underrated.

Tait's return to the study of town history was signalled by a lecture delivered to the British Academy in 1922. The first two decades of the century had been marked by an impressive volume of work on the origins and development of towns in medieval England, and by an equally striking series of misfortunes that had stricken and removed many promising talents. In particular Mary

[9]A. Ballard, *op. cit.*, p. 2.
[10]Ibid, p. 14.

Bateson, who had made a comparative study of borough custumals and shown how Norman lords had spread the customs of the borough of Breteuil through their English estates, had died in 1906 at the early age of 41, a few weeks before Maitland himself.[11] Charles Gross of Harvard, who wrote *The Gild Merchant* (1890), died in his fifties in 1910, and his pupil Morley Hemmeon, whose study of burgage tenure published in 1914[12] is still the only comprehensive work on the subject, died soon after him. Ballard had published only one volume of *British Borough Charters* before his death, at 48, in 1915, and his papers had come to Tait, who had undertaken to complete the project.

Tait took a careful measure of all that had been done, and now saw his way to elucidate the medieval borough as an institution. He published the second volume of *British Borough Charters* in 1923, and turned to his main task. In the next decade he found himself engaged in controversy with an American medievalist, Carl Stephenson. Stephenson's study of Domesday Book and knowledge of continental European scholarship led him to argue, after Henri Pirenne, that town life was a fragile and uncertain growth in England even in 1086, and that its decisive onset should be put to a later date. His *Borough and Town* appeared in 1933, and included an interesting discussion of the topography of boroughs, as well as close argument from the Domesday evidence. Tait's refutation of Stephenson's central thesis, however, was as decisive as his dismissal of Maitland's 30 years earlier. His own knowledge of the contents of Domesday Book was equal to any challenge, and his view of the Old English component in the medieval borough was penetrating and comprehensive. Stephenson's topographical approach was an unfortunate casualty of a sharp and prolonged difference of opinion between two gifted commentators, and in England a concern with the shapes of urban settlement was largely resigned to local historians until the development of urban archaeology after the Second World War.

The issue of Tait's work was the appearance of the *Medieval English Borough* in 1936. Its content fell short of the implicit promise of his Academy lecture, the text of which is reprinted as the last chapter of the book, but it remains the best account of its subject in constitutional terms. Its vindication of the pre-Conquest borough against Stephenson's dismissive arguments, and Tait's careful account of the developments in the 20 years after the Conquest, have been amplified rather than modified by all subsequent work, both historical and archaeological. Tait was fully aware of the anomalies that the use of the terms borough and burgess entail when they are applied on the one hand to the major settlements of East Anglia and the East Midlands, and on the other to the speculative enfranchisement of a handful of manorial tenants or to the little West Saxon boroughs left behind by the expansion of their kingdom. He nevertheless discerned in the evidence, and duly displayed, a complex but coherent organization itself the product of more than one culture, and developed over several centuries. The decisive change, from the inchoate to the

[11]M. Bateson, *Borough Customs* (Selden Society 18, 1899); 21, 1905; 'The laws of Breteuil', *English Historical Review* 15, 1900; 16, 1901 (6 parts).
[12]M. de W. Hemmeon, *Burgage Tenure in Medieval England* (Cambridge, Mass., Harvard University Press, 1914).

functioning town, had taken place before the Conquest. The Norman intrusions protracted rather than accelerated the next stage of development, though they brought, in new settlements and new alignments, the substance of a further advance in the twelfth century.

Tait's assessment of the material in Domesday Book was shrewd and confident. He was familiar with the entire text, and had a similar mastery of the pre-Conquest material. If *The Medieval English Borough* has sometimes been regarded as an enigmatic or disappointing book, it is partly because its matter is highly technical, and partly because in its tight and patient argument it is still really a preliminary to the more general account that Tait had originally hoped to make. It does, however, set out the institutional growth of the borough to the early thirteenth century in a manner that remains unrivalled in economy and precision. The testimony of Domesday Book is at the heart of the work, and is made to display the state of the Old English borough, the changes worked by the Conquest, and the conditions of 1086, when the combination of the sheriffs' depredations and the building of castles had imposed burdens that still bore heavily on the communities. Those were, however, the very factors that disposed the boroughs to new growth under the Angevins, when the king became aware of their potentialities, and the townsmen bargained and paid to circumvent the sheriff.[13]

Before his death in 1944 Tait saw the study of Domesday Book transformed by the work of his former pupil, Vivian Hunter Galbraith, who advanced a theory in the *English Historical Review* in 1942 which he had sketched in the Ford lectures the previous year. Galbraith's view was the antithesis of Round's. He argued that Domesday Book had been carefully planned from its inception, and that it was cast in its present form before the Conqueror died in 1087. The strength of his exposition was that it took account of all the ancillary documents, known since Maitland's day as the Domesday satellites, and especially of the Exon or Exeter Domesday, which Round had explicitly set aside because it could not be accommodated to his views. Galbraith accepted the territorial phase of the survey, with information gathered locally by the king's commissioners in separate circuits of up to five or six counties each, but then posited its reduction, also in the provinces, to regional returns of which Exon Domesday and Little Domesday were the type and antitype. Great Domesday, comprising an account of all but the four northern and the three easternmost counties, therefore represented the final and intended form of all the intermediate returns except that for East Anglia and Essex, which was probably delivered last. The northern reaches of the kingdom were occupied by, or in dispute with, the Scots, and to some extent with the English. They were probably not surveyed beyond the marcher lands of Westmorland and Furness, and Lancashire south of the Ribble, of which there are accounts under Yorkshire and after Cheshire.

---

[13]J. Tait, op. cit., pp. 139–93; on specialized functions of the courts see G.H. Martin, 'The Registration of Deeds of Title in the Medieval English Borough' in D.A. Bullough and R.L. Storey, *The Study of Medieval Records: Essays in Honour of Kathleen Major* (Oxford, Clarendon Press, 1971) pp. 151–73.

The essence of Galbraith's view is that the compilers of Domesday Book knew what they were about, and that, though they experienced difficulties in marshalling the material before them, they arranged and presented it in a manner that was intelligible and they deemed to be useful. It would follow that its text should tell us what it was that the king wished to know, and in that sense what was of consequence in England 20 years after the Conquest. The prospect is not altogether clear, for whilst Domesday may be a rich mine, as a book it is a more formidable proposition, subtle in plot and enigmatic in detail. Galbraith was mindful of the detail, and pursued practicality in the plot. He developed his theory in *The Making of Domesday Book* in 1961, which reviewed the survey as an administrative exercise, and argued back from the manuscript texts to the proceedings of the king's commissioners. His discussion of the Kentish satellites in particular went far beyond that essayed by their individual editors, Ballard and D.C. Douglas,[14] and demonstrated that the successive stages of sworn inquest and seignorial testimony that can be discerned in the Exeter Domesday is strongly borne out by the details of the Domesday Monachorum and the texts preserved by St Augustine's abbey, Canterbury. He subsequently extended his argument in *Domesday Book: its place in Administrative History* (1974), in which he sought to show how the two volumes of Domesday had been used in the business of government. Much of the book is again concerned with the mechanics of the survey, but to Galbraith Domesday's vital feature was that it was a record of feudal society, and continued to serve as a work of reference in the Exchequer far beyond the twelfth century, when the first notices of its administrative value occur.

The two decades of Galbraith's intensive work on Domesday were marked by a number of other important studies. His major thesis was powerfully supported by the discoveries made when the two volumes were rebound in the Public Record Office in 1951–2, and the deliberate nature of its layout and handwriting examined for the first time.[15] R. Weldon Finn published a series of handbooks on the manuscripts of the survey, of which two, on Exeter Domesday and Little Domesday, are particularly useful.[16] In the meantime a general study of critical importance was also in progress, and resulted in the seven volumes of Professor H.C. Darby's *Domesday Geography* (1952–80), five regional studies, covering successively eastern England, the Midlands, the south-eastern counties, the south-western counties, and northern England, with a gazetteer and a general survey. It represents the largest and most consistent extension of work on Domesday since the translations begun in the Victoria County History in 1900. The object of the series is to reconstitute the raw material of Domesday Book in terms of the land and its human occupation, a work complementary to but largely independent of the close analysis of the mechanics of the inquest. The additional evidence of the satellites is, however, consistently related to the main text.

[14] A Ballard, *ed.*, *An Eleventh-Century Inquisition of St Augustine's, Canterbury*, published as Part 2 of N. Neilson, ed. *A Terrier of Fleet, Lincolnshire*, (British Academy 1920); D.C. Douglas, *The Domesday Monachorum of Christ Church, Canterbury* (London, Royal Historical Society, 1944).

[15] Public Record Office, *Domesday Re-bound* (London, HMSO, 1954).

[16] R.W. Finn, *Domesday Studies: the Liber Exoniensis* (London, Longman 1964); *Domesday Studies: The Eastern Counties* (London, Longman, 1967).

The *Domesday Geography* therefore deploys a systematic rearrangement of the information that the commissioners gathered in, and their clerks refined towards the feudal directory that the king had ordered. It is particularly valuable in its attention to towns, rehearsing not only the entries for the acknowledged boroughs, but also the fragmentary and often enigmatic notices of burgesses, urban properties under various names, markets, and other resources which suggest the presence of trade and crafts, and of urban life. As the contributors to the series are concerned with the functions rather than the status of settlements, they have extended their view beyond that of most specialized commentators, and the General Editor's account of 'Boroughs and towns' is the most comprehensive survey of its kind, presenting in a small compass the gatherings of the five regional surveys. It accepts a total of 112 boroughs, which is a conservative and readily defensible estimate: on existing indications the number could be advanced to 120, and probably beyond. Most of the examples are signalled by the presence of burgesses, or tenements (*hagae*, *masurae*) of the kinds found in accounts of the larger towns, some by other characteristics, such as properties formally associated with rural manors in the hinterland, as at Wimborne in Dorset. The total is an impressive one, and accounts for more than one-tenth of the estimated population of the kingdom in the eleventh century.[17]

Throughout the work, however, its compilers regularly express dismay at, and dissatisfaction with, much of the material that they have extracted. The regional survey of the south-west covers five counties, and four have substantial sections on town life. Wiltshire had at least 10 boroughs in 1086: 'the information about all 10 boroughs is extremely meagre, especially for those other than Malmesbury'. Dorset had five: 'the information about all . . . is very meagre, and we can only conjecture about their economic life'. In Devon 'the information relating to all five boroughs is very scanty and we can form no clear picture of their respective economic activities'. It comes as no surprise to learn that 'the information about urban life is the least satisfactory part of the Somerset record'. The fact that Bodmin, which is not called a borough, actually had 68 burgesses makes it seem almost well-documented.[18] At the other end of the kingdom the information about the two boroughs in the East and the two in the West Riding of Yorkshire is judged uniformly unsatisfactory; similar comments occur throughout the series.[19]

The sense of disappointment in the face of such a variety of material is readily understandable. Domesday Book is replete with information. It names people and places, and rehearses facts and figures. Although it nowhere defines a manor, it leaves us in no doubt of a manor's physical resources and the uses to which they were put: tenants, ploughteams, arable and pasture evoke clear enough images, even though their details and the arithmetic of valuation leave scope for argument. For the boroughs and their inhabitants there is only a

[17]H.C. Darby, *Domesday England* (Cambridge, CUP, 1977), pp. 289–320.
[18]H.C. Darby and R.W. Finn, eds, *The Domesday Geography of South-West England* (Cambridge, CUP, 1967), pp. 51, 117, 279–80, 196, 339–40.
[19]H.C. Darby and L.S. Maxwell, *The Domesday Geography of Northern England* (Cambridge, CUP, 1962), pp. 75, 225.

shifting nomenclature, a scatter of uncertain information within narrow limits, a studied silence on matters which we might deem essential but in an historical context can hardly dare to take for granted. If the king and his advisers knew what they wanted at large, what they wanted from the towns remains mysterious. Yet the answers are there in the text, and the questions must lie behind them in the survey.

The Domesday survey was commissioned in Gloucester at Christmas 1085, and seems to have been substantially completed before the end of 1086. Its returns cover the entire kingdom of England from the Channel to the Ribble and the Tees in the north, county by county, with notices of all the major towns except London and Winchester. It was accomplished by the king's ministers working through the apparatus of local administration, and the two volumes of Domesday Book with their congener Exeter Domesday are an impressive testimony both to the driving force of the Conqueror's will and to the efficiency of the system of government that he had acquired. Although it seems that nothing had ever been attempted on the same scale, the means to produce the survey was there before the Conquest. There is good reason to believe that the collection of the tax known as the geld and probably other fiscal operations were aided by the existence of written documents, lists of tenants and estates, which were used in the compilation of local returns, and the evidence of the Anglo-Saxon Chronicle suggests that the survey of the king's lands and dues in the shires preceded, and was conducted separately from, the inquest into the holdings of the tenants-in-chief.[20]

The diverse nature of the texts now known collectively as the Domesday satellites enables us to reconstitute the successive phases of the survey, and also to recognize that the commissioners, and the local officials upon whose knowledge the commissioners drew, probably followed different procedures in the early stages in different circuits. A broad outline nevertheless emerges in a form significantly different from the *omnium gatherum* which Round supposed to have been boiled down, in a mood of mounting desperation, at Winchester. Using lists of holdings afforced by the testimony of lords, tenants and communities, including the boroughs, the commissioners proceeded to compile returns for some seven, perhaps eight, circuits, of which Exeter Domesday and Little Domesday represent two, covering the south-western peninsula and East Anglia with Essex. They also reveal different techniques and preoccupations, notably in the sense that the Exeter text includes documents concerned with the assessment and collection of the geld, and takes stock of royal and some baronial estates across county boundaries, whilst Little Domesday ignores the system of leets by which the geld was levied in Norfolk and Suffolk, and deals with each of its three counties as an entity. It seems likely, however, that the two texts also represent two stages of recension, and that the south-western material in Great Domesday was taken from a refinement of the Exeter text, more closely matched to the form of Little Domesday.

Scholarly attention has focused upon the two regional returns, of which that

[20]S. Harvey, 'Domesday Book and its Predecessors', *English Historical Review* 86, 1971, pp. 753-73.

for Essex, Norfolk, and Suffolk, probably because of its scale and complexity, was eventually put beside, instead of being incorporated into, the larger volume of Domesday Book. Their survival is an extraordinary fact, presumably attributable to the existence in the one instance of a fair copy despatched to Winchester which allowed the Exeter text to be preserved locally, and in the other to the late arrival in Winchester of the return for the easternmost counties, which resulted in its acceptance as it stood, to allow the formal completion of the survey. Behind them the other satellites afford glimpses of the earlier stages of the proceedings. The most striking of them are an elaborate territorial survey of the Cambridgeshire hundreds in the *Inquisitio Comitatus Cantabrigiensis*, a return of some of the manors of St Etheldreda's, Ely, in the *Inquisitio Eliensis*, and a composite record of land-holding in Kent in the records preserved in the *Excerpta* of St Augustine's abbey and the *Domesday Monachorum* of Christ Church, Canterbury.

The text of the *Inquisitio Eliensis* includes a list of the questions asked of each estate 'by the king's barons', to which most of the entries in both volumes of Domesday Book closely correspond: most, but not all. The questions begin with the name of the manor, and of its lord in 1066 and 1086, and ask what its assessment is, what numbers of various categories of tenants it comprises, what are its physical resources, and what its value. The catechism is searching enough for a rural estate, as its outcome shows, but it says nothing of towns, or of the activities associated with them. What is more, it appears from the material that was returned for the towns that there was no other set of questions that could be applied to them: by inadvertence or calculation they were ignored when the survey was planned.[21]

For a substantial proportion of the places deemed boroughs the omission was of little consequence. Where a borough was subsumed in a manor, as it was at Steyning or Okehampton, its burgesses were simply returned as a class of manorial tenants and their renders noted, or not, as an additional resource. In some places, as at Leighton Buzzard and Luton in Bedfordshire, only a market is mentioned: it seems unlikely that it would have existed on an estate entirely devoted to agricultural pursuits, but no tenants who might have served it as traders or craftsmen are recorded.[22]

Such entries are anomalous only in isolation; taken together they imply an institution to which in their diverse ways they can be related. Manorial burgesses as a group are tenants who have an affinity with the inhabitants of a borough, and although the scheme of Domesday directs our attention to their status, that status is informed by their function. They are engaged in, or are intended by their lord to engage in, activities appropriate to townsmen, and whether or not the community of which they are part is called a borough depends on their lord's, or the commissioners', perception of their relative importance.

Of the total of more than 100 boroughs in Domesday Book, however, 32 are distinguished by being placed at the head of their county sections, above or

[21]DB IV, p. 497.
[22]Steyning, DB I, fo. 17; Okehampton DB I, 105 v. Leighton Buzzard, DB I, fo. 209; Luton, ibid.

apart from the standard list of land-holders and the opening entries describing the royal demesne. The descriptions of the 32 are very various in their scope and their details, but their principal shared characteristic, next to a substantial royal interest, is the quality that Maitland called their tenurial heterogeneity: the presence of a number of magnates amongst the holders of property in them, and frequently an explicit connexion between their tenements and rural manors elsewhere in the county – a connection that on occasions, as between Oxfordshire and Berkshire, and Essex and Suffolk, can extend over the county boundaries.

That differentiation of entries is a conspicuous and significant feature of the manuscript text. The most striking characteristic of Domesday Book, which is lost in a printed version, is the careful organization of the entries on the page, and its executant's efforts, without extraneous decoration or even great variety of script, to arrange its information in a readily intelligible manner. The opening page for each county is an important element of what might today be called the presentation of the text, and in general, except for the special cases of Middlesex and Hampshire, where spaces seem to have been left for London and Winchester, and the overloading of Wiltshire with afterthoughts, it is a notably successful one.[23] The major boroughs therefore have a commanding place in the scheme of Domesday Book, and the question of how they came by it is an interesting one.

It is an unfortunate accident that the surviving satellites, which afford such strong clues to the general conduct of the survey, have comparatively little to say about the treatment of towns. Only two of the five counties in Exeter Domesday offer clear examples for argument. The Wiltshire text is incomplete, in Somerset the entries for Bath are dispersed whilst Taunton is submerged in an episcopal manor, and in Cornwall Bodmin is not referred to as a borough although it appears to have had burgesses amongst its population. Only in Devon and Dorset are there clear references to boroughs as distinct communities, and the accounts of Exeter and the leading four boroughs in Dorset are substantially the same in the Exeter and in Great Domesday, where they show only minor rearrangement and stylistic changes.[24] We cannot say that whoever directed the making of Great Domesday was satisfied with the return for boroughs in the south-western counties, but at least he was not disposed to reject what he was sent. On the other hand the entries are quite brief, and there is nothing in their acceptance to suggest that the much fuller accounts of the eastern boroughs in Little Domesday, and especially the entries for Colchester, would not have been extensively edited if they had been formally incorporated in the main text.

Nor is the argument much advanced by what survives from the earlier stages of the survey. The *Inquisitio Comitatus Cantabrigiensis* and the *Inquisitio Eliensis* cover only rural manors, except for the fee of Ely abbey in Cambridge.[25] The Kentish documents, and particularly the *Excerpta*, show some editing of the

[23]Middlesex DB I, fo. 126; Hampshire, DB I, fos. 37–8. For Wiltshire see n. 31 below.
[24]For the entries for the south-western boroughs in both texts, see *The Domesday Geography of South-West England*, 1967, pp. 50–60; 117–22; 196–205; 279–85; 335–6.
[25]See n. 38 below.

accounts of Dover, Canterbury, and the smaller boroughs which is displayed conveniently and discussed by Ballard in his edition of the St Augustine's text. His examination is minute and useful, but the changes are not of as far-reaching a kind as he suggests. In one or two instances compression of the text has produced an error or a misleading emphasis, as in the account of the bargain struck between the king and the burgesses of Sandwich over their service at sea. The description of Canterbury in Great Domesday omits a passage about the management of the stream between the mills on the Stour. The wording is obscure, and an opinion upon it in Domesday would have been welcome, but the matter appears to be of only local significance.[26] At the same time the Domesday text adds a detail to the account of the burgages in Canterbury held by Ralph Curbespine which is analogous to the way in which the entries for rural estates have been filled out elsewhere in the Kentish text. The *Excerpta* represent, in other words, the product of one stage of the inquiry, and not a general review from which an essence could be extracted. Its assessment was a critical process, and it drew as a matter of course upon other material, gathered notably from the landholders, themselves, or their agents.

At this point we must turn again to the general question of the regional returns. The presence in both Exeter Domesday and Little Domesday of returns of livestock on individual manors is a symbol of the condensation and refinement of the main text. The shamelessly minute enumeration of pigs, an aspect of the inquiry which particularly scandalized the author of the Anglo-Saxon Chronicle, was retained to the very last stage of the survey, and abandoned only as the great feudal directory emerged. At the same time both the differences between the south-western and the East Anglian returns and their resemblances remind us that the regional work on Domesday was by no means a simple matter of assembling data to be evaluated elsewhere. The systematic construction of standardized entries and the essential organization of the returns by fiefs was necessarily entrusted to the commissioners on circuit, and Little Domesday shows how well they understood their task.

The accounts of the major boroughs in Great Domesday, various as they are, actually reinforce the point. At first sight they lack internal consistency, and seem by their careful treatment in the final text eloquent of the designer's ability to make the best of a bad job. They range between a perfunctory statement of the assessment of Bedford as a half hundred, with a word on an encroachment by the bishop of Lincoln on St Paul's church, and the accounts of the judicial and other customs of Chester and Shrewsbury, or the details of the shires or wards of York, and the complex of royal and baronial holdings in Leicester and Northampton.[27] All, however, have something to say of the king's rights, and most something of the pattern of lordship over the population of the borough. Customs occur often enough to suggest that they were a particular object of inquiry, and disputes, and to a lesser extent grievances, such as the specific complaints against Picot the sheriff at Cambridge, and the

---

[26]A. Ballard, *op cit.* (n. 14, above), pp. viii, xxiii–xxvii.
[27]Bedford, DB I, fo. 209; York, DB I, fos. 298–98 v. Leicester, DB I, fo. 230; Northampton, DB I, fo. 219.

grievous incidence of customary dues on the reduced population of burgesses at Shrewsbury, are also as prominent as might be expected of so comprehensive a review.[28]

Those features all accord with the broad outline of the survey. The commissioners must have turned to the major boroughs for statements in amplification of what the sheriff or other lords had told them. The townsmen, who for all their vulnerability to the sheriff were familiar enough with the processes of sworn testimony, then produced both confirmation of total dues and some details which on occasions, as at Canterbury, went beyond what was desired or could be adequately assimilated. The standard form of the inquiry into conditions 'now', 'when the king gave it', and in King Edward's day, naturally invited comparisons which would often enough be odorous. The townsmen's resources and organization were probably as various as the returns themselves, but whilst the statement of market tolls at Lewes is no doubt the merest small change of oral tradition, the length and nature of the list of the king's burgesses at Colchester suggests a document, and perhaps one based on a street-by-street survey like the so-called Winton Domesday. The customs of trade at Chester, which have some affinity with the twelfth-century statement from Newcastle-upon-Tyne, may also have been offered in a written form. Those disparate matters, however they came to hand, all presented practical problems as they were assessed and transmitted.[29]

Other problems appeared as the returns for each shire took shape. In all the boroughs eventually placed above the line, except for Dover, Bedford, and Shaftesbury, and in up to a dozen others not so differentiated, there were the holdings of other lords, amounting in Warwick for example to almost one half of the recorded total of burgesses and houses: 112 out of 242. In Warwick that total comprises both tenements returned under the borough itself, and burgesses or urban properties recorded amongst the details of individual manors outside. At Hertford the properties are enumerated only under the borough, but elsewhere, as in Dorset, they appear only in the manorial entries. In a few instances the borough itself is represented only by such incidental references. London and Winchester are the pre-eminent examples, but another is Hastings, which may have been intended to fill the blank space at the head of the entries for Sussex, its fellows Arundel, Chichester, Lewes, and Pevensey having been distributed under individual fees at large in the county.[30]

Such vagaries might be thought to reflect the difficulties of the final recension of the text, and indeed Galbraith spoke of the untidiness of the first folio of Wiltshire as proof 'that the attitude of the compiler of volume I (Great

---

[28]Cambridge, DB I, fo. 189; Shrewsbury, DB I, fo. 252.

[29]Colchester, DB II, pp. 104–6; Winchester, M. Biddle, ed., *Winchester in the Early Middle Ages: An Edition and Discussion of the Winton Domesday* (Oxford, Clarendon Press, 1977). Chester, DB I, f. 262 v. Newcastle, G.H. Martin, 'The English Borough in the Thirteenth Century', *TRHS*, 5th series, 13, 1963, p. 129.

[30]For the Warwick entries, see *The Domesday Geography of Midland England* (Cambridge, CUP, 1971), pp. 305–6. For Sussex, DB I, fo. 16; fo. 23 (Arundel and Chichester), fo. 26 (Lewes), and fo. 20 v (Pevensey).

Domesday) regarding the recording of boroughs and towns was at odds with that of the *legati* in circuit 2', that is to say in the south-west.[31] As we have seen, however, the boroughs for which we have entries in Exeter Domesday are presented in substantially the same form in Great Domesday, where no attempt is made to gather the manorial properties together under their respective towns. In a number of the Midland boroughs the information is divided as it is at Warwick, whilst at Chester and Worcester it appears only under the entries for individual magnates.[32] Either the compiler of the final text showed an uncharacteristic inconsistency here, or he accepted what he had been offered in the circuit return as he did with the engrossment of Exeter Domesday. He did, after all, impose a rule of his own, which was to elevate the eponymous shire towns to the beginning of each section, and to associate with them those which he judged most like them.

The decision to distinguish some boroughs may even have been prompted by representations from the circuits, rather than made at a later stage. It had certainly been decided before the final recension began. In any event, it seems to justify Maitland's observation that 'throughout the larger part of England the commissioners found a town in each county, and in general one town only, which required special treatment. They do not locate it on the *Terra Regis*; they do not locate it on any man's land. It stands outside the general system of land tenure'.[33] To Maitland that notion was an interesting but if anything aberrant by-product of Domesday as a survey for the assessment of the geld. If, on the other hand the text is accepted as the feodary which it undoubtedly is, the distinction becomes even more striking. The inquiry used the existing system of local government because it provided a competent means of collecting and marshalling voluminous evidence. The evidence was arranged by fiefs, beginning with the king's own lands, and descending close to the level of ordinary freeholders, because what the king desired and needed was an account of his total resources and the manner of their distribution, but it was presented as an arrangement of fiefs within shires because that, and not a hierarchy of feudal assemblies, provided the means by which the kingdom was governed, or perhaps more precisely, managed.

William had ruled from the outset as King Edward's heir and successor, and although he and his followers had transformed aristocratic society in England there was no advantage to him in transforming the territorial system of government. The elements of that system were the shire, and the shire court meeting in the shire town. Another two centuries passed before the territory of the borough was separated from the administration of the shire, but in the meantime the shire court and the more dimly perceived burghal community were

[31]V.H. Galbraith, *Domesday Book: its Place in Administrative History*, p. 154 and nn. The entries of fo. 64 v comprise an account of Malmesbury written above the list of the holder of lands, with brief notes below on Wilton, the king's dues from Wiltshire, Salisbury, Marlborough, Cricklade, and Bath, followed by further notes on Malmesbury. The statements of the 'third pennies' due from Salisbury and Marlborough are the only evidence of their formal status as boroughs in 1086. The apparent loss of material for Wiltshire from Exon Domesday makes it difficult to reckon the provenance of the additional material, which perhaps came from testimony in the shire court.
[32]H.C. Darby, *Midland England*, pp. 262-3; 305-6; *Northern England*, pp. 378-9.
[33]F.W. Maitland, *Domesday Book and beyond*, p. 178.

facts. It seems certain that the commissioners came upon them together. The customs of Berkshire, Herefordshire, East Kent, and Nottinghamshire are related to the accounts of their boroughs, and the boroughs of Derby and Nottingham appear to have been noted together, at the head of Nottinghamshire, because their counties were united.[34] The statement of shire customs, however, whether or not it was asked for, was noted much less consistently than were the distinctive features of the towns.

That the commissioners came to conclusions of their own can be deduced from the material in the satellite texts. The gap between the *Inquisitio Comitatus Cantabrigiensis* and the Kentish surveys and Great Domesday cannot be bridged by any surviving document, but some of the differences between the *Excerpta* and the finished text are suggestive. Thus on the first folio of Great Domesday the entry for Dover is followed by a statement of the customs of the lathes of East Kent and by a list of the lands of the canons of St Martin's, Dover, which is broken on fo. 2 by the account of the city of Canterbury and a brief note of Rochester. Dover begins with a bold initial D, set into the text as the most emphatic *incipit* in the book. It suggests, especially in conjunction with the banded sequence of counties in the bound volume from south to north, that it was conceived as the first entry. If that were so, it would be strange if the block of material attached to but not formally associated with the principal boroughs of Kent was taken up with them by the compiler himself. The slight but distinct changes in the handwriting between the entries for Canterbury and Dover and the rest of the material suggests some reflection on the best use of the available space. Nevertheless it seems more likely that Dover, St Martin's, the customs, and Canterbury had been grouped together in the engrossed regional return than that they were taken up piecemeal, and St Martin's gratuitously removed from the general company and from the list of landholders, only at the last moment.

The arrangement of the boroughs in the two surviving regional returns, which has sometimes been taken to show an uncertainty of purpose, points to a similar conclusion. In Exeter Domesday the boroughs of Devon and Dorset are treated simply but consistently, and in groups. In Little Domesday Colchester, which ranked as a hundred of itself, is removed from the royal lands and put at the end of the whole text for Essex after the disputed cases or *Invasiones*. In Norfolk, Norwich, Great Yarmouth, and Thetford are placed together at the end of the royal demesne, as is the main entry for Ipswich in Suffolk. Ipswich was a dower borough, and its territory had been divided before the Conquest between the queen and Earl Gyrth; Sudbury and Dunwich, both mediatized, are left at large under their current royal keepers.[35] There appears throughout to be a sense that the boroughs have more in common with each other than with any ordinary estates, and what boroughs the eastern counties had to offer

[34]Berkshire, DB I, fo. 56; Herefordshire and Archenfield, DB I, fo. 179; East Kent, DB I, fos. 1–1 v; Nottinghamshire and Derbyshire, DB I, fo. 180 v. Nottingham and Derby are together on fo. 180.

[35]Colchester, DB II, pp. 104–7; Norwich, Yarmouth and Thetford, DB II, pp. 116–19; Ipswich, p. 290; Dunwich, DB II, pp. 311–12; Sudbury, DB II, p. 286. There are further entries for Ipswich and Dunwich under individual fiefs; H.C. Darby, ed, *Eastern England*, pp. 193–4.

would have come readily enough to the compiler's hand if their returns had been formally incorporated in the final text. It is interesting to note, however, that the references to crafts and trades under the entry for Bury St Edmunds, which is not referred to as a borough and is bedded in the extensive returns of the abbey's eight hundreds, are like those which St Augustine's included for Canterbury, and which were taken out in the final recension. Religious houses, though mistrustful of townsmen and municipal self-consciousness, had a more explicit interest in the economic functions of towns than did the king's minsters, intent on their own brief.[36]

The indications in Great Domesday are that the commissioners made broadly similar provision for the boroughs in other circuits, and there is almost certainly more to be teased from the details of what they presented. The variations in the treatment of places like Leicester and Oxford, in which the seignorial holdings are noted partly under the borough and partly under the estates of individual lands, and those like Hereford and Chester, in which they appear only in the rural entries, are more likely to reflect the text of the circuit returns than choices made in the final recension. At the same time, it is worth noting that in every case in which the magnates' urban properties are listed under the borough, the order in which they appear departs, and often differs radically, from the order in which their fiefs are ranked in the county at large. The brevity of some of the lists and the compactness of the grouping does not suggest, like the returns from Colchester, that the basic is topographical, but the apparently random order is as likely to reflect some account offered by the townsmen themselves as one compiled by the circuit clerks.

There are four towns in Eastern England, apparently in two separate but adjacent circuits, which are distinguished by references to internal territorial divisions. Cambridge is said to have ten wards, and Huntingdon four quarters or *ferdings*. Stamford has six wards, five in Lincolnshire and one beyond the bridge, in Northamptonshire, which paid all customs with the rest except rent (*gablum*) and toll which went to the abbot of Peterborough. York has seven shires or shares, one being the archbishop's and another laid waste by the castle.[37] We know from the *Inquisitio Eliensis* that the return for Cambridge was based on a list of the wards, one of which is named there, but not in Great Domesday, as the Bridge Ward.[38] It seems probable again that the structure of each return has been determined by the borough's own response, and that would be borne out by the differences in the general treatment of the four places. However, the later prevalence of wards as units of police in boroughs has led to various suppositions that these were early examples of that general development. The arguments are deeply entangled. If the size or sophistication of the community were a factor, Lincoln, Norwich, and perhaps Colchester should at least have kept pace with Huntingdon and Cambridge,

[36]Ballard, *op. cit.*, p. viii; DB II, p. 372. Ironically the account of Bury is the only urban entry to win praise from the Domesday Geography: *Eastern England* (Cambridge, CUP 1952), pp. 197–8.

[37]Cambridge, DB I, fo. 189; Huntingdon, DB I, fo. 203; Stamford, DB I, fo. 336 v; York, DB I, fos. 298–298 v.

[38]DB IV, pp. 507–8.

whilst if Scandinavian influence were decisive, Lincoln and Norwich again might have been of the number. On the other hand if the determinant were the commissioners' own scheme of work it might also have raised echoes in the returns for Nottingham and Derby, which were also reckoned with Stamford, Lincoln, and Leicester as the Five Boroughs of the Danelaw. Eventually we may be driven to accept three layers of evidence, as often as not laid unconformably: what the towns offered, what the commissioners added and took away, and what the author of Great Domesday selected and revised.

Urban topography in its various manifestations is a matter of particular interest to us, with our destructive power over our surroundings, and of a lesser concern, or a less self-conscious concern, to the eleventh century. One reason for its uncertain figure in Domesday lies in the inchoate quality of arrangements to which we attach importance because of what we know they later portended. Domesday makes many and largely mysterious references to the incidence and proceeds of jurisdiction, expressed in terms of sake and soke over burgesses, or as enjoyed by some burgesses, such as the hereditary lawmen of Stamford, over their own tenants and households. In the twelfth century such rights find expression in territorial terms, by the process that by 1189 had converted the bishop of London's four acres and 14 houses within the walls of Colchester in 1086 into a soke associated with the advowson of St Mary's church and containing the town school. As private jurisdiction by that time was fading into the more vigorous system of municipal courts, conducted by townsmen themselves as they gained communal liberties, there is a temptation to suppose that the earlier sokes lay stronger and better defined somewhere behind the clipped phrases of Domesday Book. If the returns for Winchester and London had been incorporated into Domesday we should certainly have seen something more of the private soke, and might have found it depicted more robustly and informatively.[39] Even with more information, however, it is likely that the reality would have remained elusive. The soke more probably evolved between the eleventh and twelfth centuries as did the parish over the same period, from a complex of rights better defined by practice than by theory, into a territorial institution of a more apprehensible but also subtly different kind.

The same considerations apply to nascent municipal organization. There are various traces of gilds, ranging from the gild-hall that the burgesses of Dover had lost by 1086 to the thegns' gild of Cambridge, and the properties held in their gilds by both townsmen and clerks in Canterbury. On Gross's hypothesis that the gild merchant was a creature different from other gilds, and one which appeared in England only after the Conquest, those were tantalizing references that seemed to reflect the backwardness of English institutions and

[39]On Colchester, see DB II, fo. 11; G.H. Martin, *The History of Colchester Royal Grammar School* (Colchester, Benham, 1947), p. 6; C.R. Hart, *The early charters of Essex: the Norman period* (Leicester, Leicester University Press, 1957) pp. 38–39. See also H.W.C. Davis, 'London Lands and Liberties of St Paul's, 1066–1135', in A.G. Little and F.M. Powicke, *Essays in medieval history presented to Thomas Frederick Tout* (Manchester, Manchester University Press, 1925) pp. 45–59, and G.A. Williams, *Medieval London, from Commune to Capital* (London, Athlone Press, 1963), pp. 6–7, 81.

their uncertain movement towards Continental patterns. In fact it was the ubiquity of the gild, and its indispensable function as a means to common action of any kind that accounts for the rarity of such references to it. It would play its own part, still most imperfectly discerned, when municipal institutions of every kind and the occasion to record them multiplied together in the twelfth century.[40]

The search amongst the riches of Domesday Book for a clear statement about the nature and functions of the borough has frequently been mis-conceived, though Tait's patient argument and the instructive material assembled by Professor Darby and his colleagues show in widely different ways what rewards a systematic appraisal can win. In the nature of things, the essen-tial contribution of towns to eleventh-century society, which was to maintain the network of markets both for local and long-distance trade, was likely at the time to go unremarked in any formal scheme. There might well be more to a burgess than met the eye, but so there was to a sokeman or a bordar. All were tenants with duties and rights that were the business of their lords, but were fit to be measured only in terms of the income that they produced. There was therefore no more need to dwell upon the context in which a townsman plied his business than upon the widely various customs of the manors under which rural tenants lived and laboured.

If that were the reasonable assumption of the king's advisers at Christmas 1085, however, the material that accumulated on the circuits soon prompted some further thoughts. By the time the final version was in hand the business of identifying boroughs as communities with a public role, defined only by casual interaction but striking in its effects, had become an essential part of the scheme. The consequences are to be sought in the following century, as systematic records developed in the wake of Domesday as instruments of government. Domesday Book was constantly consulted, and its treatment of the boroughs was as constant a reminder of their peculiar status. Perhaps it was more than a reminder, and a positive influence in itself. Almost 90 years ago Maitland drew attention, as he turned to the boroughs, to their appearance in the Pipe Rolls of 1130 and 1156, and the manner in which they rendered so-called aids and gifts to the king.[41] He emphasized that the list of places taxed is not a simple tally of the principal merchant communities, but a list much like that of the boroughs above the line in Great Domesday, with some of the addi-tions, such as Guildford and Southwark, that we might divine from what Domesday says about them. To Maitland what was interesting about them was an archaic flavour and the neat roundness of the sums at which they were assessed. He detected in them the lingering traces of the historical pattern that he sought to reconstruct. Those were not necessarily misleading indications, but the significance of the ordering was also not exclusively historical. The king's tallages and levies on the boroughs were evidence of his rights and power, and of the townsmen's unchallengeable duties, but he taxed them as communities rather than as tenants. In that there lay the beginnings of another

[40]C. Gross, *The Gild Merchant*, pp. 2–4. For a recent review of the evidence, see G.H. Martin and S. McIntyre, *op. cit.* (n. 2 above), pp. 297–300.

[41]F.W. Maitland, *Domesday Book and Beyond*, pp. 174–8.

order of things, in which the boroughs not only paid but bargained as communities, to buy their way around the sheriff to privileges, to independence of practice, and to a new status.

In that movement all manner of factors old and new played their part. Courts offered experience of delegated authority and communal deliberation, gilds the protection of artificial brotherhood and communal anonymity. Established customs could provide the matrix for new practices; the profits of trade rose on a growth of population that transformed the whole of western Europe. The tentative and affirmative judgements of Domesday Book made one factor amongst many, but within the circle of the king's household, the seat of government, it was not the least of them.

The power of the written word is a recognized force in human affairs, and a book has a talismanic quality of its own. In Domesday that has if anything intensified with age, but the text had a practical purpose and its effects cannot have been disappointing to those who planned it. The Conqueror had not a long time in which to satisfy the curiosity which was the imperative force at Gloucester in 1085, but his successors reaped an enduring benefit from the material which the survey captured and displayed. So in a variety of ways, and as ever at their own costs and charges, did the boroughs.

CHAPTER NINE

Domesday Book and the Computer

John Palmer

The fundamental reason for computerizing Domesday Book was stated long ago by Maitland. If we are ever fully to understand the statistics of Domesday Book, he argued;

> it is necessary that we should look at the whole of England. Far be it from us to say that microscopic labour spent upon one county or one hundred is wasted; often it is of the highest value; but such work is apt to engender theories which break down the moment they are carried outside the district of their origin. Well would it be if the broad features of Domesday Book could be set out before us in a series of statistical tables.[1]

For without such tables the 'mass statistics' of Domesday – and hence the national picture – are all but impossible to assimilate. As Baring observed,[2] even a single feature of a single county is difficult enough to grasp by simply reading the text. Yet despite the desirability of a systematic tabulation of Domesday manor by manor, fief by fief, and county by county, Maitland's successors have generally ignored his plea, preferring to indulge in 'the many pleasures of hypercriticism'[3] at the expense of the statistics rather than labour to use them. With the honourable exception of Professor Darby's team of geographers, little or no advance on a national scale has been made since the late 1890s, despite some useful work at the local level. The first benefit that the computer will confer upon Domesday scholars will be the realization of Maitland's dream on a scale for which he could scarcely have dared to hope. Within the year, all the major statistics for every manor on every fief in every county should be available for the asking.[4]

[1] F.W. Maitland, *Domesday Book and Beyond* (Cambridge, CUP, 1897), p. 407.
[2] F.H. Baring, *Domesday Tables for the counties of Surrey, Berkshire, Middlesex, Hertford, Buckingham, and Bedford and for the New Forest* (London, St Catherine Press, 1909), p. ix.
[3] G. Bois, *The Crisis of Feudalism: Economy and Society in Eastern Normandy c. 1300–1550* (Cambridge, CUP, 1984), p. 14. Bois rightly castigates such 'obscurantism', arguing that 'Even rough and approximate quantitative formulation . . . is preferable to the absence of any statistical treatment'.
[4] They will shortly become available by courtesy of the Santa Barbara project for computerizing Domesday under the direction of Warren Hollister and Robin Fleming.

This is only the first of a number of advances which the computer will allow in the next year or two. Perhaps its single most valuable contribution to Domesday studies will prove to be its ability to restructure information rapidly and with complete accuracy. The need for such restructuring is obvious enough. The uneasy combination of geographical and feudal principles upon which Domesday Book is organized is ill-adapted for the purposes of almost any kind of research. As Maitland prophetically observed in his last words on Domesday:[5]

> A century hence the student's materials will not be in the shape in which he finds them now. In the first place, the substance of Domesday Book will have been rearranged. Those villages and hundreds which the Norman clerks tore into shreds will have been reconstituted.

The utility of a Domesday Book arranged upon geographical principles is fully borne out by the past record of Domesday scholarship; for what many would consider to be its two greatest achievements are the products of just such a reorganization. It will be recalled that Round's crucial discovery of 'a vast system of artificial hidation, of which the very existence has been hitherto unsuspected',[6] was first suggested to him by the *Inquisitio Comitatus Cantabrigiensis* (ICC) which provided – as the famous opening sentence of *Feudal England* declared – 'the true key to the Domesday survey, and to the system of land assessment it records'. Round unearthed supplementary evidence for his thesis in the Lindsey and Leicestershire surveys and in the Reverend William Airy's *Digest of the Bedfordshire Domesday*, all of which, like the ICC itself, were arranged on geographical principles. Similarly, a geographical rearrangement of Domesday Book was, of course, indispensable to Professor Darby's magnificent enterprise; and one must presume that much of the four and a half decades spent on that project was devoted to the huge clerical labour of reconstructing the Domesday villages. The obvious utility of a geographically arranged Domesday has prompted scholars and antiquaries to labour at this task for over a century, urged on by researchers such as Round insisting – 'at the risk of wearisome iteration'[7] – on the need for a Domesday structured along the lines of the ICC. But after a century of such efforts, the results have been meagre. The published reconstitutions account for only about a dozen Domesday counties, few of which can be considered to meet the standards of modern scholarship.[8]

Moreover, invaluable though it would be, a Domesday in an ICC format would satisfy the needs of only one particular group of researchers, though admittedly a substantial group. But neither the existing organization of Domesday Book, nor its reconstitution by villages, would be of much

[5]Maitland, *Domesday Book*, p. 520.
[6]J.H. Round, *Feudal England* (London, 1895 n.e. Greenwood Press, 1979), p. 49.
[7]Round, p. 98.
[8]Notably, G.H. Fowler's *Bedfordshire in 1086: an analysis and synthesis of Domesday Book* (Apsley Guise, Bedfordshire Historical Record Society, 1922). Other such efforts are usefully reviewed by H.C. Darby, *Domesday Geography of Eastern England* (3rd edn, Cambridge, CUP, 1971), pp. 13ff.

assistance to a student of the Anglo-Saxon nobility. There are perhaps six major ways in which the statistics might usefully be organized:

1 in Domesday format – the least useful!
2 geographically
3 feudally, by tenant-in-chief
4 by landlord, at the demesne level, for 1086
5 by landlord, at the demesne level, for 1066
6 by Anglo-Saxon overlord

These will be the indispensable research tools of future generations of Domesday scholars. There is every prospect that the computer will make them available in permanent, published form as standard works of reference in the near future, perhaps for 1986.[9] And these six structures are far from exhausting the possibilities of this particular computer application. There are literally thousands, indeed millions, of ways in which the statistics may be meaningfully structured and tabulated, this being limited only by the nature of the problem under investigation and the imagination of the research worker.[10] But even a single such restructuring is a painfully slow and error-prone process if done manually. With the aid of a computer it is painless and without error, however many times the process is replicated. By relieving the student of the labour, tedium and error inescapably involved in rearranging what King William's clerks have bequeathed to us, the computer will surely provide an enormous stimulus to research of the kind for which Maitland contended.

Finally, of course, computer packages[11] not only facilitate restructuring of the statistics but also make available every statistical procedure that could conceivably be of use, from the simple calculation of totals, percentages and averages to the more complex tests of correlation and regression. That such statistical techniques will not appeal to every one is perhaps the most confident prediction that can be made about the future use of the computer. But as John Hamshere has rightly observed, most statistical work on Domesday has been naive to the point of being meaningless. Yet some of the tests on the data can, as he has also shown, be extremely illuminating.[12]

These facilities, which have been available now for many years, are routine applications in computing terms, requiring no programming skills and only

[9]Harvester Microform are considering publication on microfiche.

[10]E. Shorter, *The Historian and the Computer: A Practical Guide* (Englewood Cliffs, N.J., Prentice-Hall, 1971), p. 7 suggests as a rule of thumb that the number of tables that the researcher might wish to see would be half the square of the number of variables involved, which might mean several hundred on a given Domesday project.

[11]I have tried to avoid jargon but some words are unavoidable. In lay terms, a package is a collection of computer programs dedicated to a particular task. For the historian, the most useful of such packages is the Statistical Package for the Social Sciences (SPSS). It is documented in *User Guides* published by McGraw-Hill. The *Guide* to the latest of the ten 'releases' – called SPSS^x – was published in 1983.

[12]J.D. Hamshere and M.J. Blakemore, 'Computerizing Domesday Book', *Area*, vol. 8 (1976), pp. 289–94; J.D. Hamshere, 'A computer-assisted study of Domesday Worcestershire', in T.R. Slater and P.J. Jarvis, eds., *Field and Forest: an Historical Geographical of Warwickshire and Worcestershire*, (Norwich, Geo Books, 1982), pp. 105–24.

moderate acquaintance with the computer and a suitable package.[13] The only real deterrent to their use – apart from ignorance – has been the considerable labour involved in extracting the statistics from the text and typing them into the computer; and even this obstacle will shortly be removed when the Santa Barbara data base becomes available. In future, only masochists will approach Domesday's statistics without the aid of a computer.[14]

But there is more to Domesday Book than its statistics. Despite Maitland's appeal quoted at the beginning of this essay, the overwhelming emphasis of Domesday research since his day has been on *textual* analysis, as work associated with the names of Round, Stenton, Douglas, Galbraith, Finn, Sawyer, Cameron, Jones, Harvey, and even Lennard, will immediately suggest. And if anything, this catalogue understates the importance of the textual approach, since much work of an apparently statistical nature depends upon prior analysis of the text in which the figures are embedded.[15] At the moment, computing facilities are still inadequate for research of this kind,[16] and the textual approach to Domesday will remain the last refuge of those anxious to postpone that 'painful process of retooling in the struggle to avoid technological obsolescence'[17]·with which the historical community has been chillingly threatened.

But not for very much longer. Domesday is such a unique record, used by so wide a community of scholars, that it deserves, and is receiving, special treatment. The entire text of Domesday Book – every word – has been computerized; and this will become available in the not too distant future, together with a package of programs dedicated to the analysis of Domesday Book and Domesday Book alone.[18]

A machine-readable text will offer many advantages. In the first place, curiously enough, it will allow a more accurate and sophisticated calculation of the statistics. For even the simple addition of figures in Domesday is neither simple nor just a matter of addition, due to the ambiguity of much of the textual context. As Maitland observed with his usual incisiveness:[19]

[13]The amount of time and effort required to learn the use of packages such as SPSS for those totally unfamiliar with computers is perhaps comparable to finding one's way around an unfamiliar archive. It would require considerably less effort than, say, mastering a new language. Courses to assist beginners will shortly spring up, but at the moment the only one that I know of is the Hull one year MA in Historical Computation.

[14]Shorter, *Historian and the Computer*, is the best introduction to using the computer for statistical purposes for those with no experience at all of computers, though the technology he describes is all but obsolete. Recent work using computers in History is most conveniently found in the journals *Computers and the Humanities*, and *Le Medieviste et l'ordinateur*. *Computers and Medieval Data Processing* describes current research projects and publishes an annual bibliography.

[15]R.W. Lennard's work on the Domesday peasantry is a particularly clear example: 'The economic position of the Domesday *villani*', *Economic Journal*, LVI (1956), pp. 244–66.

[16]The earlier releases of SPSS, for instance, make even the handling of simple names awkward enough.

[17]*The Washington Post* for Tuesday 9 March 1982, p. C15.

[18]Briefly described in J.J.N. Palmer, 'Le Domesday Book', *Le Medieviste et l'ordinateur*, XI (1984), pp. 2–4. See appendix below for further detail.

[19]Maitland, *Domesday Book*, p. 407. Variations of formulae are not, of course, the sole reason for differing totals. Maitland mentions faulty arithmetic and the difficulties of complex entries as

two men not unskilled in Domesday might add up the number of hides in a county and arrive at very different results, because they would hold different opinions as to the meaning of certain formulas which are not uncommon.

And what is true of the hides is true to some degree of all the statistics. On circuit III, for instance, three values are usually recorded: for 1066, *quando recepit*, and 1086. Occasionally, however, a value is given by the formula *valet et valuit*. The *valet* presents no problem; but does the *valuit* refer to 1066, to *quando recepit*, or to both? A difference of opinion on this single point will make an appreciable difference to the totals calculated. And this is only one problem among many, and a particularly simple one. That is why it is possible for any number of researchers to fail to agree upon a single total for a single category of information, as the following table illustrates:[20]

Some Bedfordshire Statistics

	Hides	Teamlands	Teams	Population	Value 1086
Maitland	1193	1557	1367	3875	1097
Baring	1229	1579	—	3507	1180
Fowler	1210	1581	1401	3723	1033
Darby	1186	1588	1405	3591	1164
Palmer	1206	1560	1403	3527	1041

The figures are not even consistently inconsistent. Maitland has the highest total for population but the lowest for teamlands and teams; Baring the lowest for population but the highest for hides and values; Darby combines the lowest count of hides with the highest tallies of teamlands and teams; while Fowler records the lowest total for the values for 1086 after achieving near maximum figures for the remaining statistics.

There are three possible approaches to this problem posed by the ambiguity of King William's clerks. The first is to accept the discrepancies as unavoidable, taking comfort in the generally small percentage differences between the highest and lowest counts. For as long as the figures had to be calculated manually, such an attitude was probably inevitable. But with the computer in mind, the Santa Barbara team have adopted a more sophisticated approach, in which separate totals are kept for each formula, the user himself deciding which might be appropriately combined. In the case of the *values* on circuit III for instance, it would be open to the user to choose whether the totals for TRE or *quando recepit* should comprise only those unambiguously declared to be such, or should include the *valuit* or *semper valuit* cases as well.

From the student's point of view this is a considerable advance. But though the methodology is a marked improvement upon current practices, its imple-

---

additional reasons, and could have added duplicate entries and the problem of properties which 'lie in' one county but geld or are valued in another.

[20]Maitland, *Domesday Book*, pp. 400–1; Baring, *Domesday Tables*, p . 179; Fowler, *Bedfordshire*, p. 5; H.C. Darby, *Domesday England* (Cambridge, CUP, 1977), p. 359.

mentation may raise problems of its own. The statistics are compiled manually by the Santa Barbara team. By multiplying the number of categories of figures, they also multiply the possibilities of clerical error in compiling them. In the case of the *values* discussed above, for instance, my description considerably simplifies the process. There are not four but about a dozen formulae to keep track of, or nearer two dozen if the peculiarities of the royal estates are included. To compile the figures for plough teams, almost 20 formulae are required. In an average county where Domesday may record about 30 pieces of information for the majority of properties, 200 or so formulae may well be needed. The patience of Job and the skill and concentration of the most dedicated worker will not, in these circumstances, be enough to avoid a considerable crop of errors in compilation.

With the entire text of Domesday Book in machine-readable form, however, this source of error can be eliminated by taking the process of automation one stage further. The computer itself can compile the statistics. The formulae can be selected, and the figures allocated appropriately, under program control. However many formulae are involved, however fine the distinctions between them, however large the number of manors to be processed, the computer will not grow weary, lose concentration, or turn its attention elsewhere. It will keep track of 5,000 categories as accurately as one, that is with 100 per cent accuracy.

A more obvious advantage of a machine-readable version of the record is that the text itself can be analysed with the aid of the computer. The ramifications of this simple fact are considerable. To begin with, the Domesday scholar will have available an index to every single word in Domesday Book. It is equally possible to generate a concordance of any or every word, using another general-purpose computer package, the Oxford Concordance Program.[21] There can scarcely be a research project of any nature which will not benefit from one or other or both of these new tools.[22]

But it will be the prospect of exploring the formulae, rather than the words, of Domesday which is likely to attract the greatest attention. For despite the considerable effort which has gone into the investigation of 'the making of Domesday Book', the text of the Exchequer Domesday has contributed little to the debate, even though it is the only text available for most of the country. Now that the 'satellite' texts appear to have yielded up most of their secrets, Domesday itself will be increasingly placed under contribution. J.S. Moore and Professor Darby have given some indication of the possibilities of this approach in their analysis of one particular formula on a fief-by-fief basis.[23] The method should be extended to encompass a range of formulae, analysed

[21]Henceforth, OCP. There is a useful *User Guide* by S. Hockey and I. Marriott, published by the Oxford University Computing Service (1982). Susan Hockey has also written a lucid introduction to most forms of computer-aided text analysis: *A Guide to Computer Applications in the Humanities* (London, Duckworth, 1980).

[22]Linguists and lexicographers should find a crop of words and usages to include in the *Dictionary of Medieval Latin from British Sources*, ed. R.E. Latham (Oxford, OUP & British Academy 1975-).

[23]J.S. Moore, 'The Domesday Teamland in Leicestershire', *EHR.*, LXXVIII (1963), pp. 696–703; Darby, *Domesday England*, pp. 109–10, 347–51.

by fief, by sub-tenancy, by hundred and vill, and perhaps by Anglo-Saxon tenurial groupings. Despite successive layers of revision and editorial intervention, the Exchequer Domesday might in this manner be persuaded to reveal, if only in palimpsest, the administrative techniques by which it was produced. And such an approach would have the further advantage of revealing such county, circuit, and regional variations in the making of Domesday Book as may be presumed to have existed but which have been rather ignored in the debate to date.

A related topic which invites investigation is the question of the writing of Domesday: was it the work of one man, of several, or of many? In the present state of technology, the computer can give no assistance with the handwriting or inks;[24] but it can analyse variations in the use of particular words, symbols, formulae and abbreviations, on a folio-by-folio, and quire-by-quire basis. By these and other techniques,[25] it should be possible to separate random scribal variations from more regular patterns of usage, and hence detect the 'fingerprints' of the individual scribe, or scribes.

There is one other area of textual analysis in which the computer will make a significant contribution, that is with the problem of identifying individuals. As is well known, the majority of individuals in Domesday Book are identified only by their christian names. Faced by 20 occurences of the name 'Robert', therefore, we may be dealing with a single individual who owns 20 manors, 20 individuals owning a manor apiece, or any number of individuals between one and 20 holding varying numbers of properties. Before an attempt can be made to analyse almost any aspect of the social structure of Anglo-Saxon or Anglo-Norman England, or to investigate the impact of the Conquest upon the landowning classes, this uncertainty in the identification of individuals must first be reduced to tolerable proportions, though we know that it can never be entirely eliminated.

Until recently, such a task was too vast to be contemplated. Even an accurate index and count of the Anglo-Norman tenants-in-chief – who are fully identified – has yet to be compiled, despite Round's insistence that such a compilation would reveal that 'the vast total given by Ellis and others' would be reduced to 'a mere handful' of names once the official index of Domesday had been replaced by a more accurate one.[26] His belief has yet to be put to the test.

The computer can assist with this problem in two ways. In the first place, it is possible to link names automatically on the basis of certain assumptions which Domesday scholars traditionally make. For although there is no certain test by which we can identify one 'Robert' with another unless the record explicitly tells us that they are identical (as it occasionally does by the use of such phrases as 'the same Robert'), students of Domesday do not in practice treat every occurrence of a particular name as being equally likely or unlikely to refer to a separate individual. When we find, for instance, that on the fief of Hugh de

[24]The Kurzweil Data Entry machine will read crisply typed or well printed texts but the days when a device of this kind can read manuscripts of any kind are still some way in the future.
[25]Miss Hockey gives a useful overview: *Guide*, especially chap. 6.
[26]J.H. Round, *The Commune of London and Other Studies*(London Constable, 1899), pp. 37–8; *VCH Hampshire* I, pp. 422–3.

Beauchamp in Bedfordshire the Anglo-Saxon owner of 15 of his properties had been named 'Askell', we do not assume that Hugh had 15 predecessors named Askell. Instead, we assume that Hugh had inherited 15 of his properties from a single individual named Askell. Similarly, if we find a man of the same name holding a particular manor in both 1066 and 1086, we assume that he is the same man on both occasions, even though we are not told so explicitly. And if, on a given fief, there are several mentions of an 'Aelfric, Burgraed's man', we again assume that all refer to the same two individuals, Aelfric and Burgraed, and not to several pairs of Aelfrics and Burgraeds. In all these cases, I use the word 'assume' advisedly. For although there are general grounds for believing these conclusions to be true, there is no conceivable way in which it could be proved to be so in the vast majority of cases. If we had to rely upon proof, we would treat the 15 occurences of Askell as 15 individuals. But we do not succumb to such nominalism. Whether consciously or not, we rely instead upon the laws of probability rather than on the usual criteria of proof.

I have made this point at some length because many will instinctively distrust the idea of 'decisions made by machines'. But it is not, of course, the machine which makes the decisions but the person who constructs the algorithm upon which the machine operates. The algorithm itself merely makes explicit the assumptions upon which a scholar would instinctively make his decisions. It would not therefore treat *all* occurrences of a particular Anglo-Saxon name on the fief of a given Anglo-Norman tenant-in-chief as *always* referring to a single individual. For while such a rule might be reasonable in Bedfordshire, it would be most unreasonable when applied to Yorkshire, Cheshire and Cornwall, where the Conqueror had created fiefs which bore more resemblance to Capetian counties than to the tenurial patchwork observable in most parts of Anglo-Saxon England.

On the other hand, the algorithm should identify as a single individual one 'Leofeva, commended to Earl Waltheof', the Anglo-Saxon predecessor of Hugh de Beauchamp at Apsley Guise, and 'Leofeva, King Edward's man', the Anglo-Saxon predecessor of Countess Judith at Bletsoe, despite the different forms of the two names and their occurrence of different fiefs in widely separated parts of the record. It should do so on the grounds that the name is unusual; that Waltheof and Judith had been husband and wife; and that the fiefs of Judith and de Beauchamp were interrelated in a number of other respects.

The automatic linkage of names, therefore, attempts to reproduce the mental processes of the Domesday scholar, merely making them explicit. The benefits of using the computer to do this lie not in the nature of the decisions made but in the fact that they can be made on a scale which the individual scholar could not contemplate. The advantages of the computer are 'all clerical, not intellectual'.[27] The results will be built into the Hull data base.

These results, moreover, will be open to inspection, for the grounds upon which they have been made will be recorded in a file which is linked to the names. This linked file brings us to the second way in which the computer will,

---

[27]Shorter, *Historian and the Computer*, p. 8.

in future, assist with the problem of identifications. There are, of course, methods of identifying individuals other than on the basis of the information in Domesday Book itself, and these methods are generally more secure. The two most obvious of these are the additional information recorded in some of the satellite texts, and the subsequent descents of Domesday manors held by men of the same name to one family. The results of identifications of this type are unfortunately scattered in hundreds of books and periodicals published over the past century, requiring a considerable research effort to bring them together. The obvious place in which to gather these identifications will in future be the Hull data base, where they will then be available for the whole scholarly community. This is not a result which will be achieved in the next year or two. But the ultimate benefits of centralizing the accumulated expertise of generations will make the effort and delay worthwhile.

Finally, linked files of a similar nature can and will be used for purposes other than the collection of references. A further use will be to establish connections between different words. In its very simplest form, all words in the text will be linked to their dictionary lemma, making it possible to access the occurence of every individual form of a particular word. Similarly, all place-names could be categorized by type, thereby enabling the student of place-names to obtain sorted lists of any and every type of place-name in a particular area, or for the country as a whole, with or without their associated statistics. It would be equally feasible to attach to each place-name data from geological surveys and drift maps, thereby making it possible to select manors for analysis on this basis. Personal names could be treated in a similar way and categorized on racial or linguistic grounds, or even by sex. A particular example of this approach which is currently being built into the data base is the categorization of all landowners according to the nature and date of their tenancy, thus making it possible to produce a more accurate and more detailed version of all of Ellis's indices. In other fields, experts will no doubt be able to suggest desirable additions which will make the analysis of Domesday Book more sophisticated, or less arduous, or both, to future generations of Domesday scholars.

All this is looking no more than three or four years into the future. Beyond that, prophesy is hazardous, given the speed at which computer technology is changing.[28] It is probable, though, that the satellite texts will be computerized, and programs developed to permit the texts of Domesday and the satellites to be analysed concurrently, each being used to interpret the other. Other major sources of social and economic history will be similarly computerized – the Hundred Rolls are an obvious candidate – and programs developed to facilitate comparisons between these different sources. All this is a little speculative. But although the precise manner in which computer applications in this area are liable to develop cannot be predicted, we may assume with confidence that within the next decade the use of computers in the Humanities will become

[28]The single most desirable technological development from an historian's point of view would be the ability of computers to read text directly from the sources; but there are at present no certain indications as to how long we shall have to wait for this breakthrough.

commonplace and that at the end of the decade – to adapt Maitland – the Domesday scholar will find neither his materials, nor his methods of study, 'in the shape in which he finds them now'.

APPENDIX:

The Hull Data Base

The main stages in the creation of the Hull data base have been outlined elsewhere,[29] and this appendix simply aims to explain the reasons for the methods adopted, as simply as possible.

The Hull data base has been designed for inter-active use at a terminal, which means that speed and efficiency are among the most important of the design criteria. With a text of the size of Domesday Book – some two to three million words, perhaps 12 million characters – even a large mainframe computer will take a measurable amount of time to perform the simplest analysis – to locate occurences of a particular word, for instance. Anything more complicated than this – and most analyses will be considerably more complex – may well take hours of computer time.[30] This would make inter-active work impossible.

To improve speed and efficiency, the text of Domesday Book has therefore been pre-processed. To begin with, it is sorted alphabetically. Searching a sorted list produces dramatic increases in efficiency in two major respects. First, a search program no longer has to inspect every word, but only every *different* word. In the case of the Domesday text for Bedfordshire, for instance, there are a little under 30,000 words of text but rather less than 1,300 different words. Roughly speaking, only one word in 23 is a new word; or, to put it another way, each word occurs on average 23 times. Furthermore, because these words are arranged in alphabetical sequence, a program does not have to inspect every word in order to locate any particular one. What it does it to inspect the word in the middle of the list; test to see whether this is higher or lower in the alphabetical order than the word for which the search is being made; then discard the half of the list in which the word cannot occur. It then continues to halve the area of search in this way until it locates the word it is looking for or discovers that it does not occur in the text. This process reduces search times very considerably. To locate a particular word among the 1,300 or so in the text for Bedfordshire, for instance, would require *at most* 11 comparisons using this technique of the 'binary chop'. If we assume that the text of Domesday Book as a whole contains roughly three million words, and that

---

[29]Above, note 18.
[30]To produce a concordance of even a moderate-sized text such as that for Bedfordshire will · take several hours even on a fairly powerful machine.

there are approximately 100,000 different words – both assumptions being on the generous side – then the maximum number of comparisons needed to locate a particular word in a sorted version of the entire text would be 17. The comparable figure for a search on the whole unsorted text is, of course, 3,000,000. An improvement of the order of 3,000,000:17 is worth achieving!

Further improvements in efficiency have been achieved by compacting the data and by indexing every occurence of each word both in the text itself, in the sorted list, and in its stored position in the computer. The relationships are shown in Figure 9.1. The data base itself is just a series of numbers, each one of which is an index to the position of a word in the sorted text. For instance, the first number in the data base is 311. This means that the first word in the Domesday text for Bedfordshire is, alphabetically speaking, the 311th; and if we examine the alphabetical listing we will find at position 311 the word '209a', the folio reference with which the text for Bedfordshire begins. By these means it is possible to store the entire text of Domesday Book in a highly compact form, which means in turn that it may be kept in the main memory of the computer (instead of disk or other storage devices), all of which increases the speed of access. This, plus the use of multiple indices, means that any part of the text can be accessed virtually instantaneously. Any type of analysis will be correspondingly rapid.

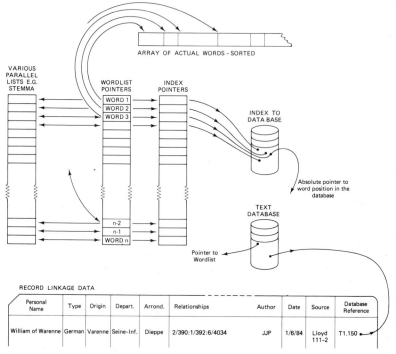

Figure 9.1: Domesday — an overview
To locate a word the ARRAY OF ACTUAL WORDS is scanned using the wordlist pointers. Finding the word, the same element of the INDEX POINTERS contains the required reference to the INDEX TO DATABASE. This index is read and contains a list of absolute pointers to every occurrence of the word in the TEXT DATABASE.

Index

Numbers in italic refer to illustrations.

175

passim, 66n, 67; rolls, 58, 59, 62, 172; sessions 61, 63

Huntingdon 124, 160

Huntingdonshire 35, 36, 66n, 70, 72, 76, 91 99, 113

Ilchester (Somerset) 64

Ingleric, priest 121, 132

Innocent III, pope 138

Inquisitio Comitatus Cantabrigiensis 57, 70, 155, 159; dual purpose of Ely compilers 53; and Round 62; and names in DB 72; as satellite 53, 58, 62, 154; as 'true key' to Domesday survey 1, 165

Inquisitio Eliensis 22, 53, 55, 58, 68, 69, 70, 154, 155; dual purpose of compilers 53; and Cambridge wards 160

Institutio Canonicorum 117

invasiones super regem 66 & n, 70

Ipswich 33n, 159

Irminon, abbot of St Germain-des-Prés, *see* polyptych

Itlay 9, 11, 13, 22, 23

iugum, iuga, in Roman Empire 8−13 *passim*, 24, 92, 96, 101

Jones, A. H. M. 8, 10, 92, 167

juries, *see* hundreds

Keisby (Lincs) 97

Kent 3−4, 34, 35 & n, 36, 54, 59, 73n, 82n, 99, 112; P (satellite) 59, 60, 64; land-holding in 154−60 *passim*; lathes 58 & n; 59 & n, 159; sulungs 69, 92−3, 101; *see also Excerpta*, Domesday Monachorum

Ker, N. R. 30−1, 42−3

Kingston-on-Thames (Surrey), church 112

Kirkdale (Yorks), church inscription 121

Kirtling (Cambridgeshire) 88

Kreisler, F.F. 59

Kurzweil Data Entry machine 170n

Lancashire 57, 150

Lanfranc, archbishop of Canterbury 69

lathes *see* Kent

Laxfield (Suffolk) 75

Leatherhead (Surrey) 126

leaves in Domesday MSS 29−34 *passim*, 40−9 *passim*, 63−4

Leicester 147, 156, 160, 161

Leicestershire 35, 36, 61n, 74, 76, 77, 90n, 92, 112, 165

Leigh (Churstow, Devon) 72

Leigh (Staffs) 95

Leighton Buzzard (Beds) 154

Lennard, R. V. 3, 167; and Bath A 60; and minsters 105

Leodmaer (landholder, Herts) 77

Leofric, bishop of Exeter 123, 127, 132n

Leofric, earl 121, 123

Leofric, son of Leofwine 74

Leofstan, abbot of Bury St Edmunds 55

Leofwine, father of Leofric 74, 77

Leominster (Herefords) 121

Lewes (Sussex) 157

Liber Exoniensis, see Exon

Lichfield (Staffs), church 132

Lincoln 160−1; cathedral or chapter 126, 131, 141

Lincolnshire 3, 35, 36, 40n, 58, 66nn, 67n, 70, 72, 74, 75, 76−7, 81, 83, 97, 99, 124, 126, 160

Lindsey, ridings of 53n, 58, 73, 165

Little Domesday Book (LDB) 28−56 *passim*, *44*, 62−4, 68, 106, 144, 150, 151, 153, 155, 156, 159; as satellite 50; arrangement of text 37; re-bound 32; special status 51; *see also* Domesday Book, leaves, quires, *and* rubrication

livestock (various) 14, 51, 60, 71, 87, 89, 93, 94, 96, 97, 98, 100, 102, 127, 156

Lobbes, *see* polyptych, 'lesser'

London 32, 121, 123, 153, 155, 157; episcopal manor, 79−80, 161; St Martin-le-Grand 132

Longnon, A. 14

Losinga, Robert of, bishop of Hereford 64 & n, 66, 126−7, 132; quoted 100

Lot, Ferdinand 22−3, 101

Loyn, H. R. 51n

Luton (Beds) 154

Lydbury North (Salop) 94, 113

Maitland, F. W. 1−2, 4, 79n, 87, 88, 90, 97, 146−50, 155, 158, 162, 164, 165, 166, 167 & n, 168, 173; *Domesday Book and Beyond* 1, 78, 164

Malmesbury (Wilts), abbey of 80, 158n; borough of 152

Mandeville, Geoffrey de 73, 74, & n, 77, 79 & n, 84, 126

manors: administration 54, 55, 60, 68, 69, 89; role in Domesday survey 55; and Bath A 60; of Burton abbey 95; boroughs subsumed in 154; churches of 119, 123, 125 & n; and Evesham A 61; and Evesham K 62−7 *passim*; and Evesham Q 65; and Exeter Domesday 60; and GDB 158; at Gillingham, Kent 93; grouping of, in DB 55 (under abbeys), 54 (within counties), 58, 61, 63, and 84 (in or within fiefs), 67 (within hundreds); and *Inquisitio Comitatus Cantabrigienses* and *Inquisitio Eliensis* 53, 62, 154−5; and sequence within fiefs 63−5

Marston (Beds) 76

Matilda, queen 69n, 72−3 & 73nn

Maurice, bishop of London 132

Mercia 113, 114n, 116, 118, 121, 136

Merleswein (landowner) 76, 83

Mersey, river 35, 36, 57

Middlesex 35 & n, 36, 75n, 77, 78, 79, 84, 87, 93, 99, 106, 155